Strange but true stories inside.

- Contenders for the title "Most Traveled Man"
- With only 150 countries under my belt, I'm still trying to catch up
- The real island paradise "Bali Hai" of *South Pacific* fame—found
- Adventures on Pitcairn Island of the HMS *Bounty*, Robinson Crusoe island, Haiti, Guam and other exotic islands
- The ballerina-spy who recently became First Lady of the world's newest nation
- Burmese leg-rowing—don't try this at home
- Visiting the royal patron of the Knights Templar at her huge castle
- "Psst, wanna be a spy?"—the Russian secret service tries to recruit me as a secret agent
- Sailing the high seas on tall sailing ships
- The Bridge on the River Kwai—the real story of the Railway of Death
- The search for Brian Boru, High King of All Ireland, and my 29th great-grandfather
- The ten myths of natural disasters at home and abroad—what you don't know could kill you
- Wanna lose weight? Slap your belly 20,000 times
- Visiting six countries no one's heard of in six hours
- And 50 other amazing stories from every continent.

The Most Traveled Man on Earth

The Most Traveled Man on Earth

Llewellyn Morgan Toulmin

The Village Press
Silver Spring, Maryland

Biography

Lew Toulmin is a travel columnist, advisor to foreign governments, and adventurer. Each month he writes "The Cruising World" for *International Travel News* and "Travel Tales" for the *Montgomery Sentinel* (of Maryland). He has traveled to over 150 countries and sovereign territories, and has worked in 30 less-developed countries for the World Bank and U.S. Agency for International Development on projects in telecommunications, disaster relief, public administration and e-government. He holds a B.A. from Eckerd College in St. Petersburg, Florida, a Master's in Public Administration from Syracuse University, and a Ph.D. in public administration and economics from American University in Washington, D.C. He has worked as a letter carrier, burger flipper, budget and financial analyst, professor of government, private detective, and labor organizer. Recently he was elected to the prestigious Explorers Club.

Dr. Toulmin is also active in the Travelers' Century Club, the Descendants of the Signers of the Declaration of Independence, the Jamestowne Society, and numerous other heritage organizations. He is the vice president of the Hereditary Order of the Families of the Presidents and First Ladies of America. He is a Knight Chevalier of the Sovereign and Military Order of the Temple of Jerusalem (the Knights Templar). His hobbies include collecting military medals, genealogy, sailing tall ships, and of course, traveling. When not on the road, he lives with his wife Susan in Silver Spring, Maryland and Fairhope, Alabama.

Dedication

To my wife Susan, mother Mary, and father Harry—
without them my life would not exist.

Contents

Section 3 Hollywood vs. History

Section 4 Boats, Ships, and the Sea

Section 5 Clients and Other Disasters

Section 8 Pink Belly

Section 9 This Sceptred Isle

Section 10 It's A Wild Wide World

Section 11 Six Countries in Six Hours

Section 1

The Most Traveled Man

on Earth

The Most Traveled Man on Earth

Mirror, mirror, on the wall, who is the most traveled of them all? The Pope? Nope. The President? No way. The Secretary of State? Not even close. According to the Travelers' Century Club and Guinness World Records, which keep tabs on these weighty matters, the most traveled person on earth is John D. Clouse, a 69-year-old practicing lawyer from Evansville, Indiana. He has visited all 308 countries and dependencies recognized by the Club, including such inaccessible spots as Tristan de Cunha, Nauru, North Korea, Kyrgyzstan, and the Russian Antarctic base at Bellingshausen. He has visited all 50 U.S. states and all 13 Canadian provinces. He has crossed the Atlantic 102 times and the Pacific 42 times. And he did it all as a hobby, with no international road warrior job to assist him.

John Clouse on remote, uninhabited Jarvis Island south of Hawaii, accessible only by permit. Note the "No Trespassing" sign

Clouse got his love of travel from his father, a native of East Prussia who moved to Evansville in search of a better life and found the Depression instead. "Dad had the wanderlust but no money, so we would sit out on the porch and he would bark at us kids, 'What's the capital of Bolivia? How deep is the Mariana Trench?' He always said, 'When times get better I'll take you to Europe.' But he died in 1939. Once he was able to take us to Henderson, Kentucky, ten miles down the road—and that was the greatest travel thrill I've ever had."

Clouse joined the infantry in World War II. "I finally got to see Europe, but under adverse circumstances—the damn Germans kept trying to kill us." Clouse got severe frostbite and woke up in a hospital in Paris. "From the hell of combat to the heaven of Parisian girls and restaurants— Paris has been my favorite place on earth ever since," says Clouse.

After the war Clouse began traveling as a tourist in 1958. "I stayed cheap and ate rich. But back then even eating rich was cheap. A whole dinner with wine at the Tour D'Argent restaurant in Paris cost $35. Now the salad costs that."

"After traveling four months a year for pleasure for many years, I joined the Travelers Century Club in 1970. One day I looked at the TCC list of 300-plus countries and realized that I could maybe visit every one. That's when the mania really hit me. I've spent over $750,000 on foreign travel since 1958, and almost as much again on travel in the U.S. How do I know? The IRS wouldn't believe that I have no investments or money saved, so I had to prove to their auditors how much I've spent on travel."

How does Clouse prove he has been everywhere? "The TCC is self-certifying. But Guinness is much more demanding. Ideally you must produce an immigration stamp in a passport. This is often a problem. For instance, in

East Timor I asked for a stamp and caused a big fuss. Officials there feel strongly that East Timor is *not* a separate territory—it's part of Indonesia. So they refused to give me a stamp. Finally I had to settle for a picture of me and a local landmark. For uninhabited islands I get an affidavit from the ship's master."

John Clouse in the doorway of Sir Ernest Shackleton's hut in Antarctica

Is Clouse competing with other TCC members for top honors? "I didn't start traveling for competitive reasons. And the idea of traveling as a competitive sport is sort of ludicrous. But I do want to visit every place listed. And I'm very strict in my standards—no cheating. I have to actually set foot on each territory, no matter how inaccessible. What's kind of annoying is that Guinness keeps changing its list, almost as if they don't want anybody to get to all their places."

Nicholas Heath-Brown of the Guinness staff confirms that the competition at the top is close. John Todd of Britain is one country behind Clouse and Parke Thompson of Akron, Ohio is two behind. The most traveled woman is probably part of the "most traveled couple"—Carmen and Robert Becker of East Northport, New York. But Guinness has not gotten detailed enough confirmation from various women contenders to definitively list this category. Although the Guinness list is different from TCC's, Heath-Brown says that Guinness works closely with the TCC in identifying the world's top travelers.

Clouse feels that using the TCC and Guinness lists adds some discipline to his travels. He says there are many interesting places, like Georgia and Armenia, that he would never have visited without prodding. But once he got there, they were quite absorbing.

The TCC and Guinness rule is that to "count" a country you only have to visit the airport. Clouse thinks that, "It may seem like a silly rule but it's the only way to get to a lot of places. For example, Johnston Atoll, a chemical weapons facility southwest of Hawaii, is run by the U.S. government and Raytheon. They don't want you to visit in transit and if you do, they don't want you to touch the tarmac. Of course I did. But the only way to really see the island is to get a degree in chemical warfare and join Raytheon."

How does Clouse manage to leave his local criminal and divorce legal practice for months at a time? "I have a great staff—they do much better when I'm away."

Why does a world connoisseur live in Evansville? "I was born and raised here, built my law practice here, and never thought of living anywhere else until it was too late. But you can say this for the folks here—they pay their bills. Of course the climate is horrible—sort of like Washington, D.C. "

Clouse has had six wives and six divorces. "Do my divorces have to do with my travel? Of course!" he says. "I'll meet a wonderful lady who says she likes to travel. We get

5

married, but her idea of travel is Claridge's Hotel in London or the George V in Paris. The reality is some tiny, hot copra boat headed for Tuvalu with a dirty crew, stinking bilges, horrible food and big waves."

Clouse has some treasured souvenirs of his travels, including a collection of palyks, painted and lacquered boxes purchased in Russia. Clouse says, "I also recently started collecting little blocks of wood. I used to bring home more things, but I found that my ex-wives got all the good stuff in the divorce settlements."

Clouse's hobbies complement his wanderlust. He says, "I love reading and books—I've got thousands. You have to read like crazy to appear even half smart. I also love good wine and food. But don't say I'm a gourmet—in the Midwest 'gourmet' is synonymous with 'pretentious asshole.'"

Has he ever had any health problems? "Lots. The worst was in Zambia in '68—it was like six diseases in one. I was attacked by a swarm of insects that looked like flies from hell. Within a few hours I had a fever of about 110 degrees. I flew to London where a doctor said I had had a heart attack and shouldn't fly. So I flew to Indiana and the dean of the IU medical school said I had an African disease called 'The Devil's Grip.' I called on the CDC in Atlanta and they said I had a heart attack and dengue fever simultaneously. I asked a noted epidemiologist and he said I had sleeping sickness caused by tsetse flies. Whatever it was, I feel fine now."

Clouse has had some people problems, also. He says, "I was arrested in Tajikistan basically because I wouldn't go on the tour. I insisted to the 'Comrade Guide' that I wanted to go on my own. I saw a particularly ugly building and took a picture. Turned out it was the local intelligence HQ. The cops arrested me and took me to a cell, where I had a chance to sit for several hours and contemplate the virtues of the American legal system. Eventually a big guy stormed in,

real P.O.ed, and demanded to know what I had been d
I figured if I couldn't talk my way out of this, I better tu
my lawyer's suit. So I said, 'Comrade, I am a lawyer
like the great Comrade Vladimir Ilich Lenin, the found
this great country. And Comrade, I am a great friend o
Soviet Union.' After about an hour of this soft soa
started calling me 'Comrade' and we were buddi
headed back and took the tour."

What were the toughest spots to get to? Clouse s
"Nauru, North Korea, and the Golan Heights were
compared to the British Indian Ocean Territory. That
group of islands with a super-secret US base, Diego Ga
in the middle, and basically you can't get there from h
After much correspondence I hired an Israeli yacht
sailed to Danger Island in the group, with the tacit appr
of someone in charge whom I'd rather not name. A
sailing thousands of miles we got to the island and the s
was so high that the captain, a big Israeli, refused to take
ashore. 'Screw that,' I said, 'we're going.' Since I can't sw
the engineer had to carry me 400 yards through
pounding surf. I was 66 years old but at 6'5" and 2
pounds I'm not small, so we almost didn't make it. It scar
the hell out of me."

Clouse's son George ("Chauncy") is a world travel
too. Chauncy was also once listed in Guinness as the mo
traveled child, since he had visited 104 countries an
territories before he was five. How did Clouse take a sma
child so many places? "No problem, a small baby is th
easiest baggage there is. But now at 15 he's no long
interested in travel. Can you believe it, he's discovered girl
And he's crazy about basketball, which of course is bigg
than God in Indiana. Maybe later he'll rediscover th
world."

Now that he's 69, in what beautiful spot will Clous
retire? "I can't retire! I'm raising a 15-year-old son and I'v

spent all my money on travel. I'll be able to retire in 20 years."

As an expert traveler, Clouse has some tips for fellow tourists on attitude and practicalities. "Go with an open mind and don't take a suitcase full of crap." "In a dangerous area (like Gaza or Soweto) go early in the morning. Rioters always sleep late—they're sleeping off last night's riot." "Learn 'please' and 'thank you' in the local language—it always brings a smile. With those two words, and my English and so-so French and German I can get along anywhere." "Read up on the area ahead of time. You don't want to come back and find out that if you'd walked another 10 yards you could have seen the World's Biggest Mud Pie."

Even though he has visited all 308 TCC countries, Clouse plans to keep traveling. "I'm a travel nut," he says, "and I have six more places to visit before I have been everywhere listed by Guinness as a country or territory."

The remaining six? "Kingman Reef, 1500 miles south of Hawaii, which only shows up at low tide. The Baker, Howland and Jarvis Islands in the South Pacific, which cost $2,000 per day to get to in a hired yacht. The Paracel group and the Spratly Islands in the South China Sea, which are being fought over by six countries. Queen Maud Land in Antarctica, which is always iced in. And Bouvet Island in the South Atlantic, the remotest place on earth. I got within 400 meters of Bouvet but had to turn back because of the tremendous surf. But I'll make it to all of them."

Will Clouse ever stop traveling? "Even after I visit all the Guinness list, I want to keep going. I want to walk the length of Manhattan. I want to ride the Indian Pacific Railroad across Australia. I want to take the Vonglo Express from Teheran to Istanbul. I want to visit every national and state park in the U.S. I've got a lot of places to see."

The Best and Worst of the World, from the Most Traveled Man

These are the world's best and worst, as stated by John D. Clouse:

- Best restaurant: "the Tour D'Argent in Paris—built in the 1500s, with great food and a wonderful view of the Seine and Notre Dame."

- Best hotel: "Bangkok's Oriental Hotel—they have a different concept of service in the East."

- Best resort hotel: "The Mount Nelson in Cape Town, South Africa—vast, beautiful grounds."

- Best wine: "Heitz Martha's Vineyard cabernet sauvignon wine from California—they haven't had a release for five years but it's worth the wait."

- Best beer: "Berlin's Weisse beer—a wheat beer with a dollop of raspberry syrup in it; sounds horrible but it's great."

- Best city: "Paris—a beautiful city with great food and ladies who know how to make the best of what they have."

- Best US city: "New York—the faces of the people there are so striking, bright and intelligent. If I had a whole bunch of money I'd move there right away."

- Best sights: "The Sydney Opera House and the Taj Mahal. The Taj is like a delicate ivory carving. Even the best pictures don't do it justice."

- Best airline: "Singapore Airlines—unfortunately a democracy could never create a super efficient airline like this."

- Worst airlines: "Almost all the rest—they try to do way too much, going to too many cities with too many flights. The Aeroflot pilot with the gun on his hip does stick out in my mind."

- Best research source for travelers: *"National Geographic* magazine—I have every issue ever printed."

- Most beautiful women: "California girls—they look so healthy and strong, like they could screw your brains out and you wouldn't have to do all the work!"

- Worst cities: "The big cities of Asia—Manila and Calcutta. Hot, overcrowded and dangerous."

- Worst country: "Equatorial Guinea—it took ten years to get a visa. When I got there the dictator Masie Nguema Biyogo had killed off a third of the population. He had public torturings before the national soccer matches. The streets of the capitol were deserted, because everyone was hiding inside. It was eerie."

- Favorite country: "The U.S., closely followed by France. We have tremendous beauty in this country. Of course I like the French attitude toward life— where we say, 'Gotta get the check, I have an important meeting in fifteen minutes,' the French say, 'Let's sit back and enjoy our lunch!'"

The *Other* Most Traveled Man on Earth

The pieces above were written for *International Travel News*, where I am now the cruise columnist.[1] John Clouse held the record for ten years, from 1991 to 2001, succeeding J. Hart Rosdale and G. Parke Thompson. Clouse was generally recognized by most observers and authorities, including Guinness, as the most traveled person on earth. According to Clouse, he last received a certificate from Guinness in 2001 as the most traveled man, but then Guinness "rested" (retired) the title.

A Guinness spokesman stated in 2005 that since a number of men (no women, by the way) had reached all the countries on the Guinness list, there was no one person who could be named as the *most* traveled. Guinness does not currently recognize any humans (man, woman or child) in the "most traveled" arena, although it does recognize numerous travel-related records, such as the longest walk (around the world), the longest solo Antarctic trek, longest walk by a woman, the longest lawnmower ride, the longest car journey, longest taxi ride, etc. Currently Guinness is monitoring a new travel record, which no one has achieved: traveling to all the Guinness-list countries within six months. [Good luck!]

John Clouse at age 80 is still going strong. He hasn't married again but, "I did have a 22-year-old girlfriend, a

---

[1] Llewellyn M. Toulmin, "What it Takes to Be the Most Traveled Person on Earth," *International Travel News*, June 1996.

waitress at Hooters, for a year and half. Then she dumped me a few months ago for a guy in his twenties with muscles, wavy hair, and lots of teeth—isn't that incredible? I had a crisis in my law offices a few years ago, so I fired all my legal staff and hired Hooters girls." Clouse is still working on trying to get to Bouvet Island and the Paracel Islands. He says, "I think the Chinese who control the Paracels have finally figured out that they can get some greenbacks by selling visas to Westerners, so I hope to get there soon."

Other high-volume travelers include:

- Graydon "Gig" Gwin, the most traveled travel agent. According to Gig and his website (www.gwins.com), his million dollar quest has taken him on over 2,400 flights covering 3.1 million miles, over 30 cruises, and has involved not only the usual cars and trains, but also elephants, camels, horses, mules, donkeys and an ostrich. Gig feels that *he* is the Most Traveled Man, based on two facts: first, he went to the latest "country" added to the TCC list, Nakhichevan (near Turkey, within sight of Mount Ararat), just five days after it was added to the list. Second, Gig feels that he really *travels* to these countries, and doesn't just touch down for a few minutes. "My passions are writing, tourism, and travel," he said. "As a travel agent and writer, when I visit a place, I go to see everything, including the hotels, the sights and the restaurants. I have been to all the TCC countries, and been to about 160 of them at least twice. My favorite countries are the U.S., especially Hawaii, with its fabulous sun, surf, and infrastructure; Canada, with its polite people, great trains (especially the Rocky Mountaineer), and incredible variety; and Thailand, with its great unique culture, un-influenced by the West."

- Carmen Becker, now of Pompano Beach, Florida, probably the most traveled woman. She was named by Guinness in 2002 as half of the "most traveled couple" with her husband Bob. Unfortunately, according to John Clouse, Bob was trying to get to sail to Norwegian Antarctica when he had a stroke, never really recovered, and subsequently died. Extreme travel can be hazardous.

- Tony Allman of New Zealand, one of the few non-Americans on the extreme traveler list. According to Clouse, "Tony is one of the wackiest of us travel nuts. His luggage just consists of two paper bags, with some socks, T-shirts, and underwear. His wife left him in Africa, hollering, 'You're insane,' when his car stripped all its forward gears, and he tried to drive across the continent in reverse."

And then there is John Clouse's real competition: Charles Veley. Charles Veley claims to be the current most traveled man, and has even set up a Web site called "mosttraveledman.com."

According to *International Travel News*[2], Veley had only done a little foreign travel when he got bitten by the travel bug at age 34. He had become a self-made millionaire in the dot-com boom, and cashed in his shares as a software executive. He took a flight to Africa and read about the TCC in an airline magazine. He immediately vowed to become a member. Within a year he nailed his required 100 countries.

---

[2]Michael McCarthy, "The Man Who Has Been Everywhere," *International Travel News*, July 2004.

13

The Most Traveled Man on Earth

*Charles Veley, aspirant to the title of "world's most traveled man,"
with friends in Nepal*

Next he reached all the locations on the TCC list, achieving this at age 37 years, 9 months and 17 days, after only two years of concentrated travel. (Most of the other ten or so people who have reached all the TCC locations are in their 70s or 80s.) Then he went after the title of World's Most Traveled Person. Why? Says Charles:

> My motivation is a classic overachiever's response to a quota: You want me to do 100? I'll do better than that; I'll do 200. But by the time I got to 200 I knew I wasn't going to be able to stop until I had completed the whole thing. The world is the ultimate jigsaw puzzle. Every new encounter, every new interaction is a tiny piece. Joined together, they give me a privileged glimpse of the common face of humanity. Can you imagine? A total global perspective built entirely by first-hand information. And that grows just by the act of trying to

get from one place to another. Sometimes, especially because of it.[3]

One of Veley's most difficult places to reach was Clipperton Island, 700 miles off Mexico in the Pacific. After sailing for four days to reach the remote French outpost, he and his crew were unable to land, owing to the treacherous reef. "So I swam. There was nothing else I could do," he smiles.[4]

Veley recently reached the almost inaccessible Bouvet Island in the South Atlantic, which John Clouse had tried twice to visit but was never able to get ashore, due to terrible weather conditions. Bouvet is uninhabited, except for seals and sea lions, is surrounded by freezing waters, is 23 square miles of lava fields, and has some of the worst weather on earth. Getting to the island required special permission from the Norweigan Polar Institute and the South African National Antarctic Program. Veley sailed for 72 days with a party of scientists to reach the isolated island. Veley issued this announcement:

> I am pleased to announce that, at roughly 0515 Greenwich Mean Time the morning of December 16 [2003], a group of 9 people landed on Bouvet Island. Bouvet was incredibly stark and foreboding, but the seas were relatively calm and visibility was good. Even so, I was very cold and windblown after 2 hours on the island. The entire beach and rocky upslope was covered with penguins and seals. With this landing on Bouvet, I have now visited all but 2 items on the Guinness list, a record matched only by John Clouse. I have also now visited 300 of the 335 items on the Ham Radio list,

---

[3] Ibid.
[4] "The One Million Dollar Travelling Man," *The London Telegraph*, www.telegraph.co.uk, March 8, 2004.

which is several more than anyone has ever done. Therefore, I will be claiming the title of Most Traveled Man from Guinness.[5]

Veley has gone on to compile a new, "extreme" list of 570 countries, enclaves, and territories, using the TCC list, the ham radio DXCC list, the Guinness list, and other sources. He is traveling full time, despite having a wife and baby daughter at home, in order to visit all the locations on his list. At last count Veley had visited 485 of the 570 entities on the new list. Two of the ones he is missing include the disputed Paracel Islands, occupied by the ferocious Chinese Navy, and remote Peter Island in Antarctica. Veley is also trying to get validation for his list by having members of his website vote on his proposed list of entities.

But according to John D. Clouse, despite Veley's million dollar quest, Veley cannot claim the title. He "never received the title from Guinness of most traveled man, since the title was retired when I was holding it," according to Clouse. Clouse states that, "I am still the most traveled—I know that Charles has never reached remote Peter Island in Antarctica, and he is still one shy of me. You know, this competitive traveling is kind of crazy—more sex and less travel and everybody would be happier."

---

[5]McCarthy, ibid.

John Clouse and Charles Veley, top claimants for the title of "World's Most Traveled Man"

And the Winner Is...

Guinness does currently (as of 2006) officially recognize *one* most traveled individual. But it is not a human. This prodigy is Columbus Bear of Co-op Travel in Stockport, UK, a Teddy Bear who traveled 205,000 miles through sixteen countries in one year. Columbus Bear beat out Tornado Ted as the bear to cover the most distance in a year. In his whirlwind year, Columbus Bear visited Australia five times, drove through eighteen US states, and relaxed on the beach in Mauritius. He rode on the Orient Express, crossed the River Kwai in Thailand, and took a cruise ship through the Far East. According to Guinness, there were no reported romances during the year. Perhaps he was moving too fast to have a girl bear in every port?

Columbus Bear with his guide, in the Philippines

So who is the real winner of great John Clouse vs. Charles Veley (vs. Gig Gwin?) race for Most Traveled Man? Can there be a winner when there is no judge, jury or court of competent jurisdiction? And isn't the title rather arbitrary, when you think about it? I mean, look at the Guinness list—who cares if John or Charles has made it to Bouvet Island or Peter Island, where no one lives or ever will? There are 17,000 islands in the Indonesian archipelago alone, and no one will ever visit all of those. Why shouldn't *they* all be on the list? Perhaps *International Travel News* had it right, when it created a list of the 195 nation-states that common sense dictates are the way we humans have carved up our world.

Hmmm, let's see now. In that case, *anyone* could become the "Most Traveled Man," or at least one of the "Most Traveled *Men*," just by hitting all those 195 countries. What's the number of my travel agent—I gotta get moving....

The remainder of this book describes some of my travels, from Alabama to Zambia, in my race to catch up with the Most Traveled Men. With only 151 countries and territories under my belt, perhaps I'll never catch them, but it's been great fun so far—including finding the real island paradise "Bali Ha'i," learning Burmese leg-rowing, getting headhunted by the KGB, joining the famous Knights Templars, and working on every major continent. I hope you enjoy my stories as much as I've enjoyed living them.

In the Appendix various lists of "countries" are presented, so that you may count how many you have visited on the *ITN* and other lists. Web sites and other contact information are also provided. Happy travels!

The Most Traveled Man on Earth

Section 2

A Kid in Paradise

Papa Doc and His Colt .45 vs. My Papa

I started traveling before I was born. My mother, Mary Morgan Duggar Toulmin, was pregnant with me in California, but decided to fly home at the last minute, so that I could be born, in 1951, in the old family home town of Mobile, Alabama, near our *really* old home town of Toulminville. I moved six weeks later, carried by my mother to one of over thirty short governmental consulting assignments that my father was undertaking around the United States. My father, Harry Theophilus Toulmin, was advising local governments on budget and personnel matters. Each job usually lasted about two months. We lived in lots of cheap motels, and my mother learned never to acquire more household items than could fit in the trunk of a car. As I got older, I started going to kindergartens and nursery schools. Fourteen in all.

My first memory, at age four, is of laying down for a nap at the Tiny Tots Finishing School in Miami, Florida, where my father was one of the founders of the new government of Metropolitan Dade County, and was later made the first Budget Director.

In 1959 my parents and I moved to Port-au-Prince, the capital of Haiti. My dad signed up for a two-year contract with the U.S. Agency for International Development (USAID) to be the financial and management advisor to the government of President-for-Life Francois "Papa Doc" Duvalier.

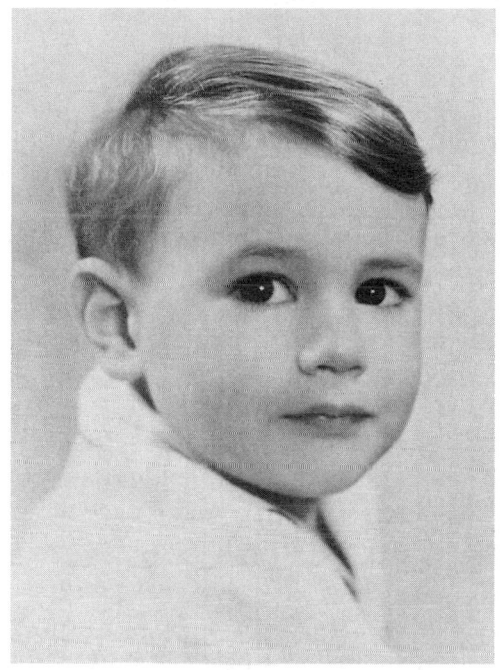

Lew Toulmin at about age four

Papa Doc was a famous and colorful character, to say the least. He intentionally dressed like the malevolent voodoo god Baron Samedi, with a thin white tie, white shirt, black suit and black pork pie hat. Most Haitians thought he *was* a voodoo god, and swore he could not be killed except with a silver bullet though the heart. They also believed that Papa Doc could easily turn any enemy into a zombie—a "living dead" slave who would be forced to do unspeakable acts.

Papa Doc robbed the country blind, supported by the tiny ultra-rich class who lived on a high ridge overlooking the sweltering slums of the capital below. He robbed the poor, the small middle class, and especially the foreign aid donors.

Papa Doc's militiamen, the notorious Ton Tons Macoutes, were on almost every street corner. They wore wraparound dark sunglasses and hefted submachine guns. Their job was to shoot anyone who disagreed with the regime. They were very good at their work.

After we had been in-country about two months, my father got a summons to come down to the Presidential Palace to meet the President-for-Life. Harry went down to the Palace, a huge white pile with a large round dome on top like a colander. At the front gate he was searched from head to toe by two Ton Tons Macoutes. Inside the gates he was searched again by two Presidential guards. Then between the two tanks in front of the Palace he was searched again, and again at the front staircase, and so on—fifteen times in all.

Finally Harry came to the large doors of the presidential office, where he was searched again, naturally. The doors opened and Harry found himself in a huge office as big as a high school gymnasium. The doors were in one corner of the office, and in the far corner he could see Papa Doc's desk, placed so the President could see who was coming, from a long way away.

As Harry approached the huge wooden desk, he saw Papa Doc in his voodoo getup, and noticed two things on the crowded desk: a piece of paper, and a Colt .45 automatic pistol.

There was nowhere to sit, so Harry stood in front of the desk. On the paper he could make out his name and several paragraphs in French.

Papa Doc perused the paper for about five minutes, before looking up and saying in a French Creole accent, "Soooo, Monsieur Toulmin, you are here to advise Haiti on how to reform eets financial management and budgeting, *n'est-ce pas?*"

"Yes, your Excellency, your Holiness," stuttered my father, "That is correct."

"Well, Monsieur Toulmin," said Papa Doc, reaching out and stroking the Colt .45, "I believe zat we have ze pretty good financial management in Haiti already—what do you sink?"

"Oh, yes, your Excellency, you have a wonderful system here," said my father quickly.

"Well, good, Monsieur Toulmin," said Papa Doc. "I am glad we had zis little chat. Goodbye."

President for Life of Haiti, Papa Doc Duvalier. Note the Colt .45 in the lower right.

Two months later the financial management project was abruptly terminated and we were sent to Thailand instead. USAID had decided the Haitian project was hopeless.

Papa Doc died peacefully in bed twelve years later and passed on his financial techniques to his son, "Baby Doc," who looted the country even more effectively. Ironically, rapacious dictators, economic chaos, deforestation, and AIDS have left Haiti in such a terrible state that the time of Papa Doc is now generally thought of as "the good old days." Having lived there, I hope both Papa and Baby Docs rot in hell for their crimes against their people.

Something good did come out of this mess. In Haiti, at age eight, I realized three things:

- Poor and oppressed people like the Haitians exist all over the world

- Some concerned citizens like my father were trying to help; and

- I should follow in my father's footsteps. And so I did.

Harry Toulmin died in June 2002, having dedicated his life to improving governmental administration in the United States and in numerous countries around the world. Like him, I became an advisor in public administration, and also in emergency management, e-government and telecommunications, eventually working in thirty less-developed countries.

Llewellyn M. Toulmin

Harry and Mary Toulmin at their 50ᵗʰ wedding anniversary party,
Fairhope, Alabama, 2001

Swimming in Green Goo, the Mother of All Mudholes, and the Citadel of Haiti

In Haiti my father, my mother, and I stayed at the Hotel Splendide. It was a run-down colonial hotel with thick walls, swishing overhead fans, and no air conditioning. It was far from "splendide," but it seemed pretty exotic to me.

The hotel's main attraction was the swimming pool, since the days were very hot and there was no air conditioning. Unfortunately, the pool was always covered with a thick layer of green goo about two inches thick. Probably algae, but who knew for sure? Being a resourceful eight-year-old, I rapidly solved this minor problem. I simply did a big "cannonball" off the diving board, which broke through the initial layer of goo. Then I swam in circles, spiraling outwards, until most of the green goo had been pushed up onto the edge of the pool. Thus the pool was cleaned and eminently usable. As the Haitians would say, "Pas de problème."

There were no English-speaking schools in the country at that time, so I was thrown into the deep end—a completely French-speaking international school. For me at least the deep-end approach did not work. I did not learn a single thing in four months, not even any French. It was a good thing we were sent on to another country, otherwise I might still be stuck in the third grade.

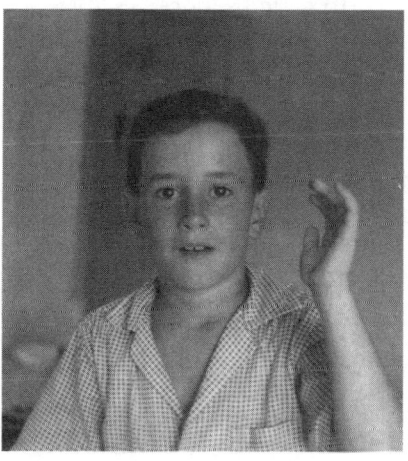

Lew Toulmin at age eight, without the green goo

After we had been in-country for a couple of months my parents borrowed a long wheelbase Jeep, and we went on an expedition up into the jungle in the mountains north of Port-au-Prince. We headed northeast on a "road"—more of a goat track—that had not been used by any vehicles for months, if not years. Our family took along one of my father's local assistants, Albert Charlot. We drove very slowly through the Artibonite river valley and central plain, a stark, denuded area that had once been productive sugar plantations. Despite the poor, eroded soil, the area was densely populated with large families living in huts.

Our mini-expedition never got stuck, except once. The track wound through a low bit of jungle that was very wet, with many small streams and of course 100 percent humidity. At the lowest point of the track was the Mother of All Mudholes. It was fifty feet wide, a hundred feet long, and probably as deep as the center of the earth. The track seemed to lead straight through it.

We stopped and watched some of the locals get through. They didn't have cars. They had donkey carts, mules, an occasional bicycle, and of course their feet. They placed boards and branches on the mud, thus spreading the weight, and usually got through. We waited for hours and asked everyone for advice, but no-one had ever seen a car or even a Jeep on this "road" before. So finally my father laid down some branches, put the Jeep in four-wheel drive, gunned the engine, and charged straight across the mudhole. He got about thirty feet before the sticky mud grabbed the Jeep in a ferocious grip. The Jeep sank deeper as Dad spun the wheels. Eventually it ended up with all four wheels totally buried, and the entire frame sunk into the mud.

We pushed and pulled on the Jeep. We got covered in mud. We asked the local villagers for help. We said that their mules and donkeys could easily pull out the Jeep. We pleaded. We offered money. All to no avail. No one would lift a finger. It was Fate—or perhaps in their minds, voodoo black magic.

After being stuck for about three hours, my father sent Albert back down the trail on foot. Miracle of miracles, he was able to locate a missionary some miles away. The missionary had a large truck with a winch and strong cable—yet another miracle. He and Albert arrived with the truck and laid the cable across the mud to the Jeep. They winched the Jeep out of the mudhole; then the missionary showed us a rough but passable trail around the hole. Thanks to the missionary, we were on our way again. Otherwise we might still be stuck in the mud. There is a God!

At Cap-Haïtien we found some of the strangest remains of Haiti's violent past: Sans Souci and the Citadel. In the late 1700s, Haiti was the most valuable colony in the world, due to its high sugar production. But its masters in France had created this wealth out of the human misery of slavery. In

1800 the slaves revolted, led by three charismatic slaves, including the famous Henri Christophe. Over the next four years the rebels managed to throw off the yoke of colonization, defeat a Napoleonic and an English army, and set up the world's first black republic.

Alas, democracy was short lived. Christophe killed one of his fellow leaders and established himself as the king of northern Haiti. He built a huge and expensive palace, which he called Sans Souci. Then on top of the 2800-foot mountain overlooking the palace, Christophe began building the Citadel. This massive structure broke the back of his kingdom and ultimately killed him.

Christophe dragooned almost the entire population of the north to work on the Citadel. At least 25,000 people perished in building the huge structure. Eventually the people revolted. They burned Sans Souci and went searching for King Christophe, hoping to kill him. But he cheated the mob by shooting himself in the head with a silver bullet. While the palace burned, his widow and a few loyal servants carried his body up the mountain to the Citadel. They threw Christophe's body into a pit of quicklime, so it could not be recovered and desecrated.

When we got to Cap-Haïtien we first wandered around the ruins of Sans Souci. It was *really* ruined—no restoration funds in the poorest country in the western hemisphere. The rooms were large and there was an air of remaining magnificence. But the animal droppings and the burned-out second floor and roof gave it an air of sadness and almost total decay. The palace is reputedly haunted by vicious ghosts who give visitors nightmares for months. Luckily we did not encounter any visitors from beyond the grave.

My father and I wanted to go up to the top of the mountain to see the Citadel. No car or Jeep could make it up the narrow track. I rented a small horse, but Dad needed something bigger. The only alternative was a big, ugly mule.

31

Dad got aboard and after a hundred yards said that, "Riding this mule is as uncomfortable as riding a McClellan saddle—it's all hard, bony, and full of holes in the wrong places."

We toiled up the mountain for several hours, until we finally emerged at the base of the huge fortress. The Citadel is 450 feet long and 130 feet high at the "prow," which looks like the bow of a giant battleship. It is made entirely of stone, and is the largest fortress in the Americas. It was designed to hold 365 cannon on three decks and thus fight off the most formidable armies in the world. From the top we could see all of Christophe's kingdom of northern Haiti.

The Citadel from above, in northern Haiti

The true heartbreaking irony of the Citadel is that the entire construction project was useless. No army or even platoon has ever attacked the Citadel since it was built. As Haiti spiraled downhill after Christophe, no one really wanted to conquer the country. The only pseudo-conquest came in 1915, when U.S. Marines landed in an effort to end years of economic and political chaos, and to protect U.S. business interests. Things were so bad that they stayed nineteen years, until 1934. But no one even thought of resisting the Marines by using the Citadel.

In many ways the Citadel has become a terrible symbol of Haiti—built out of toil, misery and despotism, a huge effort wasted, a giant sore on the face of the earth, for the rest of mankind to stare at in dismay.

Leaving the Cap-Haïtien area, we got on a good two-lane paved road leading back to the capital of Port-au-Prince. We got there in three hours—it had taken us four days to traverse the same distance using the back roads.

Daddy, Daddy, There's a Kamoy in My House!

When I was nine, my parents and I were sent from Haiti to Bangkok, Thailand, where my father helped create the new national Bureau of the Budget (similar to the U.S. Office of Management and Budget). We lived for several years in a compound across from the International School of Bangkok. In the compound were the main house with two bedrooms, a separate servants' quarters, a garage, and an orchid arbor. In the corner of the compound was a small L-shaped mother-in-law's house with a bathroom, a porch, and an open area divided into a sleeping space and study area. Since my parents each took a bedroom in the main house, I gleefully grabbed the mother-in-law's house for myself.

Our family compound was surrounded by a seven-foot wall, topped with broken glass and three strands of barbed wire. We had two large German shepherds and an internal intercom system. All these security precautions were to keep out the "kamoys"—the Thai word for burglars. About a quarter of expats living in houses in Bangkok had experienced the unwelcome attentions of kamoys. Kamoys usually stole money and appliances, and were rarely violent. Some kamoys just stole food from the expats' refrigerators. But there was always the potential for mayhem, since the normally placid Thais can be quite explosive when cornered.

In my snug little house I had a bunk bed, and, being a kid, I naturally slept in the top bed. Beside the top bunk was a shelf where I kept my alarm clock, my glasses, and a German Boy Scout knife with a razor-sharp seven-inch blade—for filleting kamoys.

One night when I was twelve, I was sound asleep as usual. Suddenly I felt a sharp pinch in my side. I woke up. *I never wake up at night*, I thought. I looked around, saw nothing, and was just drifting off when I saw something moving in the moonlight over by my desk. For a long minute I couldn't figure out what it was. Then I realized it was a man, crouched down over my desk, slowly opening each drawer. What was really scary was, that when *I* opened those drawers, they screeched like bad brakes in the high humidity. But when *he* opened them, there was not a sound.

I reached up on my shelf to get my glasses and my German knife. Both were gone. Uh-oh. So was my alarm clock. Terrified, I turned over on the other side, facing the wall, so I wouldn't have to see the kamoy.

But facing the wall was worse. I imagined the kamoy standing over me, my razor-sharp knife in his hand, about to fillet *me*. So I turned back the other way, and watched him some more. After a while I couldn't stand this, so I flipped back again. When I turned back, there was no one there—or was there? I peeked around the corner into the bathroom to see if he was there. Nothing. But was he under the lower mattress, or on the porch?

I listened for a moment, heard nothing, then stabbed at the intercom. "Daddy, daddy, there's a kamoy in my house!" I screamed at the top of my lungs—so loudly I probably didn't need the intercom.

I jumped out of bed, and for courage grabbed my white sailor's hat and jammed it on my head. I ran out on the porch, hollering all the way. My father appeared waving a flashlight on the porch of his second floor bedroom in the big house. The two German shepherds trotted up, mildly interested in all the commotion. My mother called the local police, who appeared in their usual fashion, forty-five minutes later. They found a burlap bag draped over the broken glass and barbed wire fence.

Searching my little house, we found my glasses on the floor. The kamoy must have knocked them off the shelf and into me, waking me up. He got clean away with my wallet and alarm clock, an electric fan, and of course my large German knife with the seven inch blade.

I often wonder where that knife is today—perhaps being used somewhere in Thailand to fillet a nice fresh fish? Maybe that's the best place for it, after all.

Jubilee!
Where the Seafood Jumps
onto Your Plate

A jubilee on Mobile Bay in Alabama. There is nothing like it anywhere else on earth. It begins in northern Alabama, when there is a lot of rain, and the Mobile, Tensaw, Tombigbee, Blakeley and Black Warrior rivers fill with fresh water. That water is carried down to Mobile Bay, fifteen miles wide and forty miles long, a shallow, brackish estuary filled with fish and crabs.

When the moon is full and the summer nights are long, the fresh water floods into the Bay, and other mysterious conditions are right, the jubilee occurs. The fish and crabs go crazy! They jump, they splash, they school, they party, they blow bubbles, they crawl up on the beach.

A jubilee might happen once in a summer, or dozens of times. Sometimes it happens all up and down the Eastern Shore of the Bay, sometimes only on an isolated stretch of beach. Fairhope and Daphne are the two towns where jubilees are most common. It rarely happens on the muddier Western Shore. It's apparently a completely natural phenomenon—no pollution story here—caused by lack of oxygen in the water.

Everyone wants to get in on a jubilee, but no one wants to wait up every night all summer. So many families hire a teenaged boy to stay up all night and patrol the beaches. Then if he spots a jubilee, he activates a telephone tree and the locals come running.

Although I lived on the Eastern Shore for three summers while attending college, I saw only two jubilees. The first time was on the long concrete municipal pier in Fairhope. I had walked out on the pier in the moonlight and looked back at the shore. It was thick with smaller wooden piers sticking out into the bay, almost all with a small house at the end. Many houses leaned picturesquely to starboard or port, having been sideswiped by the last storm. Some houses were boathouses, but most were just for relaxing, sunbathing, cooking, crabbing, and dreaming of jubilees.

Suddenly there was a big commotion at the end of the pier. I ran out to see what was happening. Hundreds of mullet were jumping out of the water and standing on their tails. The jubilee was localized to a small area the size of a football field, just off the northwest corner of the pier. Local fishermen tried to cast their lines into the mass of mullet and get a bite, but there were no takers. The mullet were too crazed to be interested in eating. They just wanted to jump to the moon.

One smart fisherman ran to get his casting net. There are always casters on the pier. Each has a circular net about twelve feet in diameter, with weights at the bottom. The caster laboriously straightens the net, repeatedly throws a fold of the net over one shoulder, holds another bit in his teeth, then casts the net with a swirling motion out into the water. If he does it right, a beautiful ellipse is formed, and he has a chance of catching something. If he does it wrong, a sullen knot of net and weights lands in the water with a plop, and he loses several teeth. Usually casters catch little or nothing, even if they do it right.

The fisherman hurriedly returned with his casting net, and began preparing to throw. Everyone watched and wondered if he could reach the mass of mullet, which was gradually moving away from the pier. Finally he was ready. He cast, and caught the edge of the school of crazed mullet. Triumphant, he needed help to pull up the net, heavy with scores of mullet. In one cast he had caught more fish than his total for the last year.

After a while my first jubilee faded away into the night and into memory. The mullet relaxed and swam below the surface for a while.

Then one night I was on the short municipal pier in Daphne. Again the moon was full and it had been raining in the north. There was a rising tide and a gentle wind. Suddenly mullet began jumping off the end of the pier. "It's a mullet jubilee!" hollered one fisherman, and he ran to call his friends. But he was wrong. It was a universal jubilee, with shrimp, crabs, shiners, flounder, mullet, croaker, spot, eels, bay whiffs, anchovies, needlefish, and hogchokers. And they were all moving towards the beach. The crabs hit first. They scuttled out of the water and moved drunkenly sideways up the beach.

Crabs are especially prized, since usually the only way to catch crabs is to buy some old chicken necks, let them rot a little, freeze them, thaw them, let them rot some more until they really stink, then tie one on the end of a string off a pier. The crabs love the stink, and swim over and start nibbling on the rotten chicken neck. Then you slowly and carefully pull on the string, and raise the neck near the surface, not scaring off the crab. You gently lower a crab net—like a butterfly net—and scoop up the crab. You put the crab in a tub of Bay water with a bunch of his friends. Then you whoop for joy. Crab cakes tonight!

So being able to grab crabs and just put them in a bucket, with no stink and no fuss, was wonderful. We all ran around the beach, chasing the drunken, crazed crabs and putting them in tubs. Usually crabs are vicious and can snap off your little finger with their big claws, but these jubilee crabs were so dazed that they didn't even bother to bite. Instead, they blew bubbles and seemed to be trying to breathe the air.

Then the rest of the jubilee hit. Delicious flounder flopped in the shallows and almost begged to be caught. Usually you have to wade patiently through the shallow water, looking for the incredibly faint outline of a flounder half buried in the sand. Then you gig the flounder with a trident-shaped, six-foot spear, trying not to impale your foot in the process. But these flounder tried to jump out of the water to attract attention. Mullet and eels and croaker, all prized catches, swam up on the beach and gasped for air.

After a while the jubilee wound down. The fish and crabs went sane again and swam back in the water. We headed home with ice chests and pickup trucks full of enough food to feed our families for months.

Of course the greatest satisfaction came the next day, when those of us who had participated in the jubilee were able to boast about it to the sleepyheads who had missed it. Some of the participants vigorously claimed that the fish and crabs had actually jumped right into their iceboxes, while they just relaxed in a beach chair. But I'm an honest guy. I would never, ever tell a tall tale like that. Someone might think I was telling a fish story.

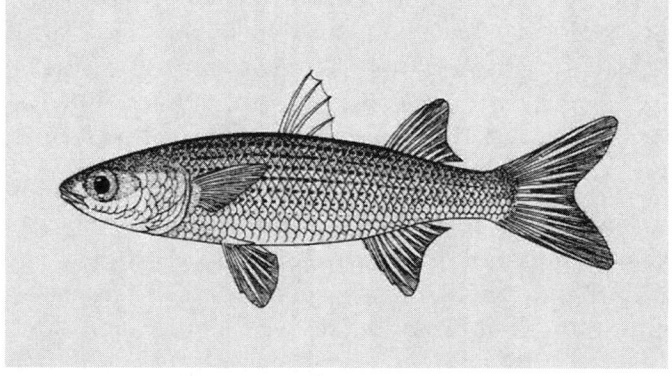

A grey mullet

Llewellyn M. Toulmin

The College Chapel and the Golden Calf

Bill and I were sophomores at Florida Presbyterian College when we worshipped the Golden Calf.

We had entered FPC in 1967. By 1968/69 the school was changing from a quiet little religious school to a noisy, radical, anti-Vietnam-war college. This didn't bother me. But it profoundly disturbed Bill, a member of the "God Squad" who as a freshman had wanted to enter the ministry. He made the mistake of studying psychology, and was caught up in the touchy-feely, Esalen, counter-cultural current of the time. He seemed to lose his faith, and somehow psychology was a poor substitute. The God Squad numbers on campus declined precipitously and the whole school changed, seemingly overnight.

Bill brooded on this change. He began to drink. A lot.

Late one night he drank a six-pack and had an inspiration. He got in his beat-up old VW convertible Bug. He drove to north St. Petersburg, about five miles away, to a Foremost Dairy. Outside was a herd of life-sized plaster-of-Paris cattle.

Bill seized one of the calves and jammed it in the Bug, with its hooves sticking up out of the sunroof. He took it back to the college Art Department, broke in, found some paint, and painted the calf a brilliant golden hue. Then he drank another six-pack.

He took the calf to FPC's unfinished chapel, which was still under construction. The chapel was hexagonal, with six Erector set–style L-shaped girders holding up a massive

41

underbelly of concrete. The students called it "the pregnant spider."

Eckerd College chapel in the sunset, St. Petersburg, Florida

Bill put the golden calf under his arm. It weighed eighty pounds. He put several beer cans in his pockets as a reserve. He began climbing up the girders toward the roof of the chapel. The first few rungs of the girder were not too tough, but higher up the diagonal rungs were further apart. Yet he managed to keep climbing, occasionally bumping the head of the calf into the chapel girders.

Eventually he reached the roof, forty feet above the ground. He marched up the sloped roof to the eight-foot-high cupola. On top of the cupola was a six-foot spear pointing into the sky. The workmen hadn't yet put on the crossbar to make it into a Christian cross. Bill drank his reserve beers. Somehow—he later said he couldn't remember how—he climbed up on the cupola with the calf, then shinnied up the shaft of the spear and lashed the golden calf halfway up the spear.

The next morning the students arose for breakfast as usual. First one, then another noticed the Golden Calf on top of the chapel. Excited students pointed out the amazing sight to each other. All immediately realized the religious significance of the event and what it symbolized: Baal had taken over as the God of Campus. Spontaneously first one and then all the students, including me, got down on our knees in prayer facing the Golden Calf. We touched our foreheads to the ground. We chanted deep, meaningless phrases to our new God.

It had taken Bill about three hours to create the Golden Calf God and raise it to the heavens. It took the St. Petersburg Fire Department three days to get it down.

By our senior year the God Squad was annihilated. Jack Eckerd of Eckerd Drugs gave the college $20 million, and the school changed its name from Florida Presbyterian to Eckerd College. On graduation day students painted "Eckerd Drug College" in huge letters on the entrance to the school, for all the parents and faculty to see. God was dead.

An American
Named Llewellyn, Ya!

I took my college junior year abroad at age 18 at the University of North Wales at Bangor, in northwest Wales. With my ultra-Welsh two first names—Llewellyn and Morgan—I was very popular with the locals. I was reminded of this literally every morning at 7 A.M., when the Welsh cleaning lady in my dorm kicked open the door to my room, where I was trying like a typical student to sleep until noon. She would stride in, mop and bucket in hand, stand over my bed, look down, and in a loud Welsh accent declare, "An American named Llewellyn, ya! I can't believe it!"

The University of North Wales at Bangor

Llewellyn M. Toulmin

I quickly learned that Llewellyn is *the* Welsh name to have. Three major Princes of Wales were named this, as well as numerous lords and chiefs. The most memorable was Llywelyn (the more common Welsh spelling) the Great, Prince of Wales from 1205 to 1240. He united Wales, helped force King John of England to grant Magna Carta in 1215, and maintained Welsh independence from English invaders. Appropriately, Llewellyn means "lion-like" or "leader of the people."

Besides Welsh history and sociology, my most memorable studies were in British archaeology. I had two professors for this class, a young Welsh woman who spoke with machine-gun rapidity, and the senior professor, an Oxford don. As senior prof he wore his full academic gown all the time, so that he floated along the college corridors like a huge bat with black flapping wings.

His entire opening lecture consisted of this, done in a high Oxbridge accent: "Todaaaaay...(pause) we are here...(pause) to study...(pause) *archaeology*. Archaeooooology... (pause) is the study... (pause) of things that are very... (pause), *very* ...(long pause), VEEEEERY ... (very long pause) ...old."

My statistics professor was an intense Englishman from Leeds who took a liking to me and kindly invited me to his home several times—quite a rare event. He had a one-year-old child and a Welsh Border Collie called Chuckles. Chuckles would constantly herd the infant around the house like a small sheep. Occasionally the professor would say to the dog in a conversational tone, "Chuckles, why don't you stop bothering the baby and go upstairs and play by yourself?" Chuckles would immediately comply. I never heard a single command like "heel" or "roll over"—just intelligent conversation as between a professor and his student. I was quite glad that Chuckles had not decided to enroll in my college statistics class, since I was quite sure he could ace me on any exam.

45

Chuckles the Border Collie, in Wales

I studied fairly hard, but most of the year none of my peers seemed to study at all. After a while I realized that this was actually very rational behavior. This was because the student's placement as "first class honours" (top 3 percent), "upper second" (next 20 percent), "lower second" (next 20—the not-so-great degree that Prince Charles got at another branch of the University of Wales) or "third class" (uh-oh) was solely determined by exams at the end of each of the three B.A. years. So intense cramming at the end of the year was the universal approach. This left lots of free time for the innumerable clubs and societies—everything from opera to mountain climbing to sailing—many more than at any American university I attended.

Of course the major student occupation was smoking and drinking. Millions of gallons of beer, mostly Guinness, were consumed by the students, probably enough to fill the Menai Straits near the college and the Irish Sea beyond.

Perhaps the students drank so much because they ate so little. The dorm food was truly terrible: two types of potatoes at every meal including breakfast, hard bits of mystery meat covered with an industrial brown sludge gravy, and invariably a rhubarb pie with a pus cream sauce for dessert.

We showed our dislike for the food in an unusual way. At the beginning of the year we were required to buy short, knee-length black academic gowns from departing students, who had moved on to full-length gowns at graduation. We were required to wear these gowns at all meals in the dorm refectory. We bid high for used gowns covered with crusted food. Then during the year we attempted to spill as much of the terrible food as possible on our gowns, adding new decorative layers of potato and gravy stains. We never washed our gowns. The most disgusting gowns would command the best prices when sold to rising new students. Ah, tradition...

My college friends fell into two easily distinguished camps—the English and the Welsh. The differences were striking. If an English friend saw me coming down the opposite side of the High Street, he would cross to my side of the street, look both ways to be sure no one could hear, then in a low undertone say, "Why, hello. Beautiful morning, isn't it?" My Welsh friends would hail me from the other side of the street, and excitedly call out, "**WELL, HELLO, BOYO! AND HOW ARE YOU TODAY?**"

Then there were the eyebrows. English eyebrows consisted of short hairs that all lay flat and pointed in the same direction. Welsh eyebrows were long, rebellious hairs that pointed in all directions, jabbing, ducking, weaving, rocketing upwards—like a Jackie Chan fight scene— symbolic of the intensity within.

The professorial theatrics varied by national origin, too. English professors spoke in perfect paragraphs, carefully modulated, with few hand movements. My Welsh sociology professor viciously jabbed the air with his pipe while making his points. After a particularly telling argument, he would stop, light his pipe with a match, fix a student with his steely gaze, then throw the match over his shoulder into the air, right into the trash can three yards behind his back. He never missed.

Years later I became interested in genealogy and to my great surprise learned that I am the lineal descendant of two of the three Prince Llywelyns of Wales, including "the Great," and a cousin of the third. I am convinced that there is some memory in the genes that draws us back, largely unconsciously, to the lands of our ancestors. That is certainly true of this American named Llewellyn.

Llewellyn Morgan Toulmin at age 18 in his junior year abroad in Wales

Llewellyn, Duke of Abyssinia

During my junior year abroad in Wales, my parents were stationed in Ethiopia. They kindly sent me an air ticket to fly down to East Africa to visit them during the long spring vac. I flew into Nairobi, and went with one of my father's friends to see the game park just outside the city.

At the gate of the park we asked a game warden where to look for lions. "Look for a circle of Volkswagens," he said in a bored tone. We drove around the park on dirt roads, and then on the horizon we saw a big tree with a circle of Volkswagen buses under it. We drove closer and saw a smaller circle of seven lions, including one big male, inside the circle of buses. The tourists in the buses were very excited and kept snapping pictures, while the lions looked quite bored. One lioness lay asleep on her back, with one hind leg waving gently up in the air. The only time the lions snapped to attention was when an excited tourist opened the door to a bus and partially stepped out to get a better shot. A guide hauled him in and berated him, saying that "the smell of the oil and gas masks your scent, but if you get out of the bus you will die."

We drove off in search of other game. We saw a herd of giraffe and I wanted to go close. My companion said, "Giraffe are more dangerous than you think. Just last week in this park a guy in a Volkswagen Beetle got too close to a giraffe. He was taking pictures, when the giraffe reared back, lifted up his leg, and impaled the guy with his hoof, down through the open sunroof." I agreed to stay well away from the giraffes.

I caught the train from Nairobi to Kampala, Uganda. The countryside was beautiful, with gorgeous green plains, tall mountains, and a big blue sky. I could see why Winston Churchill called Uganda "the Pearl of Africa."

In Kampala I spent several days at Makare University. This so-so institution was the only halfway decent university for two thousand miles in any direction. It was charged with training the future leaders of Uganda. Little did the students suspect how soon they *would* be leaders. Just a short while after I left, Idi Amin kicked all the East Asians out of Uganda. These people of Indian descent had lived in Uganda for generations, and ran virtually all the commerce, trade, and industry in the country. Because they were not black, they were forced to leave the country on a week's notice. All the black students of economics and business at Makare University were put in charge of running the economy. With little expertise, no money at their disposal, and all the investors scared off, the economy spiraled downward for thirty years, and has never really recovered.

I flew from Uganda back to Nairobi, then north to Addis Ababa in Ethiopia. I was met by a colleague of my father, who introduced me to several Ethiopians. The Ethiopians were tall and proud, with attractive slim faces and very dark skins. My first three conversations went like this, all exactly the same:

The Ethiopian: "It's nice to meet you. How did you fly to our country, since there are no direct flights from Europe?"

Me: "I flew from London to Nairobi, then up here."

The Ethiopian: "Ah, yes. Kenya. [*Pause*] The people are very black down there, aren't they?"

Me: [Speechless]

My parents were not in Addis, they were upcountry. So I flew north to Lake Tana to see them. Although this was 1970, I flew in a World War II DC-3, the pride of Ethiopian

Airways. The pilot seemed to have orders to fly exactly two hundred feet above whatever was below him. Since there were some very jagged mountains north of Addis, we had some interesting flying. Pretty soon most of the passengers, including the usual chickens, goats, and pigs, were airsick.

Finally the terrible flight seemed to be ending. By peering ahead, I could see the lake. I knew we were close. I looked for the airport's perimeter road, radar dome, red and white checkerboard buildings, and runway. I saw none of these. All I saw was a green pasture filled with cows. "We're all going to die!" I screamed, as a courtesy warning to my fellow passengers, and bent over in the Full Crash Position. We landed gently at the airfield, cows scattering in all directions. I got off the plane as fast as possible, trying not to make eye contact with the other passengers.

My mother and father met me in a Land Rover and took me up to the lake, the fabled source of Blue Nile. We took a speedboat out to an island in the middle of the lake, and saw a monastery where the Ark of the Covenant was reportedly hidden, until it was moved to another part of the country.

I wanted to see the waterfall that marked the outflow from Lake Tana to the Blue Nile. My parents had seen it, so they sent me out with a fourteen-year-old guide. Like all men in Ethiopia, he carried a rifle, to fight off "shuftas" or bandits. The gun looked like it had been made in 1600, so I am not sure exactly who was most in danger from it.

All upcountry people, including my young guide, worshipped Haile Selassie, the Emperor of Ethiopia, as a god. My guide said, "Emperor Selassie is the descendant of Solomon and the Queen of Sheba. He is the anointed cousin of Jesus Christ, and we must do what he says."

My father had a different view. Dad said, "Haile Selassie dragged his country kicking and screaming from the fourteenth century into the fifteenth century." Everyone agreed on two things: the country could not survive without the Emperor, and if anyone launched a revolt, the hill people would all come down and massacre the rebels. No one could imagine the country without the Emperor. Yet just five years later a coup d'état succeeded and Haile Selassie was smothered in his bed. The resulting "dictatorship of the proletariat" was one of the worst regimes ever seen in Africa.

Emperor Haile Selassie of Ethiopia, descendant (?) of Solomon and the Queen of Sheba, cousin of Jesus

Sixteen years later, at age thirty-four, I was teaching public administration and national politics at American University in Washington, D.C. The job lacked a little in excitement—although not in academic backstabbing—so I decided to pursue a childhood dream. I would become a private detective.

I signed up for a class in how to be a private detective. I was the only Ph.D. in the class, so perhaps it was not surprising that my teacher offered me a job as a part-time detective upon my graduation.

I worked only a few cases, mostly involving surveillance of spouses suspected of cheating. Exciting for about five minutes. Then true boredom set in.

But my teacher/employer did have one case that was very exciting and affected me profoundly. He threw a party for all his clients and invited me and the other detectives to come. I was surprised to see several Ethiopians there as guests. I was introduced to David and Ermias Makonnen. I mentioned that I had visited Ethiopia many years before, during the reign of Emperor Haile Selassie. David nodded, and said, "Yes, he was our grandfather."

Wow! You could have knocked me down with a feather. I couldn't stop asking questions. David said, "When our grandfather was killed, all of our family was imprisoned or killed. Only the two of us were saved, because we were outside the country studying. I was at Georgetown University and my brother was studying tank tactics at Fort Knox in Kentucky. All our family assets were seized by the new government, and I had to become a waiter at a restaurant in Georgetown. I have now worked myself up to manager," he said, proudly.

David was launching a movement in the United States to raise money to reinstitute the monarchy in Ethiopia, with himself as emperor. My detective boss was providing security for the movement. David favored the British form of constitutional monarchy, and did not want the power that Haile Selassie had. I immediately volunteered to help him. Together we approached the Reagan Administration, which was busy making covert or overt war on Communist regimes across the globe. Oddly, we could never interest the administration in doing anything to help launch a democratic, anti-Communist movement in Ethiopia, despite the fact that they were funding opposition movements in virtually every other Communist country.

Despite our lack of success with the Reaganites, we did build up a following. David Makonnen, possible Emperor, cousin of Jesus, made an announcement at one of the meetings of our movement. He said, "Dr. Toulmin has been invaluable to our organization. If we are successful, I am going to name him a Duke of Abyssinia." Maybe he was kidding, but it did have a nice ring....

A year later, David was visiting friends in Switzerland. He had an auto accident, hit his chest on the steering wheel, and died several days later. Authorities said that he had bruised his heart, and it gave out. It sounded to me more like the work of Ethiopian intelligence agents, who had the Makonnens as their top target. Constitutional monarchy in Ethiopia was history, even before it got started.

Section 3

Hollywood vs. History

Sailing a Tall Ship
Across the South Pacific
in Search of the Real "Bali Ha'i"

Bali Ha'i may call you, any night, any day.
In your heart you'll hear it call you, "Come away, come away.
If you try, you'll find me, where the sky meets the sea,
Here am I, your special island, come to me, come to me."

—Richard Rodgers, *South Pacific*

I grew up on those haunting lyrics from the musical play and movie *South Pacific*. When I was older I read James Michener's classic *Tales of the South Pacific* (which inspired the musical) and found it an amazing but much grittier view of World War II in the Pacific. Recently ABC-TV released a televised version of the musical.

Always I was fascinated by the real Bali Ha'i island paradise—where was it? What was it really like? In researching this, I found an old, obscure interview in a Philadelphia newspaper in which Michener said that Bali Ha'i was inspired by Aoba (now called Ambae), in the New Hebrides, a thousand miles north of New Zealand. This island group is now the independent country of Vanuatu.

I contacted Michener before he died, and he confirmed in a letter that Ambae was the inspirational island. I had to go.

I resolved to find the most fascinating vessel possible to help me in my quest. I had sailed small craft and yachts, and been a passenger on various cruise ships. But I had read hundreds of naval novels from Hornblower to

56

Aubrey/Maturin, and I wanted to move up to some real tall ship sailing. I searched long and hard to find the perfect vessel. I finally found the 145-foot square-rigger *Søren Larsen* on the Internet (at www.sorenlarsen.co.nz). Through the Web site and by contacting the ship's headquarters in New Zealand I obtained a wealth of information and pictures on the ship, its voyages to Vanuatu and the South Pacific, and its unique "voyage crew" approach.

This approach immediately attracted me to *Søren*. As voyage crew you are encouraged to have fun, learn seamanship, and stand watches when at sea. Yet you have the freedom to go ashore and enjoy ports of call while the permanent crew stand anchor watch. You have the luxury of private cabins, not hammocks or bunks on the edge of open living areas, as in many cadet sail training vessels. You are not required to climb the mast and help furl sails, although if you want to, you are encouraged to and shown how. In looking for a ship, I found that most tall ships are either military-style cadet training ships with no room for voyage crew, or are passenger-oriented luxury ships that do not encourage passengers to help out in sailing in any way. There are relatively few tall ships with the voyage crew approach, and of these, *Søren Larsen* had the best itineraries, very reasonable prices and convenient time segments—usually ten- or seventeen-day voyages in the South Pacific, and three- to five-day segments along the New Zealand coast.

I joined the *Søren Larsen* in Lautoka, Fiji, for the seventeen-day voyage through Fiji and Vanuatu, and signed the Ship's Articles as voyage crew (VC). Next we VCs were asked if we wanted to go aloft, since the ship was very steady next to the dock. Several VCs dashed aloft, while others made no eye contact, and some went sunbathing. I screwed up my courage and went up almost last of the half who went aloft. The first twenty feet were easy, just climbing up the ratlines, which leaned inboard. Then came the tricky bit, climbing up, out, and over the futtocks, which protruded three feet from the side of the mast. But with a professional crew (PC) above and below me, showing me exactly where to put my feet and giving me helpful tips like, "Drive up with your legs, don't rely on your arm muscles," I was up and over with just a little sweating and swearing. The strong safety line belted around my waist and attached to the futtocks helped my confidence immensely. Getting down over the futtocks the first time required a little faith, also, but again a PC helped literally every step of the way.

We sailed to a nearby cove for the night. Next day was my first four-hour watch. The First Mate immediately asked if I wanted to steer the ship. I accepted, unbelieving. Here I was, with no tall ship experience and only a day aboard, and already I was at the helm of the *Søren Larsen*, sailing her toward the remote Yasawas in Fiji! Admittedly, I had the captain with his piercing blue eyes and several other professional crew watching over my shoulder, making sure I made no mistakes. But I was really doing it—sailing a tall ship after years of just reading about it!

Steering the ship required concentration. She often took up to forty seconds to react to a course correction, due to her long keel. It was easy to oversteer. Keeping within five to ten degrees of the set course was an achievement.

After steering for an hour, I stood bow watch for a half an hour. Since the helmsman and afterguard cannot see directly forward due to the bowsprit and cabin, this is another responsible position.

Next I was trained by a PC on how to do a safety round. This is done every hour when under way. A round involves checking about twenty-five items throughout the ship, such as whether there are lines lying uncoiled on deck, that the anchors are still secured properly, whether there is excessive

The brigantine Søren Larsen on passage from Fiji to Vanuatu, South Pacific

water in the bilge, and noting the state of the engine and the sea in the ship's safety log. In between other duties I helped raise the sails (of which there are twelve!), wear ship, and wash down the decks. In every task I was trained by a hardworking professional who was unfailingly cheerful, polite, and encouraging. The amount I learned about real tall ship sailing in a very short time was truly amazing and exciting.

After watch I went below to finish stowing my gear. I went down a steep companionway to the main saloon, which was richly appointed in beautiful golden walnut. It was decorated with the coats of arms of numerous tall ships and warships that *Søren Larsen* had sailed with, ports she had visited, and events she had participated in. I passed one of the three heads, each with a pump toilet, sink, soap, and a freshwater hot shower (very rare on tall ships). I went past the other eight VC cabins (a mixture of two- and four-berth cabins) to my cabin. It had two seagoing berths arranged in an L shape, with beautiful woods, a comfortable mattress, sink, fan, reading lights, no porthole, mirror, and adequate but not extensive storage space. I later found that on the occasional hot nights at anchor I often slept on deck, using my folding foam mat and extra matting supplied by the ship. This was no hardship, since the stars made a wonderful canopy overhead.

I shared my cabin with Richard, a thirty-something insurance broker at Lloyd's of London, who was a classic English adventurer. He modestly mentioned his mountaineering exploits and described the "good fun" he had had in Angola, checking out insurance threats to diamond mines in the company of ex-SAS security experts. (The SAS is the British Special Air Service regiment, the world's best antiterrorist unit.)

I was to find that one of the best parts of sailing on the *Søren Larsen* was the chance to get to know other VCs and the professional crew. There was not a boring person among them, and many formed deep friendships that went beyond the usual shipboard superficialities. Their varied occupations ranged from a distinguished computer lawyer from London to a stewardess on corporate jets, an agricultural policy analyst, a fundraiser for the famous American Ballet Theater, a retired British merchant seaman, several schoolteachers, an aviation engineer, and two part-time circus performers. Especially interesting were a California couple, both senior computer experts, who had signed on as VCs for ten months to escape the corporate rat race. About half the VCs were American, and most of the rest were British, with one continental European.

The eighteen VCs on my voyage ranged in age from twenty-four to sixty, but nineteen- to seventy-five-year-olds have successfully sailed on *Søren*. The PCs included experts who had sailed on most of the New Zealand and Australian sail training vessels, as well as on merchant ships. One PC had even sailed as crew on the floating palace *Sea Cloud*, probably the most expensive tall ship afloat, but she said she much preferred the "real sailing" on the *Søren Larsen*. About half of the VCs and a third of the PCs were women, including the very competent First Mate. This was a surprising and refreshingly high percentage.

From the PCs I learned some of the fascinating history of the ship. The *Søren Larsen*'s brigantine rig was romantically named for the brigands who roamed the seas in the age of piracy. Her flexible rig has a foremast with four large square sails, and a mainmast with fore and aft sails. She was built in northern Denmark in 1949, is 145 feet long in sparred length, measures 300 tons, and is named for her distinguished builder. A product of the postwar reconstruction program, she was stoutly built with the finest oak. She was a Baltic Trader for many years, carrying valuable cargoes of lumber, coal and grain.

In 1978 the *Søren Larsen* was purchased by visionary and sailing expert Tony Davies, who refurbished her for use as the star of the well-regarded BBC-TV series *The Onedin Line*. This series, based on the real-life exploits of several Liverpool shipping families, raised an entire generation of British sailors, and hooked them forever on the Age of Sail. Later *Søren* was featured in the BBC's *Shackleton* and the Meryl Streep movie *The French Lieutenant's Woman*.

Tony Davies sailed *Søren* around Cape Horn, making her the first British wooden square-rigger to do so in living memory. He took her around the world and led the fleet in the reenactment of the First Fleet to Australia. *Søren* served as the windward mark in the 2000 America's Cup, and is now based in Auckland, New Zealand. In Auckland *Søren* is the "Flagship of the City of Sails" and has won several tourism awards. Now she sails up the New Zealand coast during the southern fall and summer. In the southern winter and spring (June through November) she cruises from New Zealand to the beautiful islands of Tonga, Fiji, Vanuatu, Solomons and New Caledonia.

The crew includes Tony Davies as owner and captain, with an unlimited sail license and enviable safety record, and eleven other professional crew with extensive experience in *Søren* and other sail training vessels. There are up to twenty-two voyage crew who pay for their experience and are encouraged to literally learn the ropes. (Of which there are at least ninety-five, depending on how you count!)

Our initial destination was the Yasawa islands, lying athwart Bligh Water northwest of the main islands of Fiji. Captain William Bligh himself and his seventeen remaining loyal crewmen sailed through these waters in 1789 in their tiny 23-foot ship's boat, after the famous mutiny on the *Bounty*. Here they were chased by cannibals in canoes from the Yasawas. There are no cannibals now, but on our third day we shared a wonderful evening with their Christianized descendents.

We anchored in a beautiful bay on the island of Waya, near the village of Nalauwaki. First the captain went ashore for *"savu-savu"*—to meet with the village chief, drink kava, and ask permission to come ashore. When permission was granted, we went ashore in a Zodiac, and entered the village. It was made of bamboo and thatch, and probably looked as it had two hundred years ago, except for the stone church at the end of the small grass mall around which the village was built. In the twilight the full moon rose between two towering peaks that loomed up over the village. The villagers trooped in wearing exotic tribal costumes, and the men chanted to the deep beat of a bamboo drum. I leaned over to Ian, one of the PCs, and whispered, "This is so beautiful it's like a Hollywood movie set, but it's real!" The evening continued with beautiful choral singing by the village women, and ended with a haunting farewell song from the whole village.

Later that evening, back on board, we were treated to a typical *Søren Larsen* meal. Created by "Squizzy," the ever-cheerful cook (and registered nurse), it consisted of a delicious roast chicken, fried plantains, salad, and a lemon pudding with bananas. Entertainment and eating dinner in the Yasawas today is much more enjoyable than *being* dinner in the 1700s!

Two days later we cleared Fijian customs and headed out to sea for the ocean passage to Vanuatu. As soon as we passed the protective reefs the wind picked up to about ten knots (Beaufort Force 3, the scale used on the ship). A lumpy cross sea made the ship roll quite a bit. The experienced PC Ian advised that I immediately take some Stugeron (cinnarizine), a wonderful anti-seasickness medicine available only in the U.K. and Europe, on the Internet, and on the ship. I did so and felt fine, despite having previously turned green in rough conditions on various cruise ships.

We sailed in rolly swells for about a day and a half, but then the wind piped up and flattened the seas, and we began some classic trade winds sailing. We set the mainsail, two jibs, the main staysail, and all the square sails—course, lower royal, upper royal, and topgallant—and bowled along at almost eight knots. Perfect—this is what tall ship sailing is all about.

Lew Toulmin (left in white hat) aloft on the main yard of Søren Larsen

While on the 4 to 8 pm watch, I took the opportunity to go right out on the jib boom to the farthest point forward. Thirty feet ahead of the ship's hull, looking up to windward, I could see lines of blue-grey rollers that probably started in the Roaring Forties. Looking back at the *Søren Larsen* I was stunned by the beauty of the shape of the sails, their golden glow in the sunset, the power of the vessel driving forward, and the sound of the crashing bow wave below my feet. I felt I was flying through the air, like a bird soaring on a fresh breeze.

Later in the watch, before moonrise, we saw three satellites in fifteen minutes. This display was followed by a fantastic meteor ten times brighter than Venus, which arched across the sky and then broke into five pieces. We thought we had seen the ultimate, when PC Lucy remarked that on *Søren* she had seen shooting stars so bright they lit up the sails!

The next day we sighted pilot whales surfing in the bow wave. Throughout the trip we saw dolphins, albatrosses, petrels, and flying fish.

Four days out we sighted Vanuatu and sailed into the unexpectedly beautiful harbor at Port Vila on Efate. I went aloft and out on the upper topsail yard to furl sail. This was the second-highest yard and gave a wonderful view of the other ships at anchor, the town, and the upscale resort on a tiny island just a few hundred yards away. Stepping onto the footropes below the yard had been a little scary at first, but after a while it became fairly routine. I still hadn't conquered the second futtocks and the upper crosstrees, though.

Vanuatu, one of the most amazing countries on earth, gave us many unusual experiences. In Port Vila we shopped for baskets, circular pig's tusks, tam-tams (wooden drums), and other handicrafts. At Ambrym island most of the VCs hiked twelve miles round trip up the 3800 foot-high Mt. Marum volcano, where they saw lava exploding thunderously in the caldera 2400 feet below them. All the VCs were exhausted upon their return. But PCs Nick and Dave climbed the volcano *barefoot*, including the ash plain and the cinder path, then had enough energy after returning to climb trees! (If you want to get in shape, become a PC on *Søren Larsen*.) Because of a bad knee, I skipped the volcano and went shopping for tam-tams, and inspected chiefs' pigs (more on that later) in two villages by the shore.

We sailed from Ambrym with cool katabatic winds gusting to forty knots (Force 8) howling down between two volcanos and driving us forward at a wonderful eight knots. At Asanvari on Maewo island we saw "custom" dancing and exotic feather costumes, swam in a seven-level waterfall, listened to a great string band, and got very happy on kava.

Finally we set sail for fascinating Ambae, which inspired Michener's Bali Ha'i. As we got closer, I first saw the huge 4,000-foot volcano which dominates the entire island. As we got closer, I was very excited to see small villages and coconut plantations on shore, hugging the lush, green, rugged coast. With the low scudding clouds and cool weather, the mountainous island looked like another line from the song: *"Someday you'll see me, my head sticking up from a low flying cloud..."*

Lew Toulmin steers the brigantine Søren Larsen along the coast of "Bali Hai" (Ambae), Vanuatu

I went ashore on Ambae, and was able to visit both ends of the island. I found a unique and little-known world that has hardly been explored since Michener's visits during World War II. (I could find no reference to any travel writer or explorer having visited the island.) Ambae is located in north central Vanuatu, about 1200 miles north of New Zealand. It is lozenge shaped, about twenty-one miles long and nine miles wide. In profile it is bowl shaped. It has a few black sand beaches (which can attract sharks) and many cliffs and rocky volcanic shores. The 10,000 inhabitants live near the shore. There are no residents inland on the central volcano. The volcano features three different colored caldera lakes.

I started my explorations in east Ambae. Stephen Vusi, brother of a local chief, kindly offered to show me around in his "ute" (utility, a small pickup truck). He took me along the dirt road that circled most of the island to the government rest house at Saratamata. (There are no paved roads or hotels, but there are three grass airstrips.) Typical of the several rest houses on the island, it was clean, had a corrugated iron roof and thin wooden walls, limited cooking facilities, several narrow beds in two bedrooms, a cold water shower, and screens (with some holes), and cost 1000 Vatu (about $7) per night.

Next Stephen organized a meeting with the friendly and accommodating Secretary General (equivalent to the Governor) of the province of Ambae, Maewo, and Pentecost islands. The Honorable Keith Andrew Mala said that, "Vanuatu got its independence in 1980, after years of joint rule by the British and French. Ambae's economy is largely subsistence, with copra and cocoa being the main cash crops. There are four native languages on Ambae, one in each corner of the island. Most people also speak Bislama (pidgin English), and many speak English. All the residents are Christians, of many denominations. There was a beautiful beach on the north shore, but it was destroyed by the rise in sea levels caused by global warming. Redcliffe in the south and Lolowai in the northeast still have good beaches."

Mala continued, "In 1995 there were some scientists' reports of a quake on Ambae, but none of us felt a thing.

Cyclone season is November to May each year. Malaria is down substantially. There are two U.S. Peace Corps volunteers on the island, one teaching English and one mechanical skills. Almost the only tourists on Ambae are yachtsmen who sail into the one very protected harbor at Lolowai. We do get a lot of tourists in April on Pentecost island (next to Ambae) to see the land diving, where local men defy death by bungee jumping head first from bamboo towers and almost touching the ground, with vines tied to their ankles."

Mala described current local initiatives. "The big program on Ambae now is to build a soccer field at Saratamata, the provincial headquarters, to get ready for next year's national championship, which will be attended by 10,000 people. We would like to attract foreign investors to Ambae. We have set aside some land near the soccer field for them to buy, but the program and prices are not yet set."

I explained my interest in World War II, and Mala confirmed that many Ambae islanders worked for the Americans on the U.S. military bases on Espiritu Santo, thirty miles to the west.

I asked about Michener's story in *Tales of the South Pacific* that there was "a small island [Bali Ha'i or Ambae]…where the French government had sequestered all the young white, yellow and black young girls and unmarried women, protected from the inroads of [the half million] American troops." This hidden cache of women was what led the curious naval officer Michener, who had a pass to go anywhere and inspect anything, to visit Ambae from his base on Espiritu Santo. This in turn inspired Michener's immortal story, in which U.S. Navy Lieutenant Joe Cable from Espiritu Santo visits the island paradise Bali Ha'i and meets Liat, a beautiful Tonkinese girl.

Mala laughed and said he had not heard the hiding story, but the people on west Ambae were lighter than the rest of Vanuatu, some people there spoke French, and the women there were more attractive. So perhaps the story was true, and the French had managed to beat out the Americans, and intermarry with the locals. The Tonkinese (north Vietnamese) had been contract workers on the copra plantations. All left Vanuatu after World War II, and most went back to Vietnam.

(Thus you could have the historical irony that beautiful Liat (or any real equivalent), the lover of USN Lt. Cable, could have been back in Vietnam in time for the Vietnam war. The *Tales* state that Liat's mother, Bloody Mary, came from near Hanoi, and Michener's autobiography, *The World is My Home*, says that the real model for Bloody Mary planned to return to North Vietnam. Perhaps the children of any real Liat even fired at U.S. Navy Phantom jets over Hanoi? Strange.)

The Secretary-General kindly arranged for me to meet several World War II participants. First was Wilson Wiri, a catechist in the Anglican church. Born in 1912, he and sixty other men were ordered to leave Lolowai on Ambae in June 1942 to help the United States build five airbases and establish a supply center on Espiritu Santo. These bases supported the battle for Guadalcanal in the Solomons, six hundred miles to the northwest. Wilson's main jobs during his six months on Santo were watering down the runways to reduce dust, unloading some of the one hundred fifty ships (!) in the harbor at Luganville, and building roads by hand in the interior. He said that "air raid warnings went off frequently, but we were never bombed while I was there." During the entire campaign the Japanese dropped only one bomb on Santo—the biggest target in the Southwest Pacific—and none on Ambae. The bomb on Santo killed a cow!

Wiri said, "I was there at Santo when the USS *President Coolidge* sank. This 650-foot troop carrier and former luxury liner hit a 'friendly' mine and then was driven ashore by the captain. Over five thousand men were saved and only two killed. I helped unload goods from the *Coolidge* before it slid back into the lagoon." (Today the *Coolidge* is one of the world's best wreck dive sites.)

Wiri said, "For recreation we saw a cinema every night." There were over forty cinemas on Santo, newly built for the troops and workers. He continued, "I was thirty years old and had never seen a movie. It was 'numbaone'!"

Later I interviewed eighty-six-year-old Chief Jacob Bue. He had been recruited for the war in a similar way and worked on Santo for six months. He said, "After the Solomons campaign, the Americans tried to sell all the remaining gear to the French at a very low price. But the French refused to pay, saying they would get it for free when the Americans left. So the Americans burned it and pushed it into the sea at 'Million Dollar Point'—trucks, jeeps, lumber, munitions, Quonset huts, beds, everything! After my service on Santo I heard about the Point. I sailed the thirty miles to Santo in my dugout canoe, picked up a large load of good hardwood there while the guards 'looked the other way,' and brought it back to Ambae. With that wood I built my house, which is still standing. Thank you, Americans!"

My guide Stephen Vusi took me to his house in the jungles of east Ambae. He told me about the amazing and bizarre pig-killing cult that is prevalent throughout the country but especially active in Ambae (and which was written up in the *Tales* in the chapter on "A Boar's Tooth"). He said, "Circular pig tusks are so important in Vanuatu that there is a tusk on our national flag. Pigs are the key to becoming a chief. On Ambae any man can become a chief if he raises and ceremonially kills enough pigs with circular tusks.

Llewellyn M. Toulmin

Chief Jacob Bue and grandson, east Ambae, Vanuatu

To raise such a pig, he must knock out an upper tooth on either side of the pig's jaw. This allows the lower teeth to curve around in a five-inch circle, over a three-to-five-year period. An Ambae chief who recently died killed a thousand such pigs at the ceremony when he reached the highest, eigthteenth grade of chief."

He continued, "A pig skull with circular tusks is so valuable that it is generally accepted as a down payment on a bride on Ambae. Such skulls are also generally accepted to fully compensate for a major crime, such as murder. If skull compensation is accepted by the victim's family, then the police are not involved and any criminal or civil case is closed. However, Mormons and Seventh Day Adventists won't take skulls, and will only accept cash and mats for brides or crimes. But Catholics and Anglicans are happy to take pig skulls!"

I bought two tusks from Stephen that were classified as "gole ala"—defined as circling around more than 360 degrees in a spiral shape. I paid with a $100 bill. He was a

71

little reluctant to take the bill, holding it up and saying, "I've never seen U.S. money before." You know you're in an isolated area when someone says that!

With Stephen's help, I hired one of the very few power boats on the island for $60 to cruise along the north coast over to west Ambae. The boat was only nineteen feet long, with a small cuddy filled with mosquitoes, but it was the largest and best available. The coast was dramatic and lush, with a few beaches and many cliffs. Dugouts were pulled up onto the huge rocks. Villages and coconut plantations clung to the slopes. The only modern-looking buildings were the few schools and churches. Below the volcano the land was so rugged that the road was reduced to a difficult footpath. We passed the only harbor on the island, which had a rocky ledge blocking most of the entrance, allowing only yachts and small boats to enter.

As we sailed along I wondered about the one remaining literary mystery of Bali Ha'i. Michener in his autobiography said the name itself came from a poor village in the Treasury group of the Solomons. He thought the name romantic and jotted it down, then used it for the island in the novel. Later in the war he saw Moorea and Bora Bora and felt they resembled what Bali Ha'i should be. (In the movie, the simpler name of "Bali Hai," with no apostrophe, was used, so both versions are right.)

I got in touch with Michener before he died, because I felt there was more to his literary creation. In the *Tales* Bali Ha'i is described as a "tiny island" lying hidden in a bay of a much larger island, called Vanicoro. Inland on Vanicoro there is a tribe that practices cannibalism and head shrinking. Usually in the *Tales* Bali Ha'i and Vanicoro are described as east of Espiritu Santo, and once as south.

Llewellyn M. Toulmin

The only harbor on Ambae island, Vanuulu

There are no small islands next to Ambae, which at twenty-one miles long is too large to meet the description of a "tiny" island. So I proposed to Michener that he had fictionally combined Ambae with one of the small islands off the north coast of Malekula. Malekula lies about thirty miles south of Santo, has seven low-lying small islands on its coast, protected by bays, and had an inland tribe of cannibals and headshrinkers, the Big Nambas. I suggested he fictionally combined Ambae's cliffs and hidden women with one of these tiny islands, injected the cannibalism and headhunting of Malekula, renamed Malekula and Ambae/Aoba, added the drama, and thus created the tiny island of Bali Ha'i and its parent Vanicoro. But in correspondence Michener insisted Ambae was the only inspiration. (I still think I'm right!)

The boat arrived in west Ambae, but there was no harbor, just a little indentation in the coast. I jumped into the water, holding my belongings over my head, and waded ashore through the surf and volcanic stones. Once I reached shore, a troop of children immediately appeared. They were fascinated by this visitor, and said that no foreigners had visited their village before. West Ambae appeared even poorer than east Ambae. The dirt road was more rutted, there were fewer utes, and almost all the houses were made entirely of bamboo and thatch, with no corrugated iron.

The children took me a mile along the road to Chief Charly Bani in the village of Nanako. I stayed in his guest house for 1000 Vatu. I explained my World War II interest, and he casually asked, "Would you like to see my crashed war plane?" Smiling at my eagerness, he showed me several parts of what looked like a single engine fighter with a three-bladed prop and told me his story. "I was twelve years old in 1943. The village was getting ready for a wedding when we heard the plane screaming down and crashing into the coconut trees behind my house. All hundred of us ran to the crash site, where the plane was burning. Then we saw the parachute drifting down to the west. The American flier was unhurt, stayed with us one night, and was picked up the next day. He said the engine failed. Later some Australian missionaries came and buried some parts of the plane."

Ambae has quite a bit of malaria, a disease that is one of the worst killers on the planet. So that night in the guest house, a small shack made of coconut leaves, I put in place my seven-layer defense against malarial mosquitoes. This involved:

- Covering all the numerous holes in the walls with duct tape (which I had brought).

Chief Charly Bani, in Nanako, west Ambae, Vanuatu. Under his left hand is the large radial engine of a fighter plane; at his feet is part of the propeller

- Tracking down and killing all the mosquitoes (and spiders) in the hut.

- Spraying the hut with bug bomb (which I had brought).

- Setting alight a number of mosquito coils (which I had brought). These are spirals of a sort of incense that supposedly repel insects. I had used them in Thailand and was never impressed. I had even seen mosquitoes flying back and forth through the smoke, seemingly enjoying the smell. But some people swear by them. So what the hell.

- Putting oily mosquito repellant (which I had brought) all over my entire body.

- Nailing a mosquito net (which I had brought) to the ceiling and draping it over the bed.

- Taking my required dose of anti-malaria medicine (which I had brought).

Of course I was hot, miserable and airless behind my numerous defenses, the smell of all that repellant was awful, and I didn't get any sleep. But I didn't get malaria!

My last experience on Ambae was an unforgettable "taxi" ride to the grass airstrip in west Ambae. I was picked up in the island's most beat up ute. There was no passenger seat in the cab, and no seat or cushions in the truck bed. I stood in the back, holding on to the roll bar. I waved royally to the villagers, who looked at me rather bemusedly. I ducked the tree limbs, bounced over the ruts, and felt the cool wind on my face. I looked at the emerald jungle and the sparkling sea and knew I would never forget the real Bali Ha'i and its sweet, gracious people.

Flying on Vanair on the way home, I passed over the *Søren Larsen*, looked down, and remembered my last hour aboard that beautiful vessel. We were anchored in our final harbor, Luganville on Espiritu Santo. PCs and VCs exchanged addresses, handshakes, and hugs all around. Most of the VCs went ashore in the first Zodiac. I had one more thing to do, though. With PC Ian kindly assisting, I finally managed to climb past the second futtocks to the upper crosstrees. The view from eighty feet up was amazing. We could see for at least thirty miles in all directions. In the distance I could just make out the gorgeous green shore of Ambae. I was reminded of a verse in the song:

> *Bali Ha'i will whisper, on the winds of the sea,*
> *"Here am I, your special island, come to me, come to me.*
> *Your own special hopes, your own special dreams,*
> *Bloom on the hillsides and shine in the streams."*

Looking down at the *Søren Larsen* far below me, and at the real Bali Ha'i in the distance, I knew I had realized my own special dreams.

A typical rocky beach on Ambae

Out of Africa:
History vs. Hollywood

On a safari/cruise to Nairobi, Kenya, my wife and I visited the house of Isak Dinesen (also known as Karen Blixen), author of *Out of Africa*. This book was later made into a hit movie starring Meryl Streep and Robert Redford. Because of the movie and book, the house has become a tourist attraction and a shrine to the literary genius of the writer and is included on most package tours and safaris of Kenya. Visiting the house and learning the true story behind the movie was a major reason we were drawn to visit Africa.

Dinesen's house was modest but beautiful, built of limestone blocks with a wide verandah, tall chimney, and inviting French doors. The house was set in ten acres of lovely grounds in the Nairobi suburbs, on level ground several miles from the foot of the Ngong hills. It was surrounded with large sisal plants, a huge wall of purple-red bougainvillea, and a thirty-foot-high Christmas cactus with a four-foot trunk and dozens of twisting branches. The house was used in many of the exterior shots in the movie, although the movie interior was "borrowed" from another, larger Nairobi house.

At the Dinesen house and through later research we learned about the fascinating true history of Dinesen's lover Denys Finch Hatton. While the Dinesen character was accurately portrayed by Meryl Streep in the movie, and the movie did beautifully convey the milieu of the period, we were surprised to find that great liberties had been taken with Finch Hatton. In the movie, Robert Redford plays the character as an antisocial American loner of unknown back-

Llewellyn M. Toulmin

"I had a home in Africa" -- the Isak Dinesen (Karen Blixen) house on the outskirts of Nairobi, Kenya

ground, who makes his living as a white hunter, learns to fly on his own, and is opposed to fighting in World War I.

In fact the Honourable Denys Finch Hatton was a much more interesting and quirky character. A Briton of impeccably aristocratic birth, he was the third son of the Thirteenth Earl of Winchilsea, whose ancestors included the Chancellor of England under Elizabeth I. He attended Eton and Oxford, and was one of the most popular and social students ever enrolled at either institution. He was a superb debater, boxer, and cricketer, who declaimed poetry by Whitman and Shakespeare and loved to sing sixteenth-century madrigals. He went to Kenya because England was too small for his large Elizabethan personality. While he did lead safaris as a white hunter, he made most of his living from flax farming and from running a trading hut and rural post office built out of wattle, daub, and mud.

Finch Hatton served in the British Army as a captain in World War I in Kenya and Mesopotamia and learned to fly in the Royal Flying Corps. He did not learn to fly on his own in a plane in Africa, as shown in the movie. He was decorated with the prestigious Military Cross for gallantly saving the life of his commanding general during a German ambush. He was certainly not opposed to World War I. In civilian life he always wore odd hats—usually a blue bowler—pushed back on his prematurely balding head. He admired the Maasai's ability to stand for hours on one leg like a flamingo, concluded that they could do this because of their squared-off toes, and had a huge pair of shoes tailor-made to square off his own toes, so he too could stand like a Maasai!

Despite his quirkiness, Finch Hatton had tremendous magnetism and physical attractiveness and was admired by all his peers. He was pursued by most of the women he met, including Dinesen and the world-famous aviatrix Beryl Markham. He had great organizational skills, served as white hunter in Kenya for the Prince of Wales (later King Edward VIII), and twice saved the Prince's life from charging rhino and bull elephant. He was called by the Prince in his private diaries "the most efficient man in the world." Finch Hatton was elusive and never married, but he inspired Isak Dinesen to flower as a writer and was the great love of her life. His death at forty-four in a tragic plane accident, as accurately shown in the movie, was a great loss to Kenya and England.

Isak Dinesen returned to her native Denmark and never again saw Africa. On two occasions she almost received the Nobel Prize for literature, only being aced out by Ernest Hemingway and Albert Camus. She wrote her wonderful book from memory, and the world is greater place for it. Could the movie have done the same, if Robert Redford had tried to play Finch Hatton instead of Robert Redford? We'll never know.

Llewellyn M. Toulmin

"Oh Dear"
The Strange Life of HMS *Bounty* Descendants on Pitcairn Island

"Land ho! Pitcairn island dead ahead." Misty and shimmering, a tiny speck of land appeared beneath a cloud on the South Pacific horizon. I sang out the cry I had been waiting years to say.

Most English-speaking peoples around the world know the famous tale of HMS *Bounty* and Pitcairn—how Captain William Bligh and his mate and friend Fletcher Christian set out from England in 1787 to bring back breadfruit from Tahiti, how Christian led a mutiny against Bligh and set him and eighteen crewmen adrift in the ship's longboat, how Bligh sailed back 3500 miles to civilization against all odds, and how Christian and the *Bounty* sailed to lonely Pitcairn in the South Pacific to hide from the wrath of the Royal Navy.

But many people don't know that forty-eight people still live on isolated Pitcairn, almost all of them descendants of the mutineers. I had read *Mutiny on the Bounty* by Nordoff and Hall as a child, had seen the three famous movie versions of the story, and wanted to get a glimpse into the islanders' strange and romantic life and history.

I reached Pitcairn aboard the MV *Discovery* on a voyage from Chile to New Zealand called "In the Wake of the *Bounty*." This graceful cruising vessel was formerly the famous *Island Princess*, and was used as a backup vessel in filming the popular 1970/80s *Love Boat* TV series. She has been thoroughly refurbished and modernized and now carries up to 650 passengers in luxury and comfort to exotic destinations in every corner of the world. It is not possible to fly to tiny Pitcairn, since there is no airstrip. There is also no scheduled ship service, so a cruise ship or freighter is the only option.

It took us three days cruising at seventeen knots to reach Pitcairn from Easter Island, our previous stop. Pitcairn is one of the most isolated communities on earth, 1,283 miles from Easter Island, 1,445 miles from Tahiti, and 3,314 miles from New Zealand.

As we approached the island, we were amazed at its tiny size. Only two and a half miles long and one and a half miles wide, most of the island is very rugged, with steep cliffs on all sides and no beaches or harbor. Three large red scars on the side of the island showed that recent landslides caused by heavy rains were gradually making the tiny island even tinier.

Discovery anchored in the open roadstead called Bounty Bay and sent ashore a Zodiac with a landing party consisting of a ship's officer and a rating, along with the ship's doctor. Soon the captain made an announcement that the surf behind the tiny protective mole on shore was so high that the Zodiac could not land, even though there was an islander on shore who needed the doctor's attention for a possible broken leg. The only alternative was to have the islanders, including the injured local, put out in their specially designed longboat.

After a few minutes, we saw a very large motorized aluminum longboat with a huge six-foot freeboard come out from behind the small mole. The longboat crashed through the surf and made it out to *Discovery*, where thirty-five islanders (including the injured man) jumped from the bucking longboat into the pilot's doorway on the side of our ship.

The thirty-five islanders—almost the entire population—set up an impromptu market in the ship's dining room and began selling beautiful carved wooden sharks, plates, longboats, and replicas of the *Bounty*. They were very friendly and charming. Chatting with them we learned some of the little-known history of the island after the *Bounty* arrived.

The famous mutiny on board HMS *Bounty* took place on April 28, 1789, about a thousand miles west of Tahiti. Fletcher Christian put Captain Bligh and eighteen loyalists into the tiny, 23-foot-long ship's launch and sent them off, presumably to their deaths. Then Christian and the mutineers turned back to Tahiti, their island paradise. But they knew they couldn't stay, since the Royal Navy would probably soon send vessels to scour the seas for the mutineers. Christian, eight mutineers, twelve Tahitian women, an infant, and six Tahitian men set sail in *Bounty* to find a hiding place. After months of searching they found Pitcairn. The island was well watered, had lots of fruit and good soil, and had no harbor and no residents. Even though it had been discovered and named after a midshipman aboard HMS *Swallow* in 1767, it was mislocated on all Royal Navy charts, over 150 miles from its true position. It was the perfect hiding place to create a little paradise.

Christian and his crew burned and sank the *Bounty*, knowing they would never see England or Tahiti again. But Christian, only twenty-six years old, then made a fatal blunder. He carved the island into nine pieces for the nine Englishmen, giving no land to the Tahitian men or women. This made them into virtual slaves. Very soon the Tahitian men hatched a mutiny of their own, and they planned to kill all the English sailors. But the plot was betrayed to Christian by his Tahitian wife Maimiti ("Mainmast"). Christian and the other sailors struck first and killed several Tahitian men. Other Tahitian men hid in caves and soon retaliated, killing Fletcher Christian and several other Englishmen.

The women, more sensible than the men, tried to leave the island, which had turned from a paradise into a hell on earth. They tore down a house and tried to build a barge to sail away. The men prevented this, so the women hatched another mutiny, to try to kill the Englishmen. This plot, too, was betrayed, and the women were forced into slavery.

One islander unfortunately discovered how to distill liquor from a local plant, resulting in a number of deaths from drink, as the islanders fell off the steep cliffs surrounding the island. Almost every cliff on the island is named for such an event: Where Dick Fell, Where Freddy Fall, Tom Off, McCoy's Drop, Break'um Hip, and the mysterious but ominous "Oh Dear." This strange name was an appropriate label for the whole island at the time.

After ten years of murder, drink, and disease, there was only one English mutineer left, John Adams. All the Tahitian men were dead, and only ten women and two children remained. Adams went to a cave, meditated, and recalled his Christian upbringing. He claimed he saw a vision of an angel and vowed to never drink again. He called the islanders together, and announced that henceforth they would all be Christians and live peacefully. He lived up to his intention.

In 1808 the island was rediscovered by the *Topaz* of Massachusetts, and word finally emerged of the fate of the *Bounty*. Over the next two centuries many islanders were relocated to Norfolk Island and New Zealand, so that there are now about five thousand Pitcairn descendants worldwide. But a number could not stay away from their isolated home, which exerts a strange pull on many people from around the world.

At the market on board *Discovery* I met the piratical-looking Paul Warren, who described some of the odd Rhode Island connections that Pitcairn has. "I am a descendant of an American whaler, Samuel Warren of Rhode Island, who came to Pitcairn after the mutiny, and of Fletcher Christian," he said. "I lived in New Zealand for several years but didn't like the hustle and bustle, so I've come home."

Paul Warren of Pitcairn Island, descendant of Fletcher Christian, a Rhode Island whaler, and royalty. Two of his necklaces include nails from HMS Bounty.

The Pitcairn Islands Study Center at Pacific Union College in California confirmed Paul's story. Samuel Warren was a whaler from Providence, Rhode Island, who jumped ship at Norfolk Island (north of New Zealand) and met and married Agnes Christian, a descendant of Fletcher Christian. In 1864 the new couple and a number of former Pitcairners returned to Pitcairn aboard the *St. Kilda*. Today the Rhode Island Warren clan includes twenty of the forty-four natives on the island, including one of the island councilors, the head of the Department of Conservation, the keeper of the John Adams gravesite, and the teacher of island culture at the grammar school.

(Later I did some preliminary research on Samuel Warren and found that he was possibly a descendant of a *Mayflower* passenger. Thus there is an odd link between two of the most famous ships in maritime history. And perhaps many of the Pitcairn islanders could qualify for membership in the prestigious society of *Mayflower* descendants. Genealogists have established that Fletcher Christian is of royal descent, as are all the current native islanders, including all the Warrens, through the Christian line.)

On board *Discovery*, after the market, Jenny Lock of the grandly titled Her Majesty's Government Foreign and Commonwealth Office (HMG FCO), the British representative on the island, gave a talk about life on Pitcairn. "Life here is isolated but interesting," she said. "There is no doctor or dentist, no beaches and no high school. Children must go away to New Zealand for high school. Most children are born in New Zealand, but recently we had the first birth on the island in seventeen years, Emily Rose Christian, who was born in October 2003. There are now six children on the island."

"Transport consists of walking or four-wheeled all-terrain vehicles, or our single home-made car, a 'Samba,'" said Lock. "Getting up the steep 'Hill of Difficulty' from the boathouse to the small 'capital' of Adamstown is the trickiest part of island transport, especially when the rain has made the dirt road slick with mud. We are seeking U.K. and European Union funding to build a better pier, protective mole, and harbor and also to build roads and an airstrip. We have had studies done by experts who built airfields in rugged Papua New Guinea, and they say it is feasible."

"There is no TV reception on the island, but for amusement there are videos, intermittent emails, and ham radio. All the islanders speak English but also their own language, which is a mixture of Tahitian and eighteenth-century English. We get our mail via New Zealand; it usually takes eight weeks to get an international 'air mail' letter!"

"Most of the islanders are Seventh Day Adventists, and so there is no drinking, dancing, or eating pork," reported Lock. "A number of islanders are postal workers, since selling stamps to collectors around the world is a big source of income. Others have paid jobs as engineers or electricians, while everyone grows vegetables and some are beekeepers. There is no taxation, but rather able-bodied islanders are expected to report for public work when needed. Electricity is available nine hours each day. All drinking water comes from rainwater. There is one dog, many cats, and many wild goats."

"There are only four last names among native islanders, and virtually everyone is related to everyone else," said Lock. "It is a little claustrophobic, since there are so few people, everyone knows everyone, and the island is so small. For any of you outsiders who think that this could be your island paradise, you can apply to emigrate to the island. If you have usable skills and can pass a lengthy trial period, you may be accepted as a permanent resident. There are not enough able-bodied male islanders now—only about nine—and medical skills are very much needed. The pastor's wife is a registered nurse, but lack of a full-time doctor and lack of means to evacuate ill persons is a major concern."

After the talk, we reluctantly said goodbye to our new friends. They jumped back aboard their longboat. Thankfully, the islander who was thought to have a serious injury had been x-rayed and examined in *Discovery*'s mini-hospital, and was found to have a strain, not a break, in his leg.

The longboat sailed toward the island in the sunset. We thought for a long time afterwards about the Pitcairn "Goodbye Song" that we had just learned from the islanders, with its last plaintive line, "We part, but hope to meet again—goodbye, goodbye, goodbye."

The entire population of Pitcairn, all in one longboat, waves goodbye. Paul Warren is on the foredeck.

Llewellyn M. Toulmin

Paradise Lost: Sex Verdicts Wrack Lonely Pitcairn

Pitcairn: island paradise or hell on earth? Recently, three New Zealand judges apparently took the latter view as they sentenced six of Pitcairn Island's few male inhabitants to two to six years in prison for numerous rapes and assaults that took place over a forty-year period, on the last remnant of the British empire in the South Pacific.

I visited the island in May of 2004, and found the islanders pleasant, cheerful, and fascinating, but bitter against what they saw as the heavy-handed and irrational British system of justice. Sentences were handed down in November 2004 to the following men, who made up almost half the adult male population:

- Steve Christian, mayor of the island, a direct descendant of Fletcher Christian, the leader of the mutineers. The fifty-three-year-old mayor was sentenced to three years in prison for five rapes against women and girls as young as twelve.

- His son, Randy Christian, twenty-eight, island chairman and engineer, convicted on four rapes and five indecent assaults, received six years in prison.

- Dennis Christian, forty-nine, the island postmaster, received community service after pleading guilty to one indecent assault and two sexual assaults.

- Len Brown, seventy-eight, was convicted of two rapes and was sentenced to two years in jail, while his son Dave Brown was convicted of nine indecent assaults and was sentenced to community service.

- Terry Young, forty-two, tractor driver, convicted of one rape and six indecent assaults, received five years in prison.

Only one of the charged men, the island's magistrate Jay Warren, was cleared of the charges against him. Six more Pitcairn men, now residents of Australia and New Zealand, face trial over similar sex charges.

The chief judge, Charles Blackie, acknowledged that the sentences were relatively light, but stated that the future of the island could be threatened by harsh sentences. He said the "sentences were tailored to Pitcairn" and "took into account factors unique to the island, such as its isolation, permanent population of less than fifty, and dependence on the manpower of its able-bodied citizens." Indeed, many residents and supporters around the world fear that the trial and the sentences may doom the island. With no airstrip and no harbor, the island depends for its entire existence on the ability of its few healthy adult men to launch a heavy fifty-foot aluminum longboat to go out to ships to pick up supplies and sell goods. If those men are in prison, the fragile island economy and society may collapse.

Some observers have stated that because of this concern, many of the men sentenced to prison may serve their terms on the island, and may be let out of jail when needed for longboat duty.

The bow of MV Discovery seems to dwarf tiny Pitcairn

The trial was one of the strangest in British history. The British delegated jurisdiction to New Zealand, despite the fact that the island is a British colony. All elements for the trial had to be imported to Pitcairn at huge expense to the New Zealand taxpayers, including judges, prosecutors, defense attorneys, police, media mavens, court reporters, and their gear and food. Most of these people and their gear had to be landed via the island longboat, usually manned by the accused! The island's population almost doubled in size. The island's community center, normally a place for sing-alongs and birthday parties, was converted into a makeshift courtroom. The accused men were offered $5 per hour to build their own jail, which has barred windows and a fifteen-foot-high wire fence. All the accused agreed to build their own future prison, since the wages were good by island standards.

None of the accusing women attended the trial in person, and all testified via satellite link from Auckland, New Zealand. Women residents of the island complained about this, generally taking the side of the accused men. Amazingly, virtually none of the islanders attended the trial unless compelled to by the court. The island is literally so insular, and it is so important not to offend the few other islanders, that almost all the residents tried to ignore the allegations and the hoopla of the huge event taking place just yards from their homes.

During the trial, prosecutors painted a picture of a male-dominated society in which underage sex and assaults on children were common. Yet defenders countered with a description of an island culture based on relaxed Tahitian mores about sex, where there was little to do except work and make love, and where the absence of potential partners of similar age meant that unusual age pairings were the norm.

The sex trial was just the latest in a series of disasters that have plagued the island since the mutiny. The worst disaster was the series of battles, mutinies, and drunken brawls among the *Bounty* mutineers that left only one alive by 1808, just eighteen years after the island was settled.

For a while the island was peaceful, but in 1832 a puritanical busybody named Joshua Hill landed, claiming to have been sent by the British government. He made himself President of the "commonwealth" of Pitcairn, expelled islanders he disliked, introduced severe punishments for minor misdeeds, and ruled in a demented fashion for six years. Finally he was removed by a British warship, whose captain confirmed that Hill had no authority from the British government.

On at least two occasions large groups of islanders have been persuaded or forced to leave the island and emigrate to Norfolk Island and New Zealand. As a result there are about six thousand people around the world who are Pitcairn descendants. But often these emigrants have been unhappy, and many have returned to Pitcairn, seeking what they feel is their island paradise.

The final twist in the Pitcairn story may be the island's strange future. Defense lawyers argued that the entire trial was illegal, because the mutiny on and burning of the *Bounty* was a declaration of independence from British authority by the Pitcairn islanders. Thus the British and New Zealand police had no authority to even trespass on, much less investigate the island. Early in the trial judges rejected these arguments, but then later reconsidered, and will hear final arguments in 2005. In the unlikely event that this reasoning is accepted, the convicted men will be free. Amazingly, troubled Pitcairn could become the latest and smallest independent country on earth!

The Real Story of the Bridge on the River Kwai

The bridge over the River Kwai lay ahead, ominous and still, silhouetted against the stars. A sentry in Japanese uniform paced across the bridge, his bayonet gleaming in the moonlight. Our bamboo raft drifted closer to the bridge, when suddenly the center span exploded with a burst of light, rockets and confusion. Machine guns fired and explosions roared.

Could World War II have broken out again in this peaceful part of Thailand? Or was this a repeat filming of the famous movie *Bridge on the River Kwai*? No, this was a very realistic sound, light, and fireworks re-creation of the true history of the infamous bridge—a history that differs significantly from the Hollywood version.

Like many travelers in Thailand, I was drawn to the River Kwai by the famous movie epic and the original Pierre Boulle novel. In the 1957 movie classic starring William Holden and Alec Guinness, a single wooden bridge over the Kwai is built during World War II by a camp of British prisoners of war (POWs) and is then destroyed by an American escapee from the camp and a team of British commandos.

In reality the bridge was part of a much larger effort—a 250-mile-long railway built in 1942–43 to create a strategic land route from Bangkok to Burma. Having just conquered Burma, the Japanese feared that the Allies might threaten the long sea supply route that stretched from Bangkok south around Malaya and Singapore to Rangoon, Burma. They hoped this proposed new land route would be much less vulnerable to Allied attacks.

The Japanese set up forty-four camps along the projected railway route, and forced 61,000 British, Australian, Dutch and a few American POWs to begin construction in September 1942. Over the critical River Kwai, one of the major obstacles on the route, these men built *two* bridges, one of wood and one of steel and concrete.

Further up in the rugged hills, where the railway followed another branch of the Kwai, the prisoners had to build dozens of smaller bridges and numerous trestles and blast out many deep cuttings.

Japanese engineers had estimated that the railway would take five years to build. Instead it was finished in sixteen months, by December 1943. The cost in lives was enormous. Of the 61,000 POWs, about 12,000 to 16,000 died of starvation, maltreatment, disease and execution. Just as tragic was the fate of the 200,000 Thai and Burmese laborers who were recruited for the project and told they would be well paid. Unpaid, starved, beaten, and sick, almost half the native workers died. Conditions were so bad that the project was called "The Railway of Death."

Unlike in the movie, no Allied prisoners escaped and returned to blow up the bridges. That honor went to the U.S. Army Air Force and the Royal Air Force, which flew hazardous bombing missions in 1944 and 1945 from over a thousand miles away that knocked out both bridges. Partly as a result, the Japanese Army in Burma, the largest Japanese force outside of Japan and China, was defeated.

Pierre Boulle, who wrote the original novel, did not work on the bridge or the railway. He served as an intelligence officer in the China/Burma/India theater and was eventually captured in Vietnam in a hare-brained scheme to float explosives down river to Hanoi. His spell in captivity was a rather cushy house arrest, and he escaped by simply walking away. No such easy fate awaited the real laborers on the Railway of Death.

Today, where the Railway crosses the Kwai, only the concrete and steel bridge remains. Reconstructed after the war, it now carries trainloads of sightseers from Bangkok across the river, up into the dramatic hills and gorges beyond, to the end of the line toward Three Pagodas Pass and the closed Burmese border.

The morning after the dramatic sound-and-light show, I sat on the high bluff overlooking the bridge, and tried to imagine the events of more than fifty-five years ago. It was virtually impossible. The river flowed quickly but quietly, creating a little wake when it rippled around the bridge abutments. Children walked across the bridge on loose boards laid on the ties, and looked down between their toes at the river forty feet below. In the distance beautiful brown hills marched away toward Burma and the Bay of Bengal.

Peace had finally come to the Bridge on the River Kwai.

The bridge over the River Kwai, in eastern Thailand

Section 4

Boats, Ships, and the Sea

Sailing to Robinson Crusoe Island: "The Most Romantic Island of All"?

Richard Henry Dana, in his classic tale *Two Years Before the Mast,* describes Robinson Crusoe Island in the South Pacific as "the most romantic spot of earth my eyes had ever seen." Visiting the island on a cruise aboard MV *Discovery* made me think that perhaps Dana was right.

Robinson Crusoe Island was originally known as "Mas a Tierra" (closer to land) in the Juan Fernandez group, named after the Spanish seaman who discovered the islands in 1574. The island gained its fame from the Daniel Defoe novel *Robinson Crusoe,* first published in 1720 and never out of print since. Defoe had learned the tale of Alexander Selkirk, a Scottish seaman who was voluntarily marooned on Mas a Tierra from 1704 to 1709, and who survived alone on the island. Defoe was fascinated by the tale, researched it, and changed the true story into the famous novel. In the novel, Robinson Crusoe is shipwrecked on an island in the southeast Caribbean near Trinidad, survives cannibal raids, meets his faithful companion Man Friday, and is rescued after an improbable twenty-eight years. The real story and the real man are actually even more interesting.

Alexander Selkirk was born in Fife, Scotland in 1676, the seventh son of a shoemaker. He was unruly as a child and was disciplined in church for having struck his brother, mother, and father. He ran away to sea at age seventeen aboard the *Cinque Ports,* a British privateer fighting in the War of Spanish Succession. The vessel sailed around Cape Horn in search of Spanish treasure. But by the time the ship reached Mas a Tierra, 416 miles west of Chile, Selkirk was sick of the captain and afraid that the vessel was unseaworthy due to toredo worms. So he asked to be left ashore, and the captain readily agreed. At the last minute Selkirk changed his mind and begged to be taken back aboard, but the captain smugly refused. Selkirk had the last laugh, however, for the *Cinque Ports* later sank as he had predicted, although her annoying captain escaped.

To survive, Selkirk had only a gun, knife, hatchet, navigation books, a Bible, and three days' rations. This was actually less gear than the fictional Robinson Crusoe, who was able to salvage much more from his wrecked ship. But Selkirk was very resourceful, and he built a hut, found parsley, watercress, and heart of palm to eat, and made fire by rubbing two sticks together. He became dejected but turned to his Bible, found religion, and "life became one continual feast." He got very fit and chased down and captured goats on steep rocky hillsides for sport and food. Once he fell off a cliff and was knocked unconscious for three days. He raised cats to fend off the rats that gnawed his feet at night. He never met any cannibals, but he did hide in a tree to escape Spanish sailors who came ashore and tried to capture him.

In February 1709, after more than four years on the island, Selkirk was rescued by Woodes Rogers and William Dampier, the famous English pirates, in their vessel the *Duke*. They describe Selkirk as a hairy creature clad in stinking goatskins, who could hardly speak English any more from lack of use. Despite his strange appearance, Rogers and Dampier recognized Selkirk's navigational skills and local knowledge, and offered him a post as mate. He readily accepted, and together they raided the port of Guayaquil (in what is now Ecuador), capturing nineteen vessels including a Manila galleon. In 1711 they returned to England, selling their spoils for 147,000 pounds, of which Selkirk got 800, a princely sum.

Despite his riches, Selkirk was not very happy. He moved into a cave near his mother's house in Scotland, bewailed the trappings of "civilization," and eventually shipped out again aboard HMS *Enterprise*. He died of a mosquito borne disease in 1721, and at the probate court hearing two women appeared, each producing papers proving that she was his wife and entitled to his remaining wealth. Apparently Selkirk took the phrase "a girl in every port" a little too literally.

I reached Robinson Crusoe Island aboard the soft adventure vessel MV *Discovery*. This graceful vessel was formerly the famous *Island Princess*, used as a backup vessel in filming the popular 1970s–80s *Love Boat* TV series. She has been thoroughly refurbished and modernized and now carries up to 650 passengers in luxury to exotic destinations in every corner of the world. Although it is possible to fly to Robinson Crusoe Island from Chile, the flight is a bit hairy, with a short landing strip at the base of a cliff, followed by a two-hour boat ride or a six-hour hike (no taxis—no road!) to the only town. A comfortable cruise ship is a much more attractive approach.

MV Discovery anchored at Robinson Crusoe Island

Going ashore, I was struck by the beauty of the steep cliffs and the tiny town of San Juan Bautista. From the ship's tender I could see much of the island's habitable area. The entire island is only about fifteen by sixteen miles, but it is so steep that it is like a piece of crumpled paper resting on the sea. The island is green, with more trees than I expected, mostly majestic Norfolk pines and eucalyptus. I stepped ashore at the town dock and was met—of course—by Robinson Crusoe! Clad in goatskins, with a baby goat beside him, he looked very authentic.

"Robinson Crusoe" and his goat

I wandered up the town's wide main street, made of dirt and gravel. A town square contained a statue of the wonderfully named Bernardo O'Higgins, one of the founders of Chile. Chile still governs the island group, and Chilean president Eduardo Frei Montalva renamed the two main islands Robinson Crusoe and Alexander Selkirk in 1966, hoping to draw in tourists.

Next I bought the obligatory T-shirt, and went in to the small post office to buy some local stamps. The postman

101

kindly offered to stamp my passport, but the ship's purser was holding it. So I came up with a scheme whereby the postman stamped a blank piece of paper with the symbol of the island and the legend "Isla Robinson Crusoe." Later I stapled the paper into my passport, proof I had visited one of the world's most remote spots.

A tour guide took me and some of the other *Discovery* passengers on a tour of the town. We asked why the town seemed partly deserted and were told that a three-day rodeo on the airstrip side of the island had attracted many of the islanders. The guide gave us some of the facts about the island group today: 500 inhabitants, only ten cars, only two miles of roads, one medical clinic, one dentist, a few shops, and 3,200-foot maximum elevation. There is a grammar school, but at age thirteen children must go to the mainland for education.

We climbed up the hill overlooking the picturesque town to Fort Santa Barbara, a Spanish fortress built of rock, with fifteen rusting cannon pointed out to sea. In the harbor below we could see numerous small fishing boats, which harvest large crayfish, the island's main export. Selkirk and his contemporaries caught crayfish up to four feet long and made "jelly" out of them. Today's crayfish are typically less than half that size.

Near the fort we inspected a series of mysterious caves cut into the cliff. Our guide said that Selkirk did not live in these caves, that these were possibly dug out by prisoners when the island was later used for a time as a prison, but no one knows for sure. We walked along the rocky beach in front of the town and were impressed with the flower gardens and attractive chalet-style cottages. Many of these cottages are available for rental to long-term visitors at reasonable rates. Other passengers hiked up towards El Mirador (1,853 feet above sea level) for spectacular views, and some walked along the beach to the right of the town, where they found playful fur seals lounging on the rocks.

We ended our tour with a delicious local drink, a pisco sour, at our tour guide's house. Like most houses, it was right above the beach. As we sat and enjoyed the view, a pair of fur seals swam by and seemed to wave their flippers at us. We smiled and waved back. A fitting end to a visit to one of the most storied and romantic spots on earth.

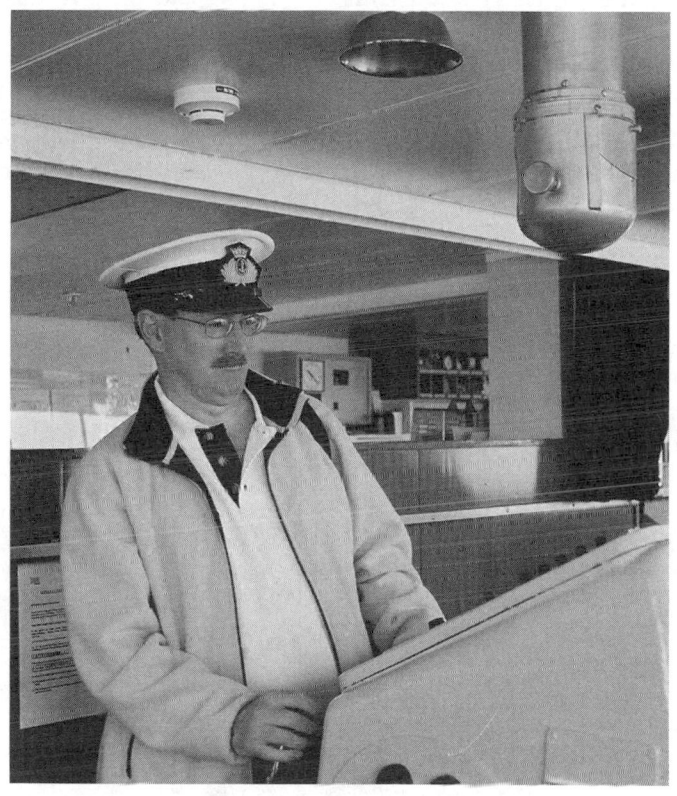

"Admiral" Toulmin steers the MV Discovery. Watch out for that iceberg!

Life of a Lady Leg-rower

At Inle Lake, 2,900 feet above sea level in central Myanmar (Burma), I was taking a fast motorboat through the marshes when I spotted one of the famous Inle leg-rowers. She was propelling her narrow wooden boat down the channel, standing erect, balancing on her bare left foot, rowing with her right leg, ankle, and hand, nonchalantly holding her baby in her free left hand. When the wake of my motorboat rocked her narrow boat, she stayed perfectly upright on her left foot and kept on leg-rowing with her right.

Wein Shwe and family, Lake Inle, Burma. Note her leg.

Knowing this is the only place on earth where leg-rowing is done, I stopped to find out more about her amazing abilities. Wein Shwe ("Fair Gold") is a thirty-year-old woman from a small village at the western edge of the fourteen-mile-long lake. She spoke in Myanma in an Intha ("Sons of the Lake") accent. Through my interpreter/guide, she answered my questions:

Toulmin: How did you learn to leg-row?

Shwe: I learned by watching my parents. They were both leg-rowers. So were my grandparents. I didn't know my great grandparents, but I think they and all my ancestors were leg-rowers.

Toulmin: Why do you leg-row?

Shwe: Leg-rowing is twice as fast as paddling or hand rowing. It is not as tiring as paddling to leg-row along our long lake. I stand up while I leg-row, so I can better see obstacles and weed patches ahead. My husband can leg-row with one hand and leg, and fish with the other.

Toulmin: Can you show me how you leg-row?

Shwe: Yes.

Toulmin: So I see you are sculling, not exactly rowing, in a figure-eight pattern. The oar is held straight up and down, and is braced by your right hip. Your right leg and ankle are wrapped around the oar, and your right heel is hooked around the shaft of the oar, just above the top of the blade. I see your right leg is well outside the boat, while you are balanced on your left foot. Most of the blade of the oar is down in the water and your right foot is about twenty centimeters above the water. You are holding the top of the oar with your right hand. It looks like you are rapidly twisting the top of the oar with your right wrist to create the sculling motion. And your right forearm is held parallel to the water, while your right upper arm is held close to your

105

body. All very complicated! Do you ever use your left hand and ankle?

Shwe: All the Intha use their right hands and legs.

Toulmin: Do the Intha people ever get back or leg problems?

Shwe: No, we are all very healthy.

Toulmin: How do you go faster?

Shwe: I put my leg farther outside the boat, and push back—or row—with my leg while I scull. Since my leg is stronger than my arm, it makes sense to use my leg to get as much power as possible.

Toulmin: Have you ever entered a leg-rowing race?

Shwe: No. My husband leg-rows faster than me but he hasn't raced either. But my seven-year-old son is very precocious and already knows how to leg-row. Maybe one day he will enter a race and win a trophy and a big 50,000-kyat [US $71] prize. Then he can earn merit by giving away most of the money to poor people.

Toulmin: When are the races?

Shwe: Every September and October we have two big Buddhist festivals. That is when the best races are held.

Toulmin: Why do you want to leg-row so fast?

Shwe: I am very busy with my farm and family. Sometimes I might paddle sitting down if I want to talk with a friend in another boat at sunset. But I almost always leg-row. All the Intha people leg-row—unless they want to go slow.

Toulmin: Tell me about your farm.

Shwe: My husband and I have a farm on twenty floating islands. Each island is about ten meters long, one meter wide, and half a meter thick. The islands are made of dried lake weed. They are staked to the shallow lake bottom with bamboos. We grow tomatoes on all our islands.

Toulmin: Have you ever lost an island?

Shwe: Yes, in the rainy season three years ago one of our islands got waterlogged and sank. We tried to recover it but it was too heavy. We lost a lot of money. Now we put more bamboos on the underside of each island to help it float.

Toulmin: How much does an island cost?

Shwe: About 100,000 kyats ["chats"—about US $143] for a good, fertile one. A poor one is 40,000 kyats [$57]. It often takes twenty years to build up a good one with nice, decomposed lake weed. It is now illegal to build new islands, so the price of existing islands is going up.

Toulmin: Can you make money growing tomatoes?

Shwe: Yes, in a good month we can make 100,000 kyats [$143]. In a bad month, 30,000 kyats [$43]. But we have lots of expenses. We leg-row our tomatoes to a broker once or twice a week. [This gross income is actually very good in a country where the average hotel clerk or mid-level civil servant makes just 3,000 kyats ($4.29) per month (*sic!*).]

[At this point the baby girl began crying, and Shwe lifted her blouse and unselfconsciously began nursing her baby.]

Toulmin: Tell me about your family.

Shwe: I have three children: this four-month-old baby girl, Sam Phyo ("Clear Abundant"); the five-year-old boy there at the other end of my boat; and my seven-year-old boy at home. We have a stilt house made of thatch surrounded by our floating islands.

Toulmin: Is your boat typical of the Intha?

Shwe: Every family in our village and on the lake has a boat like this, since all the houses are built on stilts over the water. My boat is about five meters long, one meter wide, and made of teak. It has a small platform at either end to leg-row from. We use the bow platform for fishing or spotting weeds, and the stern platform for ordinary leg-rowing. The boat only lasts about three to four years. It costs 35,000 kyats [$50] to replace.

Toulmin: Is that a special paddle you use?

Shwe: Not really. It is about two meters long, made of wood, with a round shaft and straight wooden blade at the end. The blade is about seventy centimeters long and ten centimeters wide. It looks like an oar that is used in traditional rowing boats.

Toulmin: What do you like most about leg-rowing?

Shwe: Fast rowing is the best. And I love being out on our beautiful lake.

Toulmin: Have you ever fallen in the lake while leg-rowing?

Shwe: No, I never did, even while learning.

Toulmin: Do you think I could learn to leg-row and live like you?

Shwe (*smiling*): I think that, with practice, you could learn to fall in.

A fisherman on Lake Inle shows a strong leg rowing motion

Bill Pinkney:
The *Amistad* Captain's Incredible Journey

Captain Bill Pinkney of the *Amistad* is a human dynamo. He has fit at least nine lives into his sixty-seven years, and he's working on several more.

In his current life he is the captain of the Freedom Schooner *Amistad*, the reconstruction of the famous ship that was the focus of the first U.S. human rights case and the subject of a Stephen Spielberg movie. "Our mission is to bring a message of hope, history, and racial harmony to ports around the U.S., using the *Amistad* and its amazing story as a catalyst," said Pinkney. "We work with local organizations to try to achieve tangible results in racial reconciliation and discussions about human freedom. We use the story of the *Amistad* captives—the first civil and human rights case argued in America—to spark the dialogue."

Captain Pinkney said, "*Amistad* represents the only time in the history of slavery in the Americas that prospective slaves successfully fought to go back home to Africa. As such, the ship represents a triumph of the natural human desire we all have, to live our lives free from interference or restraint."

Llewellyn M. Toulmin

Captain Bill Pinkney gestures towards the pictures of the slaves held on the original Amistad

Captain Pinkney's own life exemplifies triumphant freedom and energy. He was born in Chicago and was always interested in adventure and sailing. He served eight years in the U.S. Navy and had what he describes as a "checkered career as a high-tech mechanic, head of an electrical union, cosmetics salesman, x-ray technician, limbo dancer, stockbroker, and head of PR for a social services agency."

At age fifty-five he determined to fulfill his childhood dream of sailing around the world. "But first I had to raise the money—the sailing was easy compared to that," he says. Pinkney became the only African American to sail solo around the world via Cape Horn, and only the fourth American to achieve this feat. "In my circumnavigation I sailed a forty-seven-foot fiberglass cutter. I dodged through two hurricanes and survived two knockdowns. The main things I learned were that people are willing to help, if you ask, and that even the worst adversity does end eventually. It's your job to hold on until it's over."

Over thirty thousand children followed the circumnavigation by radio, and the voyage was written up as an inspirational first grade reading text, *Captain Bill Pinkney's Journey*, that is used in five thousand schools.

Pinkney followed up his circumnavigation with a voyage to Africa and South America to retrace the "middle passage" slave importation route. This voyage became an award-winning PBS documentary, *The Incredible Voyage of Bill Pinkney*, which aired in April 2000.

Along the way Bill picked up his Master Mariner's certificate, sailed over fifty thousand miles, and crossed the Atlantic under sail three times. He travels frenetically and has logged hundreds of thousands of air miles, publicizing *Amistad* and his other projects.

Captain Pinkney got involved with *Amistad* "when it was just a concept and a pile of logs." He was one of four key full-time staff who got the project started, and he states proudly, "I was the person who gave the order to lay the keel."

Building the ship was a massive effort, involving "over sixty thousand man-hours of labor, about a third of which were donated," according to Pinkney. "The donated equipment was amazing, and included the Caterpillar engines, beautiful top-of-the-line bronze and brass fittings, all the plumbing, and all the Raytheon navigational gear."

Christopher Cloud, President and CEO of *Amistad* America, Inc., confirms Captain Pinkney's important role in the organization. "Bill was key in designing and constructing the vessel. It was always crystal-clear that he would become the ship's first captain. His sailing and leadership skills, his speaking ability, and his capacity to deal with sensitive issues are unmatched. When he was away on his Middle Passage voyage I prayed every night that he would return safely to *Amistad*. Bill does not have a formal education. He is self-taught, although you would never guess it. *Commitment* was the name of the vessel in which he sailed solo around the world—that describes him perfectly."

Able Seaman John Kamara from Sierra Leone, a descendant of an original *La Amistad* captive who is now crewing on the recreated *Amistad*, said that "Captain Pinkney is very good at spreading our message of peace, love, and unity. We need more ambassadors of peace like him in America, Sierra Leone, and around the world."

Running the ship has been an inspirational experience for Captain Pinkney. "We have evolved into a major organization, with an incredibly talented crew of twelve, a professional home office staff, and an annual operating budget of about a million dollars." But Pinkney's main inspiration comes from the children who come to see *Amistad*. "Just a few months ago a cherubic first-grader stunned me with the simple question, 'How do you make a man a slave?' I was dumbfounded at first, but I finally came up with the answer that, 'You can enslave a man's body, but not his mind.'"

The *Amistad* incident involved fifty-three Africans who were illegally kidnapped from west Africa in 1839 and transported to Cuba aboard the Portuguese slave ship *Tecora*. In Havana, the captives were put aboard a coastwise trader, *La Amistad* ("Friendship"), for shipment to another part of Cuba. Three days into the journey, the captives rebelled and took over the vessel, ordering it to Africa. But the Spanish crew deceived the rebels and sailed north along the U.S. coast instead. *La Amistad* was seized by a U.S. naval vessel, sent into New Haven, Connecticut, and the Africans were imprisoned. The case eventually went to the U.S. Supreme Court, where former President John Quincy Adams successfully argued that the Africans had never been slaves, their capture was illegal, and they had the right to defend themselves and to return home. In 1997 the story was made into a Steven Spielberg film.

Captain Pinkney says he has had a wonderful time as captain, but "I will probably need to move on by the end of next year. I am two books behind—I want to write up my circumnavigation and my Middle Passage voyage as full-blown books for adults—and I need a concentrated dose of time to do that. I want to learn to build and 'fly' a submersible vessel. I want to become an underwater archaeologist. I've got a lot of living to do."

Captain Pinkney has a secret to his success and energy in his multiple lives. "I believe what Satchel Page said about age: 'How old would you be if nobody told you how old you are?' Everybody keeps telling me I'm sixty-seven. But they're all lying. I'm really twenty-five!"

Llewellyn M. Toulmin

Amistad: Four Days Before the Mast

The crew of the *Amistad*—including me for this leg of the voyage—gathered in the waist of the ship, joined right hands in a team star, and all shouted *"Amistad!"* together. The harbormaster called out, "Godspeed, *Amistad,"* as she pulled away from the St. Petersburg, Florida, pier. The vessel sailed out under the modernistic steel suspension cables of the Sunshine Skyway, a striking contrast to graceful rope rigging of the recreated ship. A dolphin welcomed the ship to the Gulf of Mexico with a graceful somersault.

Sailing along in fine weather, there was time for me to meet some of the fascinating and diverse crew. Recruited from volunteers, via résumés and sea education programs, crew members came from the United States, Africa, the Caribbean, and as far away as the South Pacific. They were all united by their love of the sea and their commitment to telling the story of *Amistad,* the modern re-creation of a vessel carrying slaves and cargo that became the focus of the first human rights case in U.S. ports and the subject of a Stephen Spielberg movie.

One of the most notable of the fourteen crew members was the co-captain, Mary Fenn, who was in charge of sailing the vessel on this leg of the voyage. Known affectionately as "Captain Mary" by the crew, she was forty years old and just 5'1" tall but seemed to exude authority, confidence and professionalism well beyond her physical stature.

Mary was ably assisted by her Second Mate and husband of two months, "Dash" Bien of the Marshall Islands in the South Pacific. He had gone to sea at age seventeen in a medical tall ship, and at age twenty-eight already had eleven years of tall ship experience. They had met when his vessel, the *Pride of Baltimore,* moored alongside *Amistad* in Baltimore harbor for a tall ships festival. "We keep our professional and personal lives separate," he said, which must be difficult when home is a tossing five by seven by six-foot cabin aboard a small sailing ship.

The Chief Mate was the legendary schoonerman Jon Michienzi, well known in the tall ship fleet. He was a broad-shouldered thirty-one-year-old from Mt. Sinai, New York, with ten years aboard numerous tall ships, sailing in most of the seven seas. He was the person called on in any emergency, and he managed to make a joke out of every adversity.

Amir Lee was a strong, well-spoken high school graduate from Ithaca, New York. He was quietly religious and always dependable. He wanted to "follow the sea and travel the world—I don't want to get stuck in one place." Mukanku Mkoyi, Jr., was born in Jamaica, raised in Zaire, and is now from Silver Spring, Maryland. A graduate of Howard University, he was on leave from law school. With eight months of service in *Amistad,* he had more time aboard the two-year-old vessel than any other crew member except the co-captain.

John Kamara was a native of Sierra Leone and descendant of Kali, one of the original *Amistad* captives. He first heard of the *Amistad* saga from his elders when being raised in West Africa. "We were told that our ancestors were kidnapped and taken to America, where they fought for their freedom and returned safely to Africa. But it was only when I met a delegation from America that I learned of the historic U.S. Supreme Court case that set them free," he said.

Turning northwest toward Mobile, we first encountered some great sailing, with a fresh breeze from the southwest. On a beam reach, the ship raced ahead at over nine knots, very fast for a traditional vessel. All fore and aft working sails were set, including the mainsail, foresail, staysail, jib, and jib topsail. "We're doing our fastest speed since leaving our homeport in New Haven, Connecticut," said Captain Mary.

In her speed the modern *Amistad* paralleled the original 1830s vessel, which was described in a newspaper of the time as a Baltimore Clipper–style vessel built for "matchless speed." A later owner of the original *Amistad*, who bought her after the slavery case, described how she "scudded before a northwest gale, our little clipper flying over the seas and behaving very well."

But we were destined to face more challenging conditions. Perhaps the Gulf had decided to test the modern crew and remind us that the terror of the original *Amistad* episode had occurred not far away, off the Cuban coast.

As night fell, the wind veered into the northwest and strengthened markedly. The waves became very confused, like twenty-foot moving pyramids, with only fifty to a hundred feet separating the peaks. The waves hit the boat from all directions, often with ominously loud thumps. A massive line of squalls appeared on radar, covering the screen and appearing like a giant inky fist in the already dark night sky. Captain Mary called all hands and said, "We're being hit by a brick wall of cold air. We need to lower the mainsail immediately."

All of us in the crew—African, African American, and white American- -worked together to lower the twenty-foot gaff, a heavy spar supporting the top of the mainsail. But due to the confused seas it was not safe to sail directly into the wind, which would have allowed the gaff and sail to drop directly downwards towards the deck. The gaff was lowered partway but then got stuck and wouldn't come down, despite our desperate pulling on the downhaul lines. It was slamming back and forth as the ship rolled, in a dangerous arc ten feet above the deck.

Seeing the crisis, Chief Mate Jon Michienzi swarmed up a backstay, jumped onto the gaff like it was a bucking bronco, and wedged himself between the quarterlift lines, adding his weight to the downward effort. He and the gaff slammed across the deck several times, being jerked up short at the end of the arc by the restraining mainsheet. It was a perilous moment. If Jon lost his grip he could be pitched over the side and into the sea. The chances of rescue at night in bad conditions would be slim to nil. But he held on with his legs, left arm, and chest, forced the gaff down, and coolly passed a line down around the gaff and boom with his right arm. After the recalcitrant gaff was tamed, he jumped down lightly to the deck and jokingly said, "If you'd have put another quarter in the slot, I could've had a longer ride."

With the mainsail down, the motion of the vessel eased a bit. But the seas got even more violent as the wind veered further north, creating crossing and conflicting wave trains. Half the crew was seasick, and one, Justin Smith of Gustavis, Alaska, was so violently ill that he vomited two cups of blood. Between bouts of illness Justin said, "I'm the part-time captain of a research vessel in Alaska, and I've been offshore in many oceans. This is the first time I've been seasick. I've never experienced seas like this." Despite his serious illness, Justin stayed at his post, standing bow-watch and doing hourly safety checks of the ship's systems, sails, and bilges. He received medical assistance, encouraging words from Captain Mary, and a lifebelt to prevent him from being pitched overboard as he leaned over the side.

By contrast with the interracial teamwork and good human relations of the modern *Amistad,* the original *Amistad* voyage stemmed from the worst exploitation of races for economic gain. The Africans were kidnapped from their homes, taken to a land far away, sold as slaves, and even told as a cruel joke that they would be killed and eaten. They were chained and shackled below decks, fifty-three of them in a tiny space, seasick, vomiting, with no toilets. They had to courageously rise up, kill two of their Spanish captors, and attempt to sail to Africa. After they were intercepted by a U.S. naval vessel and tried in U.S. courts, their case took two years to be decided by lower courts and ultimately the U.S. Supreme Court, in a landmark decision in 1841. The captives were freed by the Court and allowed to return to their homes in Africa.

After two days of storms, the cold front passed, the wind and seas eased, and the modern *Amistad* sailed into a cool, sunlit day. She passed between Forts Morgan and Gaines, entered Mobile Bay, and came to rest at Cooper Riverside Park in downtown Mobile.

With the voyage over and now feeling fine, Justin Smith put the contrast between the old and new best. "Our reconstruction of *Amistad* shows the power of strength in diversity. Working together as a team, with people of many countries, racial backgrounds and political viewpoints, we have created a unified crew and a strong ship that celebrates the courage of the original *Amistad* captives. That is the message we bring to Alabama and the world."

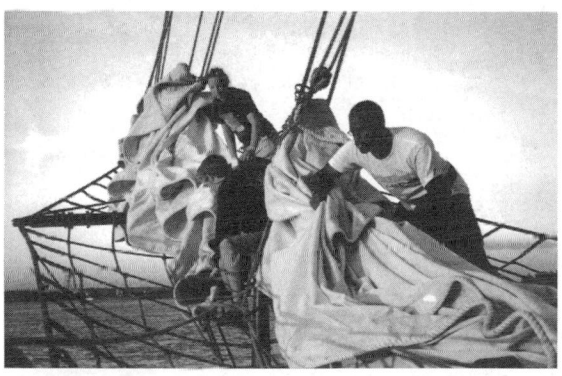

Crew of the Amistad work together to lower the jibs on the bowsprit as the ship approaches Mobile

119

Bar Crawling with the Schoonermen

Shipping as a temporary deckhand on *Amistad* on a short voyage from St. Petersburg, Florida, to Mobile, Alabama, I had survived some of the roughest seas ever dished out by the Gulf of Mexico, without getting seasick. The other hands, many of whom had gotten seasick, wanted to get their revenge by trying to get me drunk—and hopefully sick—in the bars of Old Mobile.

Out in Mobile Bay, approaching the dock, I had been quizzed intently by the Chief Mate, John Michienzi. "What is there to do in Mobile?" he said, knowing that I had been born there. "Well, there is the Museum of Mobile, the old mansions on Government Street are interesting architecturally, and the Genealogical Society is good for family research," I said, giving him the cultural highlights.

Amistad Chief Mate Jon Michienzi wills the ship forward toward the bars of Mobile

120

He looked at me like I was from Mars. "No, no. What is there to *do*?" he queried insistently.

"Perhaps you would like to visit Oakleigh Mansion, the USS *Alabama*, or take a tour of Bellingrath Gardens," I replied.

"No, you idiot," he said. "Where's the *cheap beer*?"

"Oh," I said, in a small voice. "Let's try Dauphin Street."

So on Friday night four of the crew and I headed down towards the infamous Dauphin Street, home of the original Mardi Gras (153 years older than the one in New Orleans). We found our first bar just steps from the dock, even before we got to Dauphin Street. The Mate declared, "This is perfect," and it was: a real dive, rundown and smelly, with several bikers flying their colors, and their biker chicks in tow. The crew all had *very* cheap beers. I was going to order my usual, a Sprite, when the Mate said, "You're with the schoonermen now. You can't embarrass us by not drinking booze." So I had a G&T. I hate beer. Always have. Always will. We played pool and table foosball. After half an hour it somehow became clear to our herd that it was time to move on.

This time we made it to Dauphin Street, which was still rather deserted at 8 P.M. We wandered past several upscale bars with nice décor and well-dressed people. I wanted to go in, but the Mate scoffed loudly, "Gap people in Gap bars with Gap prices—f$%# that." A few steps further on we found another perfect bar: The Seaman's Rest. There was the smell of stale cigarette butts and spilled cheap beer. Foreign flags decorated the walls. A woman broad in the beam and bluff in the bow made immediate and constant eye contact and invited us in. Other similar unattractive ladies stared at us expectantly. We settled in a booth and drank our usuals.

The walls were covered with the names, dates and ships of previous crews, written with magic markers. There were U.S. Navy, U.S. Coast Guard, Turkish, Chinese, Spanish, and numerous other vessels listed. There was hardly a blank space, except on the ceiling. I said, "We should put our ship and names somewhere—but there's no spot."

The Bosun replied, "I'm over six feet. If Trevor stands on my shoulders he can do it on the ceiling." Calling for magic markers and more cheap beer, Trevor jumped up on the Bosun's shoulders and drew a shaky three-masted topsail schooner across four feet of ceiling, and spelled out all our names. The ladies and the few other sailors in the bar admired his handiwork, but the Mate was not pleased.

"For Chrissakes," he said critically, "How much have you had to drink? We only have *two* masts!" Karen, our lone female deckhand, found a blank spot on the wall in the corner over the pinball machine and drew a better picture of our ship. We moved on to the next bar, disappointing the ladies, who were clearly on the game.

Next we found a bar with a crowd downstairs but with a second floor with no patrons and only a pool table. Cheap beer (and a G&T) were ordered and I was taught the game of cutthroat at the pool table. Naturally, I lost.

Suddenly the Mate, a bit bleary-eyed by this time, challenged the Bosun to a wrestling match. They wrestled vigorously on the wall-to-wall carpeting while we cheered them on. Natives passing by looked bemused—apparently this was pretty wild even by Dauphin Street standards. The Mate, with his broad shoulders and strong arms, won quickly, even though he was five inches shorter. Then he challenged Trevor and Karen to a match. Within a minute he had pinned Trevor's shoulders to the floor and had Karen in an inextricable leg-lock. I wisely declined a match. He was the champ.

Several of us played more pool while the Mate and Karen disappeared, apparently headed for the head. After about half an hour Trevor and I went looking for them, thinking they had been mugged. We discovered them out on the roof, again locked inextricably together, but this time enjoying a prolonged, passionate but motionless kiss. "Ah," said Trevor, and we went back inside to play some more pool. We checked on the happy couple half an hour later and they hadn't budged—clinched upright on the edge of the bar's rooftop. Finally, after another half hour the clinch of the century was over.

Perhaps their mutual attraction was their toughness. The Mate was the person on board called in any emergency, and his strength was amazing. He reminded me of the young Jack London as an oyster pirate on San Francisco Bay—hard-drinking, hard-living, and hard-working. Karen thrived in the ship's forecastle, a tiny, tossing space thirteen by twelve by nine feet, which she shared with eight male deckhands. Of all the deckhands, she was the best seaman, even though she had been on board only two months and had only a year of total sea time.

We crawled on through at least three more bars, and I can't remember exactly how much I drank. I do recall being ordered by the Mate to chug a memorable drink called a Belfast Car Bomb—a mug of Guinness with a shot glass of whiskey stuck in the middle. "To prove you're a schoonerman you have to drink the whole thing down fast," he said. "No sipping. If you sip it you'll get really sick." I sipped anyway and was called "a wuss" for my pains but managed to avoid getting either drunk or sick, despite having drunk more in one night than I usually do in a year.

By this time it was late in the evening, and a substantial rowdy crowd had gathered in the street. They clustered under a New Orleans–style second-floor balcony, on which a group of drunken men called out to the crowd. At first I couldn't figure out what was going on. Then I realized they were calling out the descriptions of passing women. "Black shirt, black shirt!" they hollered. This apparently meant that the girl in the black shirt was supposed to raise her shirt or her skirt to show the crowd on the balcony. Amazingly, it worked.

I said to the Bosun, "I was born in Mobile and never knew anything like this went on here."

He, too, looked at me like I was from Mars. He said, as if talking to a child, "Lew, our ship has stopped in every port on the Eastern Seaboard, and in every one there is a street with a crowd drinking, carousing and calling out to girls, exactly like this."

"Oh," I said in a small voice. My education as a schoonerman was clearly just getting under way.

Llewellyn M. Toulmin

A Perfect Day Sailing Aboard *Jeanie Johnston*

I am eighty feet in the air, with nothing between me and death below except my toes, a bit of rope, and my aching stomach muscles. I am untying the portside outboard gasket on the main t'gallant yard on the *Jeanie Johnston*, the recreated Irish famine tall ship. This is how I start my morning watch on a perfect day of Atlantic sailing. The sun is shining, the sky is blue, and the wind is from the southeast, blowing us straight towards our destination, the mouth of the Chesapeake, sixty miles away.

To undo that gasket I must climb up the windward ratlines for twenty-five feet, then up the outward-sloping futtock shrouds for ten feet to the fighting top, then up the remaining topmast and t'gallant shrouds for another forty-five feet. Then step out onto the t'gallant yard footrope (who ever came up with the idea of standing on a *rope*, anyway?) and drape my body over the nine-inch-thick horizontal yard, gripping the yard with my stomach muscles. I grip so hard that my stomach is bruised and aching for days afterwards. *Then*, I must inch out twenty feet to the outboard end of the yard. Yikes!

For experiencing all this terror, I do get a reward. After my task is over, I happen to look aft, and just off the stern, a huge right whale is breaching and blowing a large spout of water, as if to salute my survival. Thanks, Mr. Whale.

Lew Toulmin high in the rigging of the Jeanie Johnston

Why am I hanging off the yard? The logic is simple: to get to Washington from Charleston, South Carolina, in ten days we need to sail. In light southerly airs we need all eighteen sails, including the main t'gallant. And to loose that sail we must do it the same way the original Irish crew did from 1847 to 1858, when the original *Jeanie Johnston* carried desperate, starving emigrants away from the Great

Llewellyn M. Toulmin

Potato Famine to Baltimore, New York, and Quebec. Recreating history can be hazardous to your health!

But a little risk and some aching stomach muscles are a small price to pay for sailing aboard the *Jeanie Johnston*. The ship and her crew have given me insights into history that I never had, and have given me the chance to meet some of the greatest characters, sailors, and storytellers afloat.

Insights? Ten days aboard have made me appreciate the incredible achievements of the master and doctor of the original ship. Captain James Attridge and ship's doctor Richard Blennerhassett never lost a passenger or crew member in sixteen voyages across the Atlantic, carrying more than 2,500 souls, while many other "coffin ships" were losing up to 30 percent of their passengers. The original Jeanie carried up to 259 passengers per voyage, crammed in a small space of about 1800 square feet—less than the size of the average small house in the US. Imagine cramming 250 strangers into your house, throwing out all your modern medicines, systems, and conveniences, including your toilets, sailing your house on sixteen seven-week voyages across the dangerous North Atlantic, while dealing with typhus, cholera, and lots of seasickness! Then imagine never losing a life. Impossible. But *Jeanie Johnston* did it.

Characters, sailors, and storytellers? You be the judge.

Captain Michael Coleman of the modern *Jeanie* is fifty-nine years old and has forty-two years of experience at sea. He is from Cobh, County Cork, and has white hair and a twinkle in his eye. He was captain of the Irish sail training brigantine *Asgard II*, and is one of only three persons in Ireland qualified to captain the *Jeanie Johnston*.

Captain Coleman built his own steel yacht, a 45-foot-ketch, and sailed it to Britain, Iceland and Greenland. Seeking new cruising grounds, in the early 1990s he sailed to Russia, where he had his strangest experience. "We sailed over the North Cape of Scandinavia to the Barents Sea and to the Russian port of Murmansk. We whizzed in unannounced, right past all the vaunted defenses of Russia's biggest naval base. We were immediately arrested and questioned for three days. I told them that we were searching for new bogs of peat to fuel our Irish peat-powered submarines, and they finally released us as madmen."

A mad Irishman certainly describes the legendary ship's bosun, Tom Harding, a fifty-nine-year-old, red-haired, fierce fighting leprechaun from Cork. "My philosophy of life comes from a captain I had at age nineteen," he says. "That captain told me, 'When the grave gapes, you want to be able to say you've lived life to the fullest.'"

Tom can certainly say that already. His varied career includes sailing on *Asgard II* and on other vessels in every one of the seven seas; running with the bulls at Pamplona on fifty occasions; appearing several times at the Old Bailey criminal court in London, including one time for an ingenious bank swindle using nonexistent Greek antiquities; amassing a fine collection of first-edition maritime books; achieving a Personal Best of twenty-six imperial pints of Guinness in four and a half hours; breaking into the famous, impregnable Topkapi Palace in Istanbul ("But I was so drunk I still can't remember how I did it!"); beating the U.S. and British darts champions at their own games after just a few months of practice; being arrested in Yugoslavia for threatening the life of Tito ("I was only joking, but Communist secret police have no sense of humor"); meeting most of the British Royals; and winning all but five of his five hundred bar fights. His bar fight victories don't count a historic battle with actor Richard Harris, whom he fought for an hour to a draw. Tom's finest achievement? "Spending five dollars for every dollar I've earned!"

Hal Barstow is a fifty-seven-year-old retired petroleum distributor from Anaheim, California, who paid $160 per day to be "voyage" (temporary) crew aboard the *Jeanie Johnston* from Charleston, South Carolina, to Washington. Hal has crewed aboard eight tall ships, including the *Endeavour*, the museum-quality replica of Captain James Cook's vessel; the huge Russian sail training vessel *Kruzenshtern*; and the graceful *Christian Radich*, a square-rigged ship from Norway that was sunk in World War II and later re-floated. Hal says, "My greatest sailing experience was rounding Cape Horn on the square-rigged bark *Europa* in a voyage that recreated Richard Henry Dana's *Two Years Before the Mast*. Most modern travelers don't even know that such a voyage is possible." Despite a bad back, Hal actively participated in all *Jeanie* activities, including furling sail on the royal yard, a hundred feet off the deck; sending down the studding sail yards; standing watch; and steering the vessel through some of the trickiest passages of the voyage.

Brona McGarvey is a tiny, black-haired nineteen-year-old ball of fire from Donegal. She comes from a family of four brothers and four sisters, and gets "stuck into" every job she takes on. She was on board the vessel as a voyage crew for ten days, funded by the International Fund for Ireland (IFI). IFI paid for Brona and sixteen other Catholic and Protestant youth from Ulster and Eire to come on the *Jeanie* as part of an eleven-week program of work and training. She says, "I left my home in Donegal for the first time to come on this program. We began training and working in Orlando, Florida, in hotels, to learn the hospitality industry. After just three days I was so homesick I called my ma in Ireland to ask to come home. But she persuaded me to stick it out, and now I'm glad I did. Next year I want to visit one of my sisters in Australia for a couple of months—but I'll always want to live in Donegal."

The IFI program is designed to promote peace by building personal relationships across ethnic and religious groups. It seems to be working. Says Brona, "I am Catholic, yet I've made several non-Catholic Irish friends on the program in Orlando and on the *Jeanie Johnston* that I want to keep in close touch with when I get home. I would never have met these people otherwise."

My perfect day of sailing aboard *Jeanie Johnston* ends with a glorious 8 P.M.-to-midnight watch. The wind is now on our port quarter as we sail on a broad reach at four knots for the Chesapeake. The stars twinkle and I count three satellites in three minutes. Bright flashes of phosphorescence light up the water in all directions around the vessel.

Just at the midnight watch change, seven dolphins speed up to the bow and play in the bow wave. The phosphorescence glows around them, so we can see their entire bodies even when they are under the water. They dash past us at thirty knots, leaving twisting, glowing wakes up to a hundred yards long. They seem to be giving us a graceful, glowing escort home.

Llewellyn M. Toulmin

Cruising Up the Shannon Through the Forty Shades O'Green

I close my eyes and picture the emerald of the sea
From the fishing boats at Dingle to the shores of Donaghadea
I miss the River Shannon, the folks at Skibbereen.
The moorlands and the meadows and the forty shades o'green.
(Trad.)

As the song says, I can't stop thinking about Ireland--
the glistening River Shannon scrolling out in front of our
cosy vessel, the quiet villages, the glorious countryside, all
set amidst those incredible forty shades of green.

We began our Irish cruising adventure in Portumna, in
county Galway in south-central Ireland, at the southern
headquarters of Emerald Star lines. We were quite
surprised and impressed to see the size of the fleet—at least
40 vessels ranging in size from two berths to ten were
docked on either side of the HQ. We arrived at about 2 pm,
well ahead of the 4 to 6 pm rush. This was wise, since it
allowed us plenty of time to see the orientation and safety
film, and take our handy rental car a mile into town to shop
for provisions.

After we stored our groceries, we had a chance to
examine our boat, a Consul class, number 22. She was 34
feet in length, beam of 11 feet, V-berth cabin forward
sleeping two, aft cabin also sleeping two in a rectangular
double bed, main cabin (living room) with inside steering
position, small but well planned galley with gas stove, 4-
burner cooktop, sink and small fridge, two heads with

131

showers, sinks and marine pump flush toilets, diesel engine, and topside bridge and sitting area with an outside steering position. In a pinch the vessel could sleep one more on a convertible sofa in the main cabin. She was fully equipped with pots, pans, cutlery, lines, fuel, hot and cold water, sheets, duvets, towels, bicycles (optional) and all other necessities. She was painted in appropriate Irish colors-- green and white.

A young instructor came on board and gave my wife Susan and me a rapid-fire briefing on how to operate the vessel, and then took us for a brief spin out the marina channel and into the Shannon. He showed us how to quickly turn the vessel "on a dime" (a Euro?) by turning the wheel hard over, going ahead hard for a few seconds, then quickly using reverse, then going ahead, and so on.

We didn't want to miss the last opening of the day of the Portumna swing bridge at 5:30 pm, so after dropping our instructor and picking up some last minute supplies, we dashed into the Shannon at our top speed of six knots (about seven miles per hour). We headed south a few yards through the bridge opening, and thence into Lough Derg. We were still a bit apprehensive about maneuvering the boat and understanding the buoy system, but literally within minutes we got the hang of it and started to relax and enjoy the scenery.

And what scenery! Off to starboard in the afternoon sun was Portumna Castle, built in 1618, while opening out ahead of us was the beautiful Lough Derg, one of the largest and most famous lakes in Ireland. The gentle green hills rose up from the lake, and there was literally no ugly development anywhere in sight, just a few charming houses, churches and cottages that seemed just right for the landscape. Our position on the bridge gave us excellent all around visibility. Reading the easy-to-use chart, we spotted our destination for the night off to port, the little village of Terryglass.

Approaching the tiny Terryglass marina, we found an empty space on the quay, and easily came alongside and tied up. Late arriving vessels sometimes rafted up (doubled up) by tying on to vessels that were docked at the quay—apparently one should ask permission if the owner of the quayside vessel is on board, but otherwise, it is OK just to raft up and climb over the inboard boat.

Terryglass lived up to its billing as a lovely village, with several wells dedicated to saints, a cute Garda (police) station, and a fun pub and a restaurant. The restaurant, the Derg Inn, served a spectacular fish goujons (strips) in kattaffi pasty. The dish was wonderfully crisp with creamy white fish inside. Irish cooking has certainly improved since I last visited in 1965. At dinner we chatted with two local men who were also docked at the marina. They had rented from Emerald Star for many years, were impressed with the vessels, and eventually bought a used cruiser from the organization. Now they cruise every weekend on a different part of the Shannon. Lucky fellows.

Lew docks the Consul on Lough Ree on the Shannon

Next day, after a good night's sleep, we rose, made a quick breakfast, and got underway. The weather was sunny with a few clouds, and the temperature in early September was a very pleasant 65 to 67 degrees. We sailed south for several miles to examine the lake and catch a glimpse of Castle Clondagough. Then we turned north, and re-entered the Shannon at the Portumna swing bridge.

The Shannon starts at Shannon Pot in County Cavan in the north of the island, and heads generally south and southwest for about 200 miles through 10 of Ireland's 32 counties, and through several lakes and various locks, until it reaches the sea west of Limerick. It is the longest and most important river in Ireland.

It is also one of the most beautiful rivers in the world. Where we were sailing, it was about 60 to 100 yards wide, with very clean but dark water, rather like the Suwannee River in north Florida. Close aboard to port and starboard were restful green fields, mostly of grass to feed the numerous cattle who stared at us as we passed. The river sometimes split around low islands with small trees, marshes and beautiful cattails. We spotted herons, numerous swans and goslings, horses, many fishermen, and occasional farmhouses and picturesque ruined manorhouses. We never encountered any heavy commercial river traffic, and often had stretches of the river entirely to ourselves. Most of the other boaters were Irish, with some continental Europeans and almost no Americans.

At Meelick we encountered our first lock. We had heard from cruisers in England that these required quite a bit of work, but here in Ireland it was "easy-peasy." We simply sailed into the lock with several other recreational vessels, and looped lines over bollards at the top of the walls of the lock. Then the lockkeeper opened valves in the upstream end of the lock, the water rose, and we sailed out, eight feet higher on the new section of river. Cost? About two dollars.

Arriving at the town of Banagher, three hours cruising time north of Portumna, we stopped for the night at the free dock on the eastern shore. We walked though the town and chatted up some locals. They mainly talked about the high prices, confirming our impression that prices in Ireland were high by US and even continental European standards. This is the result of the success of the information technology-driven "Celtic Tiger," which has given Ireland one of the highest per capita incomes and standards of living in the world –higher than the US or UK by most measures.

At Banagher we examined one of many fortifications left over from the Napoleonic period. This was a "Martello tower"—a round, squat fort with firing ports for cannons. During the Napoleonic Wars the French threatened to invade Ireland on several occasions, and the British authorities thought it wise to fortify all the Shannon villages, bridges and canals. It was amazing to encounter an anti-French fort 100 miles upriver from the mouth of the Shannon, but in those days the rivers and canals were much better invasion routes than the roads.

Next morning we spent a few minutes on our daily ship's maintenance chores—checking the engine oil, radiator coolant level, water intake filter, and bilge water level. As usual, we needed to add a bit of water to the radiator; everything else was fine.

We then sailed north for Clonmacnoise, one of the premier religious centers in Ireland. It was established in about 545 AD by Saint Ciaran and seven followers. For 1000 years it was the leading monastic center in Ireland, despite over 20 devastating raids by Vikings, Englishmen, Normans and Munstermen. Although the monastery effectively closed in 1547 when it was stormed by English troops, there is still a lot to see and learn at this fascinating site. There are two of the famous "round towers"—tall, narrow towers with their doors 10 to 15 feet in the air. The towers were used for storing monastic treasures and books, as bell towers, and as hiding places during enemy raids. Clonmacnoise is the burial place of Rory O'Conner, the last High King of Ireland, who died in 1198, and various other kings. The museum houses two spectacular, nine-foot-high Irish high crosses, awesome examples of Celtic stonework.

View of Clonmacnoise from the Shannon.
Note the two round towers.

North of Clonmacnoise, we followed the twisting river around curves and through many green fields to the lovely, historic town of Athlone, where we docked across from the imposing Athlone Castle. Here we paid 10 Euros (about 14 dollars), the only time we paid for dockage on the whole trip. We walked around the old town area and the waterfront. We found a convenient and very reasonably priced pub and Internet café (about four dollars per hour for access) run by a tall Czech, where we checked our email. Our host said that over 70,000 Poles, Czechs and other eastern Europeans had come to Ireland in the last three years to live, lured by numerous job openings and high wages.

Departing Athlone, we cruised north along the Shannon, then entered Lough Ree, a 30-mile-long, beautiful, twisty, island-filled lake. The shores of the lake were almost entirely undeveloped, with green fields and even greener forests. We steamed three hours north, keeping red buoys on the left and black on the right when headed upstream, the standard practice in the Republic of Ireland. Buoys appeared every half mile in the lough (and every few hundred yards on the river) so we were always sure of the channel location.

At Lanesborough, at the north end of the lake, we went ashore, bought some groceries, had a good "craic" (fun talk) with some friendly residents, and walked through the quiet, pretty town. We knew that the next day we could loop north for a mile or two, but then would have to turn south and begin retracing our route, toward Portumna. Our week-long trip was half over, but we didn't want to turn back. We were keen to continue north as far as the Shannon Pot, and explore every Shannon tributary and side canal. No doubt about it--some Irish leprechauns had successfully beguiled us with those gorgeous forty shades of green.

Fire When Ready Aboard *Olympia*

"You may fire when you are ready, Gridley." These words launched the United States as a world power. Uttered 105 years ago by Admiral George Dewey aboard the USS *Olympia* in Manila Bay, this famous phrase began one of the most crucial and decisive naval battles in world history. Today you can stand on the flying bridge of the *Olympia* in the spot where Dewey stood and look out over the 8-inch guns that sank the Spanish fleet, gained the Philippines, Guam, and Puerto Rico for the United States, and made us into a major player on the world stage.

The cruiser *Olympia* is now moored in the Delaware River in Philadelphia. Launched 111 years ago, she is the oldest surviving steel warship in the world. Graceful and sleek, she was one of the first steel naval vessels, yet she is unmistakably Victorian.

She is 344 feet long, only 53 feet wide, and carried 33 officers and 396 men. She displaces 5,870 tons, and boasts four 8-inch guns in two main turrets, ten 5-inch guns mounted on the sides, and six torpedo tubes. She had a top speed of 22 knots (25 mph), and at that speed consumed 633 pounds of coal per minute. Recently restored to her former glory, her fascinating attractions include a beautiful mahogany officers' mess, massive coal-burning steam engines with 42-inch stroke, an operating theater ready for surgery, and a unique combined Jewish-Christian chapel. She contains displays showing her history, the life of Admiral Dewey, and examples of the Dewey Medal, now one of the rarest and most valuable of the American campaign medals. Her most distinctive features are a graceful reverse bow, designed for ramming enemy ships (!), and a beautiful Art Deco figure of a woman, done in bronze, that decorated the bridge and holds aloft Admiral Dewey's famous phrase.

The USS Olympia, docked in the Delaware River, Philadelphia, helped the US achieve status as a world power

The Spanish-American War was brought on by oppression and rebellions in Cuba and the mysterious explosion of the USS *Maine* in Havana harbor in February 1898. At the onset of war, *Olympia* and five other warships under Dewey were ordered to sail from Hong Kong to attack the larger Spanish fleet in one of the most heavily fortified ports on earth, Manila Bay. If anything went wrong, the nearest U.S. support was over 6,000 miles away. British naval observers said of the Americans, "A brave set of fellows, but unhappily we shall never see them again."

Reaching the heavy outer defenses of the Bay, Dewey called a meeting of his captains. "Gentlemen," he said, "I was brought up in the Civil War under that grand old man, Admiral David Farragut, and when he had a task like this he just went straight through and did it." Dewey took a bold gamble and ran the narrow, mined, and unmarked channel past Corregidor at midnight, slipping by the many Spanish batteries. His presence was revealed by sparks from his coal-burning vessels, but the Spanish gunners were too late and too inaccurate to stop the charging Americans.

The next morning, May 1, 1898, Dewey stood in toward Manila deep inside the Bay, and confronted the Spanish fleet. Holding his fire to conserve ammunition until the Spanish shells were bursting all around *Olympia*, he uttered his famous phrase ordering Captain Gridley to open fire. By midday every enemy vessel was destroyed or captured. While Spanish casualties were very heavy, the Americans suffered only eight minor injuries and one death from heat exhaustion in the 110-degree heat of an engine room.

It was one of the most decisive battles in naval history, and it brought Dewey instant fame. He was made a five-star Admiral of the Navy, one of only three individuals in U.S. history so honored. A medal was named for him, as were innumerable soaps, cigarette brands, cocktails, and even children. Later Dewey served as the Chairman of the Joint Army-Navy Board (a precursor to the Joint Chiefs of Staff) and even made a bid for the presidency. His beloved *Olympia* went on to serve valiantly in World War I on antisubmarine patrol, and as flagship of the U.S. Naval Academy in Annapolis. Her last official duty was to transport the Unknown Soldier of World War I from France to Washington in 1921. Decommissioned in 1922, she was rescued from destruction in 1957 by a group of civic-minded citizens. Today she serves as a fascinating floating museum and memorial to Admiral Dewey and his brave sailors.

Dewey died in 1917, just months before the beginning of World War I. His last words, prophetic about the coming war and harking back to his greatest contest, were, "Gentlemen, the battle is done and the victory is ours."

Llewellyn M. Toulmin

USS *Intrepid:* Home Is the Sailor, Home from the Sea

As the helicopter rotors began to turn, the crewman crouched, then raced across the deck of the giant aircraft carrier. He leapt into the helicopter, standing half in and half out of the door, and saluted smartly as the whirlybird lifted off. Was he headed out across the Persian Gulf to confront a foreign menace? No, this scene took place on the fantail of New York's floating museum and National Historic Landmark, the USS *Intrepid,* in the Hudson River.

The *Intrepid* has been rechristened the *Intrepid* Sea–Air–Space Museum, moored at West 46th Street on the west side of Manhattan, a short bus ride from Times Square. She is the only aircraft carrier museum in the world, with over 150,000 square feet of exhibit space. She is huge: over 900 feet long and 150 feet tall, she dwarfs the Circle Line tour boats that tie up nearby. On her enormous flight deck, more than thirty helicopters and aircraft are poised, looking ready for instant flight. Near the stern, modern Air Force and Coast Guard helicopters regularly take off and land as part of the carrier's "helicopter war" exhibit.

On the hanger deck, over 700 feet long, five major exhibit areas are devoted to telling the stories of the pioneers of flight, modern naval aviation, the aerospace technologies of the future, the Medal of Honor, and the *Intrepid* herself.

USS Intrepid museum, moored in the Hudson, New York City. During World War II she sank or damaged 289 enemy vessels.

The Medal of Honor hall is particularly moving. With a well-done film and exhibits, it tells the story of the many brave soldiers and sailors since the Civil War who have earned their country's highest award. The hall has the largest collection of Medals of Honor in the country.

The naval aviation exhibit features a Panavision film that surrounds the visitor with the exciting sights and sounds of flight operations aboard a modern super-carrier. Particularly amazing are the carrier landings at night, when the planes land in a controlled crash at 200 knots, and the pilot's only visual reference is a few lights on the stern.

Also open for inspection are the ship's bridge, the Combat Information Center, crew quarters, and the radio room. Realistic flight simulators allow visitors to get a taste of what it is like to fly a fighter plane. Alongside the carrier are a destroyer and a guided missile submarine, the only such vessel open to the public anywhere in the world. All these attractions now bring in 600,000 visitors per year.

Intrepid was not always a peaceful museum. She had to earn her quiet retirement berth. Built in Newport News in 1942, *Intrepid* was commissioned in 1943 and participated in the invasion of the Marshall Islands and the daring air raid against the Japanese fortress island of Truk in early 1944.

In October of that year, *Intrepid* had her finest hour, when her air wing sank the Japanese carrier *Zuikaku* and the super-battleship *Mushashi* during the Battle of Leyte Gulf. It was the largest naval battle in history: three powerful Japanese task forces tried to prevent the Americans under General MacArthur from retaking the Philippines. But with the "Fighting I" in the lead, the Japanese fleet was destroyed as an effective force in the Pacific.

One month later, in November 1944, *Intrepid* was almost sunk by two kamikaze dive bombers crashing into the ship's hanger deck. Six officers and fifty-nine sailors were killed as planes and ammunition exploded and thousands of gallons of aviation fuel burned on the red-hot decks. The ship was saved by putting her into a hard right turn, which increased her list and caused the burning fuel to pour over the side into the sea.

Throughout World War II, *Intrepid* sank or damaged 289 enemy vessels and destroyed more than 600 enemy aircraft. The cost was 300 of her own 3,300 men.

After the war, *Intrepid* served in the Mediterranean, off the Dominican Republic, and as a recovery vessel for astronaut Scott Carpenter. She also helped to blockade inbound Soviet vessels during the 1962 Cuban missile crisis.

In the 1960s, *Intrepid* recovered the Gemini astronauts Gus Grissom and John Young. She also served three combat tours in Vietnam, winning the Navy Unit Commendation as the designation of "best ship in the fleet."

In the 1970s, *Intrepid* was decommissioned and seemed headed for the scrap heap. But philanthropist and visionary Zachary Fisher spent $24 million of his own money in order to save the ship. With this backing, in 1982 the Navy transferred the vessel to the *Intrepid* Museum Foundation for conversion to a unique floating museum. The museum must meet set performance standards and is inspected periodically. USS *Intrepid* can even be recalled by the U.S. Navy for active duty! How many museums can boast that capability?

Llewellyn M. Toulmin

Sailing Through Five Thousand Years of History

The lady was a tad old for me—by about 3,200 years—but her beauty was enchanting. Her high feather crown and wide, heavy necklace of carnelian, lapis lazuli, and gold bespoke high birth and great wealth. She stood next to and held hands with the goddess of love, Hathor. The name in her cartouche confirmed her exalted rank: I was in the presence of Her Majesty, Queen Nefertari, beloved wife of Ramses II, the greatest of all the Pharaohs. Her stunning life-sized portrait in her tomb in the Valley of the Queens looked as though it had been painted yesterday. A visit to this just-opened tomb was the highlight of a recent seven-day cruise on the Nile, mother of civilization.

Nefertari, true Queen of the Nile

145

The cruise began in Upper Egypt at Luxor, probably the greatest archeological site on earth. We had wisely decided to come to Luxor several days before the cruise and thus had plenty of time to explore the numerous temples, monuments, and tombs in the area. The highlights were Karnak, the Temple of Luxor, the Luxor Museum, and the incomparable Tomb of Nefertari.

The Karnak temple is amazing in its immensity. It is over a mile long and half a mile wide. We visited it three times, twice on tours and once for an excellent sound-and-light show, and still saw only parts of it. The temple was added to by every Pharaoh for 1500 years, so it is really dozens of temples in one. The most awesome section is the Great Hypostyle Hall completed by Ramses II. This massive hall has over 130 huge pillars each seventy feet high, with every surface covered by hieroglyphs and cartouches (oval-shaped borders containing the name of a king or queen) proclaiming the glory of Ramses. This one hall alone is large enough to hold Notre Dame cathedral.

Oddly enough, many of the sections of Karnak *not* built by Ramses also have his cartouche cut deep into the stone. It turns out that Ramses was so vain that he ordered his name put on almost every temple in Egypt, claiming that he had built them all! Perhaps this gives some insight into the character of the man that Moses and the Israelites fled.

We visited the smaller (only a quarter-mile long!) Temple of Luxor on a night tour organized by our Sheraton ship. The massive seventy-five-foot-high First Pylon towered overhead, with huge statues of Ramses II standing guard in front. (A pylon is the high, sloped outer wall/gate that protects each Egyptian temple.) The pylon glowed in the moonlight, while behind us a long double row of sphinxes was lit by torchlight. The wonderful lighting added an air of mystery and romance that was quite bewitching.

Inside the temple, the Boat Shrine has a beautiful carving of Alexander the Great as Pharaoh, presenting offerings to Amun-Ra, the king of the sixty thousand gods of Egypt. It was awe-inspiring to think that Alexander himself had undoubtedly stood exactly where we were standing, inspecting his carving and hoping that Amun-Ra would assist him in his battles.

The Luxor Museum is an excellent museum, as much for what it doesn't have as for what it has. What it doesn't have is tens of thousands of objects (like the overwhelming Egyptian Museum in Cairo). What it does have is several hundred well-selected beautiful objects covering every period in Egypt from the pre-dynastic era (before 3000 BCE) to the Coptic Christian period (100 to 600 CE). Probably the most beautiful piece was a stunning statue in black schist of Pharaoh Tuthmosis III, from about 1400 BC. It is so unmarred and perfect that it could have been carved yesterday—except for the fact that sculptors that talented haven't carved since Michelangelo.

The beautiful Tomb of Nefertari stands head and shoulders above all the other tombs in the Valleys of the Queens, Kings, or Nobles. It was reopened in late 1995 after being closed for years. Admission is a steep $30 per person, only 150 tickets per day are offered, no cameras are allowed, you can stay only fifteen minutes in the tomb, and while inside you can't talk! But you can gasp. The life sized paintings of Nefertari, Hathor, Isis, Horus the falcon-headed god, Anubis the jackal god, and numerous other gods look like they are about to climb down off the walls and introduce themselves. It is definitely worth the price of admission.

After touring these and numerous other sites and temples in and near Luxor, we joined our Sheraton cruise vessel, tied up on the east bank of the Nile.

Our vessel, the *Tut*, was one of four almost identical Sheraton Nile Cruisers. She was built in 1978 in Norway and shipped to Egypt in a floating dry dock. She was 70 meters (about 220 feet) long, 11 meters wide, and drew only 1.7 meters. She had 80 cabins and could hold about 170 passengers. Her crew was all Egyptian. The *Tut* was last refurbished in 1990, and her deck chairs, deck coverings, and fixtures showed some of the effects of the harsh climate.

On our first day aboard we checked in and were assigned a room. Because we had had difficulty getting brochures and information from Sheraton U.S. about the sailing schedule and facilities aboard the *Tut*, the very gracious Boat Director, Mr. Tarek Taha, offered us an upgrade to a large cabin-suite. As he showed us the way, he explained that most vessels on the Nile have a boat director who serves as hotel manager and supervisor of all departments including engineering and navigation. Thus there is a chief engineer and a pilot, but no captain as such.

In the afternoon of the first day we took an included Sheraton tour of the Karnak and Luxor temples (described above). Our guide was a very knowledgeable Egyptian with a Ph.D. in Egyptology and a good command of English.

That night we had our first dinner aboard. The food on the *Tut* was plentiful and good. Breakfasts and dinners had open seating and buffet-style service. Lunch and dinner had two seating times that were chosen in advance. Lunches were multi-course sit-down affairs. Typical dishes at lunch or dinner included tehina (ground sesame seed paste—very tasty), local breads, Windsor salad, oxtail soup, veal escalope, and even an excellent Baked Alaska.

On the second day we took a long included tour of the West Bank of Luxor. We covered three tombs in the Valley of the Kings; one of the tombs of the Nobles, Ramose; the tomb of Prince Amunherkhepshep in the Valley of the Queens; the two Colossi of Memnon; and an alabaster factory. A long day but very rewarding. The Prince's tomb was unusual and a bit sad, since it showed the dead nine-year-old prince being escorted through the Book of the Gates (obstacles and tests one must pass before resurrection) by his father Ramses III. Of course, the ancient Egyptians, who believed they would achieve an afterlife after three million years of lying in their tombs, felt that death was not sad but a wonderful passage to paradise.

The tombs of the kings were interesting in the consistency of their painting style. Only the earliest, that of Tuthmosis III (1479-1425 BCE), was different, with many figures done in a sort of Magic Marker, small stick-figure style. Soon after that period the Egyptians adopted a naturalistic if slightly stiff style and stuck with it for over 2500 years. The same amazing consistency is found in their temples and architecture—virtually no major changes for 2500 years. When you consider that today art and architecture change almost weekly, such longevity of style is hard to imagine.

In the late afternoon of the second day the ship's crew cast off and headed south, thirty miles upstream to Esna. While under way, a tour of the *Tut's* engine room and bridge provided some surprises. The distinguished looking pilot, Mohammed, was dressed in a galabia robe and a turban, and spoke in Arabic through an interpreter. He said that the vessel has three 70-centimeter propellers tucked up under the stern, and that each propeller is hung on a vertical pylon and can rotate horizontally through 360 degrees. The *Tut* is steered entirely by the propeller direction, like an outboard motor that could rotate in a circle. Hence there is no rudder. In the bow a small transverse thruster assists in maneuvering.

The three Mercedes diesels for the engines each have twelve large cylinders and develop 450 horsepower, and there are three other identical diesels for generating electricity and one extra diesel as a backup. The *Tut* has a top speed of twenty kilometers per hour with a cruising speed of sixteen. The engine room was so noisy that we had to wear ear protectors as we walked between the huge diesels, each as big as a family sedan.

Pilot Mohammed had an impressive knowledge of the river. "I must know every centimeter of the Nile," he said, "from the Mediterranean to Aswan. And I have to know all 1,000 kilometers at night and in the daytime, and at every flood stage from low water in the winter to the spring and summer levels that are twelve meters higher." He had twenty-five years' experience on the river and had innumerable cousins, friends, and relatives among the other three hundred-odd river pilots.

Cruising south toward the Esna lock and barrage, the water was very low, since we were sailing at New Year's and the spring runoff was months away. Several times we felt the boat shudder slightly as it pushed over mud banks and sandbars. This set the stage for the most amazing bit of ship handling we have ever witnessed.

The *Tut* was cruising along, second in a line of five similar hotel ships. The *Tut* suddenly pulled out of the line of ships, nudged its bow into the bank, and swung its stern into the current. Swinging further around, the pilot pulled the bow off the bank, headed the stern up river, and *backed* up the river for over two miles! I asked the boat director what was happening, and he laughed and said, "Only on the Nile will you see this! It is technically against regulations, but the water is so low that we have to do it. We only have about ten centimeters (six inches) of water under the keel. We back upriver over these mud banks because our three stern props actually cut a new channel through the mud. If we went bow first, our bow or midsection might get stuck before the props could wash the mud away!" What made the feat even more amazing was that the pilothouse was not raised above the deck, so that pilot Mohammed had to steer blind from the bow, relying on assistants leaning outboard looking aft and calling to him on where to weave between the shoals. At one point the pilot steered blind and backwards between a rock shoal and a moored boat, with about two feet of clearance on either side!

Throughout the voyage we passed numerous vessels similar to the *Tut*. There are over two hundred ships in operation on this short stretch of the Nile. Most are fairly full, even though the American tourists have not come back in force. Most passengers on the *Tut* were European, particularly Italians, Spaniards, French, and English. There were also many Japanese, some Americans, and a sprinkling of at least ten other nationalities. The main competitors for Westerners' business are other hotel chain boats, especially the Meridian with a new vessel, the Hilton with three older vessels, and the Oberoi, Movenpick, and Sonesta boats.

On the third day, sailing south to Esna, I had a nasty bout of Nile Belly, the local version of traveler's diarrhea. It was probably brought on by dehydration, the ubiquitous Nile bacteria, and/or overaged pastry cream. Our Lonely Planet guidebook states that "almost every traveler who stays in Egypt for more than a week seems to be hit by 'Pharaoh's Revenge,'" and the guidebook seems to simply accept this situation. Local doctors and persons who bring many Americans to Egypt do not accept this inevitability and recommend the following precautions to minimize your risk: drink *none* of the local, over-chlorinated tap water, even as ice or while toothbrushing or showering or on the boat; drink *lots* of bottled water, even in winter, preferably with a rehydration mixture added (some salt, sugar, and vitamins—available at pharmacies); avoid leafy and unpeeled vegetables; and take two Pepto-Bismol tablets before every meal. The latter technique worked well for my wife, Susan, and was recommended by her doctor.

If you do get the Curse of the Pharaohs, call the onboard nurse immediately, and drink plenty of clear fluids (again with an added rehydration mixture) at a replacement

151

volume ratio of at least two to one. Failure to do this may lead to painful stomach distension and cramps caused by salt loss and dehydration. A nasty topic but a potentially vital one for traveling in Egypt or anywhere in the developing world.

We rested on deck and enjoyed the beautiful passing scenery of rural Egypt—groves of date palms, fields of sugar cane, blue skies, sand dunes and rocky desert marching right down to the river bank, and little children running along the shore waving at the boat. The cool weather of December was perfect for traveling—seventies and low eighties during the day dropping to the fifties at night.

On the fourth day we arrived at Aswan, Egypt's southernmost city. Here we explored the town and had a drink at the lovely Hotel Pullman Cataract, named for the cataract which blocked navigation upstream for early explorers and conquerors. The hotel was used in filming *Death on the Nile,* and Agatha Christie once stayed and wrote here. Late that evening we boarded a felucca, a twenty-foot sailboat with a large lateen sail, and drifted downstream past the rock walls of the gorge, back to the *Tut,* gazing up at the desert stars.

On the fifth day we took a taxi to the Aswan airport and flew the 150 miles to Abu Simbel on Lake Nasser. We chose to fly rather than drive three and a half hours each way through the desert. Our Egypt Air plane was full of other travelers who made the same choice.

Abu Simbel was built by the indefatigable Ramses II in 1250 BC to solidify his conquest of the gold mining region of Nubia. Outside the temple are four huge sixty-foot statues of Ramses. At his feet are much smaller statues of his mother, his wife Nefertari, and some of his children. Beside the entrance are scenes designed to impress the commoners, showing Ramses smiting his enemies from Africa and Asia and dragging captured enemy chiefs through the streets with ropes around their necks. Inside the entrance, in the area of the temple reserved for nobles, are scenes of Ramses making offerings to the god Amun. In the innermost sanctum, reserved for the high priest and the Pharaoh, are four statues including one of Ramses. The clever Egyptian architect-priests managed to cut this huge temple from the living rock in such a way that at dawn on the birthday and coronation day of Ramses, the sun flashes down the long dark corridor to the inner sanctum, and shines on his face.

Between 1964 and 1968, all of Abu Simbel was moved in an incredible UNESCO rescue operation to save the temple from the rising waters of Lake Nasser. Looking at the temple from the front, one would never know what happened, but a small side entrance leads inside the "mountain," which is revealed to be a huge concrete dome covered with rock and rubble.

We flew back to Aswan later the same day and rejoined the *Tut*, where new northbound passengers were boarding the vessel.

On the morning of the sixth day we took an included tour of the Aswan dams and the beautiful temple of Philae. The Aswan High Dam was particularly impressive. Standing in the middle, the far ends were so far away, over a mile, that they were hardly visible. The dam contains eighteen times the material used in the Great Pyramid at Cheops, and has created the world's largest manmade lake, Lake Nasser, which extends for over 250 miles into southern Egypt and the northern Sudan. The dam is the top military target in Egypt and is swarming with soldiers. Visitors are forbidden to use video or long-lens cameras on the dam. If the dam was ever bombed and destroyed, the entire country would be swept away, and water would be standing six feet deep in the streets of Cairo, over 250 miles away.

The beautiful temple of Philae was also rescued from rising dammed waters. It is on an island in the lake behind the older, low dam, and is dedicated to the goddess Isis. Isis was the goddess of motherhood, purity, and sexuality. She was one of the most popular of all the gods, and the cult of Isis lived on at Philae and in parts of the Mediterranean basin well into the sixth century CE.

Part of Isis's attraction was her tragic life story. Her husband Osiris was murdered by Osiris's evil brother Seth. Seth cut Osiris into forty pieces and buried a piece in every province of Egypt. Isis spent forty years searching for the pieces, finally found Osiris' heart at Philae, and through her powerful love resurrected her husband. With Osiris at Philae she conceived a son, thus founding the first real family. She then sent her son Horus, the falcon headed god, to seek out Seth and kill him. Horus almost succeeded in killing Seth, but at the last minute Seth changed himself into water and mixed himself with the Nile. Since all Egyptians drank from the Nile, evil thus entered people for the first time.

Later on the sixth day we cruised north from Aswan to Kom Ombo. Here we toured the dual temple that honors the gods Sobek, the crocodile god, and Horus, the elder falcon god. The temple was built here to appease the many crocs that once basked on a sandbank in a wide bend in the river. A very odd attraction at the temple is an exhibit of four mummified crocodiles dating from about 30 BCE. The Egyptians mummified just about everything that moved, not just Pharaohs, and archaeologists have found mummified dogs, cats, and even huge bulls.

Cruising north for several hours under blue skies we reached Edfu, a small town on the west bank of the Nile. Here we boarded horse-drawn carriages for a canter through the streets of the town to the very well preserved Temple of Horus. At Edfu Horus the falcon god fought the evil Seth. The temple was built by the Greek Pharaohs, the Ptolemies, from 237 to 37 BCE. It shows the classic Egyptian temple layout, with a pylon and inner court with huge carvings to impress the commoners, a hypostyle hall for the nobles, an inner hall for the priests, and an inner sanctum for the high priest, Pharaoh and gods.

The most interesting item here was the world's earliest typo! The Egyptians always smoothed the limestone blocks of their temples, drew on a grid in red, drew the hieroglyphs and carvings in black within the grid, then did the carving to the black lines. In one corner of the temple a hieroglyph speller made an error and it is still clearly crossed out in black and the correct carving made instead.

That night was New Year's Eve and the *Tut's* crew put on an enthusiastic Nubian dance and music show. For this party all the guests dressed in Egyptian, Pharaonic, or Arab attire. Top prize went to a Japanese tourist dressed as King Tut, with a full Pharaoh's crown and headdress.

We cruised north to Esna and stopped for a brief tour of the Greco-Roman temple of Khnum, which sits in a deep pit excavated in the middle of the town. The chief attraction here were the very inexpensive shops on the way to the temple—we were offered a galabia robe for only five Egyptian pounds; about $1.50!

On our last, seventh day we sailed north back to Luxor. As we docked we watched the sun set over the Nile. We thought of the more than one million sunsets that have come and gone since Queen Nefertari walked this land, and we wondered about future royalty and travelers one million sunsets from now.

Lock onto One of the World's Seven Wonders

As dawn broke over the mountainous coastline of Panama, I worried about what this day would bring. I was scheduled to transit the famous Panama Canal, an engineering marvel of the first magnitude. But in recent months, world attention had focused on General Manuel Noriega, the dictator of Panama. The United States was threatening to overthrow his government and prosecute him for corruption and drug dealing. It did not seem like an auspicious time to go to Panama.

The voyage had been fine so far. The *Cunard Princess* had good accommodations, a friendly international staff with charming British officers, and an interesting itinerary. Ports of call included the prosperous island of Grand Cayman, the Mayan ruins at Tulum, Mexico, and the old Spanish treasure town of Cartagena, Columbia.

It was in Cartagena that I had my only minor problem so far. My wife and I took the standard city tour. Our guide was an attractive but terribly bored young woman named Maria. This was her entire tour of the city:

Theese is the the castel of San Phillipe. We build it long time ago. Then the Breetish knock it down. Then we build it again. You got 15 minutes.

She was the worst guide I've ever had. But I must say, while I've forgotten most other tours, I still remember every word of hers!

Llewellyn M. Toulmin

As we approached the canal we saw helicopters hovering over the entrance, and some passengers were a bit worried that the rumored invasion had started. We were reassured that it was just routine maneuvers and patrols, and so it proved.

We began our transit of the canal by picking up a pilot from a launch off the breakwater at Colón, on the northern, Caribbean end of the canal. (As any good student of geography remembers, you get from the Caribbean which is generally east, to the Pacific, which is mostly west, by going from the northwest to the southeast through the canal. Odd but true.) Pilot and captain George Wagner, a master mariner since 1949, had piloted more than 1500 vessels through the Canal. He assumed operational control of the ship under the watchful eye of Captain Ronald Warwick, himself a master mariner with thirty years' experience, a Falklands veteran, and author (of *QE2*), with thirty-seven Panama Canal transits to his credit.

Our first stop in the canal was the impressive Gatun Locks. From seaward the locks look like a side-by-side set of three massive stair steps, each stair 28 feet high, 1,000 feet long, and 110 feet wide. We slowly entered the first lock, attended on each side by two electric "mules"—55-ton locomotives that carefully kept the ship positioned in the middle of the lock, using thick steel cables. The massive, 690-ton doors at the end of the lock closed behind us, 26 million gallons of fresh water from Lake Gatun boiled up from 100 holes in the lock floor, and we rose gracefully at three feet per minute to the level of the next lock. After three such operations we had risen eighty-five feet. When the final doors swung open, we emerged onto the waters of beautiful Lake Gatun.

This lake of 163 square miles was the key to U.S. success in building the Canal. Created by building the massive, mile-long Gatun Dam, the lake flooded much of the isthmus

157

and eliminating the necessity for digging a fifty-one-mile, sea-level ditch from coast to coast.

We cruised slowly across the lake for about twenty-four miles, wending our way between jungle islets. Overhead the sun shone down on the vibrant green vegetation, and puffy white clouds dotted the sky. On shore monkeys and birds called out in the jungle that came down to the water's edge.

After several hours the lake narrowed to a 500-foot channel with its banks covered in silver-gray, five-foot-high pampas grass. This nine-mile stretch of canal is known as the Gaillard Cut, after its chief builder, Col. David Gaillard of the U.S. Army Corps of Engineers. It was a heartbreaker. A literal mountain was moved here—more than 96 million cubic yards of dirt, rock and mud—enough to build a wall twelve feet high and twelve feet wide, all around the earth! More than 150 trains ran ten hours per day for seven years to take out the spoil. Constant mudslides inundated men and machines. Of the 25,000 men who died building the canal, most died here.

Today the Cut is a quiet, lovely place that gradually rises to a steep climax at the Continental Divide. Here a plaque commemorates the enormous sacrifice of the men and women who worked and died on the canal.

Leaving the Cut, we went through a series of locks that lowered us thirty-one feet to the two-mile-long Miraflores Lake. This manmade lake, surrounded by lush hills, turned a steely gray as we cruised under a threatening afternoon thunderhead. At the end of this lake we descended fifty-four more feet through two locks. We left the canal by passing under the massive Bridge of the Americas, a cantilever bridge that links the two continents severed by the canal.

As the pilot was leaving the ship, I eyed his wonderful baseball hat, which said "Panama Canal Pilot" and had a distinctive red-and-white pilot's flag on it. I was just about to offer to buy it off him, when another passenger said to the pilot, "Wanna swap hats?" The pilot grimaced and said, "Well, okay. I lose about a hundred hats a year this way!" Missed my chance. Darn!

After our nine-hour transit, the *Cunard Princess* lay peacefully at anchor in the Gulf of Panama, part of the Pacific Ocean. We sailed on to Mexico, and it was not until several months later that Panama was finally invaded by the United States. Our timing had been fortunate, and it was certainly worth a little risk to see one of the seven modern wonders of the world.

Adventurer Richard Halliburton swam the Panama Canal in 1928. It took him ten days and cost him a transit fee of 36 cents. The boat with armed guards is to protect him from alligators and crocodiles.

Sri Lanka to Kenya: Indian Ocean Odyssey

The best chicken satay in Asia. A baby elephant orphanage in Sri Lanka. The sensuous sand of the Seychelles. A Sultan's Palace in Zanzibar. Mating lions in Kenya.

Until now it was almost impossible to combine all these travel highlights into one cruise vacation. But aboard the *Marco Polo* we saw all this and more in a three-week voyage across the Indian Ocean.

Our odyssey began with a three-day pre-cruise package in Singapore, the vibrant hub of southeast Asia. Here the highlights were a visit to the Satay Club and a city tour arranged by Orient Lines.

The Satay Club has the best and probably the cheapest satay in Asia. Satay is chicken, beef, or pork strips on a bamboo skewer, cooked over hot coals and dipped in peanut or fish sauce. Sounds strange but it's grrrrreat! The Satay Club is an open air cluster of thirty stands near the downtown hotels and the Cricket Club. Each stand has different satays and an owner extolling the virtues of his or her food. Perhaps it is the competition that drives the excellence, but whatever it is, it works.

The chicken was tender and juicy, with a wonderful aroma of charcoal grilling, and the peanut sauce added the perfect tang. Each delectable skewer was thirty cents U.S.— so our huge meal cost only about $4.

Later in our stay we went on the included city tour, where we learned many surprising things about this booming and controversial island nation.

Most surprising was the cost of cars. To hold down the number of vehicles, the government levies taxes and duties and auctions off car permits, so that a luxury car that might cost $40,000 in the United States costs $300,000 in Singapore! Perhaps this throws a new light on the controversial caning of Michael Faye—it certainly wasn't clear in the Western press that his car vandalism was so expensive.

Housing is also highly regulated. To promote ethnic harmony, each government housing project (where 95 percent of the population lives) must have exactly the same ratio of 76 percent Chinese, 15 percent Malay, and 9 percent Hindu and miscellaneous residents.

In Singapore the law and its enforcement is strict: no chewing gum, no littering, no jaywalking, no spitting, and (according to many signs) no urinating in the elevators! (Darn!)

All this discipline has led to immense economic progress. The harbor is full of hundreds of ships, unemployment is virtually nil, all slums have been replaced by owner-occupied modern flats, and the Singaporean plan to exceed the United States in per-capita income by the year 2010 is ahead of schedule!

After a short flight to Colombo, Sri Lanka, we boarded the *Marco Polo*. Our "B" class cabin was light and airy, with blond woods and attractive, coordinated pastel curtains and bedcovers.

The next morning featured a tour of a delightful baby elephant orphanage. Set up by the government in the lush green hills near Kandy to preserve elephants orphaned by poachers, the facility houses twenty elephants ranging from three months to several years old. Passengers were able to feed two of the smallest babies, one three months old and three feet high and one eight months old and four feet high. The correct way to feed a three-foot, 500-pound, hungry baby elephant? Put a bottle of warm milk in his mouth, squeeze the bottle hard, and hold on to your hand!

Returning to the *Marco Polo*, we toured the ship's public rooms. The ship is decorated in an Art Deco style done in etched glass, pastels, and chrome, supplemented with Thai and Burmese antiques. The public rooms include a large formal dining room and a second, informal dining room. The ship's cuisine features menus and dishes planned by Wolfgang Puck, TV personality and "restaurateur to the stars."

The ship itself is a lovely vessel with balanced, traditional lines. Just over 578 feet long and 20,500 tons, she carries 600 to 800 passengers in 425 staterooms. She was originally built in East German yards as the *Alexandr Pushkin* for the Soviets in 1965, as a cruise liner to earn hard currency. She was one of four sister ships whose additional missions were to serve as ice-strengthened troop ships and as spy ships, intercepting Western signals intelligence. She was put up for sale in 1991 after she entered a Singapore yard for a minor refit and the Soviets couldn't pay the bills!

Purchased by Orient Lines' CEO Gerry Herrod for about $25 million, she was completely rebuilt and transformed into a luxury liner in two years, at a cost of $61 million. She began her new life in 1993 and is now registered in the Bahamas.

With a very strong hull originally designed to withstand ice floes and Arctic seas, the *Marco Polo* is one of the few cruise ships to receive permission to cruise the Antarctic.

The next morning we left Colombo and sailed southwest for the Maldives. A group of 1,192 coral atolls, the Maldives were named for the Arabic word for cowries, which served as the money in the Indian Ocean region for hundreds of years. Imagine being able to beachcomb your

162

way to a fortune just by picking up shells! The islands are still a paradise for shell collectors and snorkelers.

We got up at dawn to see the *Marco Polo* pass through a narrow gap in the northern string of Maldive atolls, and turn north toward the lovely resort island of Lohifushi. As the sun rose, the ship anchored in beautiful blue-green water, and we went ashore in one of the ship's high-speed tenders. We walked around the entire island in about forty-five minutes, finding it complete with a lovely reception building, multilevel pool, about a hundred small bungalows, excellent snorkeling right off the pier, and a mosque. The Maldives have retained their Moslem heritage and have opened only this island and sixty-seven others to tourists; on the rest of the islands the traditional way of life is religiously pursued. An interesting and practical cultural compromise.

After a dip in the refreshing Indian Ocean and a delicious beach barbecue prepared by the ship's friendly Filipino staff, we reboarded the *Marco Polo* for the thousand-mile sail to the famous Seychelles.

On the way we got to know some of the ship's passengers. Most were retired American and some British couples, many of whom had been on numerous other cruise ships and were now seeking an unusual itinerary at a reasonable price.

Children are rare aboard the *Polo* but as a result are treated like royalty. On our cruise the only child on board, a precocious twelve-year-old, was given free run of the bridge, allowed to steer the ship, toured the engine room, and was given a ship's uniform complete with officer's hat, engraved nametag, and commander's stripes!

We met this prodigy at lunch when he was asked by an elderly lady what he wanted to be when he grew up. "Would you like to be a fireman, or perhaps a cowboy?" she said sweetly. Fixing her with a steely gaze, he replied, "I will be a veterinary herpetologist."

Of course I knew exactly what he meant. But after checking with twenty-seven passengers, the captain, the ship's physician, and four reference sources, we confirmed what I already knew, that he was going to be a snake doctor.

One of the high points of the voyage was the arrival of the *Marco Polo* in the beautiful Seychelles. The islands are dramatically high and lush and are granite peaks formed sixty million years ago when the Indian tectonic plate broke off from Africa and headed north. As we approached the main island of Mahe we could see thousand-foot granite cliffs reaching up to the clouds, forming a terrific backdrop for the picturesque capital of Victoria. To our left and right, small islets floated like emeralds on a sea of turquoise.

Our two-day stop in the Seychelles gave us plenty of time for snorkeling on pristine reefs, swimming off windy deserted beaches, touring the islands by helicopter, and visiting the unusual palm rain forest of the Vallee de Mai.

In Victoria we sampled the local French Creole cuisine ashore at the restaurant Marie Antoinette. This restaurant is in a hundred-year-old traditional white clapboard house, with a friendly proprietress and leisurely service. The food was worth waiting for, with an amazing number and variety of dishes for the prix fixe of just $19. We had Chinese cabbage soup, fish stew, hot chicken curry, eggplant fritters (wonderful!), fried parrotfish, grilled red snapper, tuna steak, slaw salad, and fried rice. Most of the dishes were quite spicy, and all were excellent, reflecting the many culinary threads of the Seychelles' history.

The next day we attended several of the ship's "Workshops at Sea." These are series of experts in every field who involve passengers in improving their skills and expanding their horizons. One of the best was Dr. Donna Pido, an expert in East African art and culture. She had lived with the Masai for six years and described some of their fascinating customs: starting the day with a breakfast of blood and milk ("not too bad with lots of sugar!"), houses made of cow dung or crocodile skin, and warriors who demonstrate their strength by jumping straight up five feet in the air. One of her most interesting stories was about the most common problem with weddings among the Masai. It seems that many weddings are held up for hours by the bride just before taking the vows, while she negotiates a higher bride price. This price is paid to her in cattle and goats.

Another expert was Dr. Kathleen Bates Mayer, a certified gemologist. With great enthusiasm she described the gems of the Indian Ocean basin, giving tips on how to find unusual stones like Tanzanite, Tsavorite, rhodelites, peridots, and malachite at reasonable prices. She had many amazing facts and stories about gems. For example, "the Cullinan diamond of 1,450 carats was discovered in South Africa and given to the mine superintendent. Thinking it too huge to be real, he threw it out the office window! Recovered by another employee, it was eventually cut into numerous small and three very large finished stones, two of which are now in the British Crown Jewels."

Another workshop leader who really increased our "life skills" was John Jeung, an expert in t'ai chi and origami (Japanese paper folding). John emphasized the calming, reflective, spiritual side of both arts. He provided a warm, encouraging, noncompetitive atmosphere for t'ai chi, and demonstrated each of eighteen moves with grace and clarity. This was enough for a twenty-minute stretch and workout. John provided diagrams of each move and appealed to passengers from coach potatoes to athletes.

We sailed on to Mayotte, a French-owned island in the Comoros group off Madagascar. Here we encountered a real French Foreign Legionnaire. The Legion protects the island from the acquisitive intentions of the Islamic Republic of the

Comoros, which occupies the rest of the island group. We approached the Legion post, chatted up the guard, and persuaded him to let us take his picture. He was reluctant at first, but the phrase, "La Legion, c'est magnifique!" did the trick.

The most exotic attraction in our next port, Zanzibar, was the "Beit al-Sahel," or Sultan's Palace by the Shore. Within walking distance of the moored *Marco Polo*, the Palace was built in 1828 by Seyyid Said, Sultan of Zanzibar and Oman. The Sultan's beautiful daughter, Princess Salme, lived in the palace and wrote her memoirs, giving us the earliest portrait of women's life in Zanzibar. She describes a life of luxurious boredom, in which she wrote out the entire Koran in tiny script in an octagonal book three inches wide and three inches thick, received long milk baths and massages from Circassian slave girls, and looked longingly out at the sea beyond the harem's verandah. She eloped in 1866 with a German trader, moved to Germany, and lived as a middle-class housewife for the rest of her days. But she found European life hard to adjust to, with no slaves and bathing in water instead of milk!

The last stop on the cruise portion of the trip, in Mombasa, provided a chance for some unusual shopping. For sale were East African ebony woodcarvings of busts and animals, West African masks and totem figures, Tanzanian and Kenyan gems, bold TingaTinga paintings and T-shirts, and antique silver Omani daggers. Our best purchase was a silver-nickel Ethiopian cross, two feet square, looking like a beautiful giant snowflake.

Up country in Kenya the optional three-day excursion to the Masai Mara gave game lovers in our group one of the rarest sights of all—lions mating in the wild. On four long game runs through the beautiful green hills of the Mara we saw three separate pairs of lions.

In each case the male and female sat a hundred yards apart, and at first feigned indifference to each other. Then the lioness walked over and switched her tail, hitting the male in the face to get his attention. They coupled for a few seconds, growled at each other, and then separated and pretended indifference again. Our expert guide said they would keep this up every twenty minutes for ten days! We drove back toward our hotel and the waiting plane for home, looking rather thoughtful.

Mating lions in Kenya

A Cruise from Petra to the Topkapi Dagger

Petra, the lost city of stone. Luxor and the Valley of the Kings. The triumphant Suez Canal. Passages through the strategic Dardanelles and Bosphorus. The mysterious city of Istanbul and the emerald-encrusted Topkapi Dagger. These were just some of our memories of an amazing voyage from Jordan to Istanbul.

Petra in Jordan was a wonderful way to start our odyssey through history. Built by the Nabataeans about two thousand years ago, it was a hidden city that dominated the trade routes of ancient Arabia, levying high tolls on passing caravans laden with frankincense, myrrh, Indian spices, silks, ivory, and animal hides. The city was eventually abandoned and lost when the trade routes shifted and was rediscovered only after a thousand years in 1812 by Swiss adventurer Johann Burckhardt.

Approaching the region of the city, we were puzzled how the city could be "hidden" in the rolling hills and steep wadis (gulches) of the arid Jordanian plateau. We understood when we saw in the distance the incredibly jagged rocks of Petra, over which no army could possibly march, and behind which the city sheltered in a concealed valley.

Getting to the valley was one of the most amazing parts of Petra. We walked down a sand-filled wadi to the entrance of the Siq, a narrow, winding gorge cut through the beautiful rock for almost a mile. The Siq was delightfully cool and mysterious, with amazing water channels cut along the walls, which caught and fed the rare rainwater falling on the rocks into the city. Above us the rock towered as much as two hundred feet, and in places the gorge narrowed to just eight feet wide. On every precipice were the remains of human work, and it became clear that in its heyday every high prominent surface would have been covered with tombs, carvings, statues, and inscriptions. We were amazed to learn that the Siq was cut not by water action or by man, but by a huge earthquake, which tore in two a huge rock over a mile square.

About halfway through we noticed a pathway overhead, about thirty feet up. This was probably an ingenious defensive, dead-end path leading out from the city into the Siq, to be used by soldiers to hurl missiles down on intruders below. No invaders could use the elevated path because it was inaccessible except from the city. Beneath our feet were occasional Roman paving stones—the Romans under Emperor Trajan conquered the Nabataeans in 106 CE and added their own touches. We always hear of the civilizing virtues of Roman roads, but I would hate to cross the Roman Empire in an unsprung chariot on those stones.

Eventually we emerged into the light, facing the fantastic Treasury. It is beautiful in pink stone, cut right out of the living rock, much larger than it looks (over 90 feet wide and 130 feet high), perfectly proportioned, and celebrated by Hollywood in films such as *Indiana Jones and the Last Crusade*. No one really knows what it was used for, or whether the now-plain interior rooms were lavishly decorated. Two double rows of square holes running up either side of the facade made me imagine vertical races of acolytes dashing up the front of the temple—but no one knows.

Further down the valley lie a huge amphitheater with wonderful acoustics, a Byzantine church with beautiful mosaics, an attractive small museum, innumerable small and large tombs, and several other Siq-like passages leading to other temples and tombs. It would take a week, and a lot of climbing, to do it all justice. We'll be back.

Leaving Petra, we drove on to the base camp of Lawrence of Arabia, at Wadi Rum, about forty miles away across steep wadis and sensational landscapes of abrupt mesas. At the entrance to Wadi Rum we spotted the famous "Seven Pillars of Wisdom," a great cliff with seven natural towers, after which Lawrence named his autobiography. Lawrence used this wadi to launch raids against the Turks, their German allies, and their railroad, which runs from Damascus in Syria down to Medina in Arabia. Lawrence described this area lovingly in his book:

> The hills grew taller and sharper and drew together until only two miles divided them: and then, towering gradually till their parallel parapets must have been a thousand feet above us, ran forward in an avenue for miles. The crags were capped in nests of domes and gave the finishing semblance of Byzantine architecture to this irresistible place: this processional way greater than imagination.

We hired an aged Land Rover in the small settlement of Rum and found Lawrence's camp and spring in the Wadi. We reread his exploits and were again amazed to learn that, unlike the tall actor Peter O'Toole, who played Lawrence in the 1962 movie, the real T. E. Lawrence was 5'3" and weighed ninety-seven pounds when he took Damascus. We laughed at critics who accused Lawrence of being vain or humorless. They can't have read his account of his Aqaba campaign.

Lawrence acquired an expensive female racing camel, named her Naama (the "Hen Ostrich"), and attacked Aqaba from the rear by riding across the trackless, deadly desert. At a decisive moment outside Aqaba he and his men charged down on the Turkish enemy, shooting with their pistols. He said it was:

...a cataract of men and camels. The Turks fired a few shots but were not very harmful, for it took much to bring down a charging camel in a dead heap. Suddenly my camel tripped and went down upon her face, as though pole-axed. I sailed grandly through the air for a great distance, and landed with a crash which knocked all the feeling out of me. Eventually I sat up and saw the battle over. My camel's body lay behind me. In the back of its skull was the heavy bullet of the fifth shot I fired.

We reached Aqaba, fifty miles south of Wadi Rum, under more peaceful circumstances, and boarded our vessel, the *Marco Polo* of Orient Lines, for the voyage through the Red Sea, Suez, and Mediterranean.

One of the most interesting passengers we met on board was Harry Rutstein, an expert on Marco Polo who had been asked by Orient Lines to join the ship and lecture about the famous traveler. Polo published his famous *Travels,* the world's first travel book, in 1299, seven hundred years ago, and Orient Lines was celebrating this great anniversary by having the ship sail roughly along the route Polo took when returning home from China. Rutstein is the only person to have established exactly where Polo went on his outbound trip along the Silk Route, how he returned via Siam, Burma, India, and the Middle East, and to retrace all of Polo's route. It took Rutstein ten long years, much of which was consumed wrestling with Chinese and other bureaucracies who tried to prevent his travels. Polo himself had no such troubles, once he was appointed an agent of the Khan. He carried a gold plaque that signified the Khan's authority and allowed him to smite any petty official who barred his way. Wouldn't it be nice to have one of those, next time you must wait in a long immigration line?

From Aqaba the *Marco Polo* sailed down the Gulf of Aqaba and across the Red Sea to Safaga, the port for Luxor and Upper Egypt. The night was clear and cool, with

171

beautiful stars and twinkling lights on land as we passed the shores of Jordan, Israel, Saudi Arabia, and Egypt.

The next morning in Safaga we boarded buses for the three-hour drive to Luxor, where we stayed overnight. The incredible Nile Valley has more than half of all the manmade relics on earth that are more than two thousand years old, and Luxor is the crown jewel of the Nile. We visited three well-preserved tombs in the Valley of the Kings, saw the temples of Luxor and Karnak, and attended the excellent sound-and-light show at night at Karnak. But for us the highlight was again the small but wonderful Luxor Museum, with some of the best-preserved and most elegant statues in Egypt.

We cruised north from Safaga to Suez over night. Since we had been to Cairo many times, we skipped the ship's excursion to Cairo from Suez, stayed on board, and read about other travelers who had been there. One of the most entertaining was Mark Twain.

Twain came to Egypt with a group of American tourists, *The Innocents Abroad*, in 1867. He was pushed and pulled to the top of the Great Pyramid by baksheesh-demanding locals, "as all tourists are." (It is officially forbidden now, but the *Lonely Planet* says ominously that "each year a few people fall off and are killed.")

Once on top Twain was approached by an Egyptian youth who bet he could run down the Great Pyramid, across the three hundred yards of sand to the Cephron Pyramid, up Cephron to its slippery tip, back down, across, and back up to Twain, all in nine minutes by the clock. For one dollar. Twain took the bet and the man dashed off, "bounding down like an ibex," and "waving his scarf from the top of Cephron." He was back in eight minutes and forty-one seconds. Figuring he was tired, Twain bet him double or nothing he couldn't do it again. He did it again—and again! If you have ever seen the pyramids, you know this is one of the greatest athletic feats of all time. Of course, Mark Twain was also one of the greatest liars of all time!

The daytime transit of the Suez Canal was one of the highlights of this cruise, and indeed ranks with the Panama Canal transit as one of the most fascinating experiences possible on any cruise. The Suez Canal is one of man's greatest achievements—something that people dreamed of for thousands of years until it was finally realized in 1869. It cuts four thousand miles off a sea journey from Britain to India, provides Egypt with one of its major sources of revenue, is one of the world's most strategic "choke points," and has been the focus of several wars.

The Canal was the result of one man's determination and drive—Vicomte Ferdinand Marie de Lesseps, born in 1805. By the 1850s De Lesseps was an unemployed, impoverished French ex-diplomat who had no resources except his brains, his grit, and connections, from his diplomatic days, with the ruler of Egypt, Said Pasha. Said was a three hundred–pound man with enormous appetites for food and French mistresses, who claimed the throne in 1854 when his nephew was poisoned by his own slaves.

De Lesseps had always felt that a canal was technically feasible, despite mistaken engineering studies that showed it was not. He persuaded his friend Said Pasha to float a company, buy 44 percent of the shares, and begin construction in 1859. The canal was to be 104 miles long, 26 feet deep, and 310 feet across. (It has since been widened to 55 feet deep and 1,360 feet across.) The canal took advantage of several shallow lakes that already existed along the route. These lakes were flooded, deepened and joined to become the Great and Small Bitter Lakes of today.

Next, long straight cuts were dug through the sand in the blistering heat by thousands of ex-slaves, who were paid so little that they must have thought they were slaves still. Water was carried in by thousands of camels. A cholera epidemic caused thousands of deaths, and the workers fled in panic. De Lesseps lost his favorite grandchild to the disease. Sponsor Said Pasha died (hence the city named Port Said) and was succeeded by his shifty, unreliable, extravagant son, the Khedive Ishmael. Yet through all the difficulties De Lesseps and his workers persisted, and eventually Africa was severed from Asia with a mighty roar, as the waters of the Mediterranean embraced those of the Red Sea.

De Lessups and Khedive Ishmael were so ecstatic that they threw one of the greatest parties of all time, a costly mistake. They invited all the crowned heads of Europe to the official opening in November 1869, and they built two palaces in Cairo for the royals to stay in (you can stay there yourself now, at the Marriott in central Cairo and the Mena House Hotel near the Pyramids). Khedive Ishmael was particularly entranced by Empress Eugénie of France. Especially for her he built the Mena House palace and the road to it. Perhaps like his father he wanted a French mistress! Fireworks, food, French royal palaces, free trips, balls for six thousand persons, and weeks of fabulous fêtes enormously increased the cost of the Canal, which until then had been quite cheap due to the use of semi-slave labor. As a result of these extravagances, the Khedive went bankrupt in 1875.

The British, who had always opposed the canal as a French venture dangerous to Britain's control of the world's seas and strategic choke points, acted swiftly. The crafty Prime Minister Disraeli borrowed four million pounds from the House of Rothschild, and bought the Khedive's 44 percent ownership in the canal for a tenth of its value. He thus introduced British influence into Egypt and the Canal, which remained until the canal was nationalized by Abdel Nasser in 1956.

Our transit of the canal aboard the *Marco Polo* began early in the morning as our northbound convoy of twenty-one ships got under way from Suez, passing the town, dry docks, a beautiful mosque, and the Sinai desert stretching off to the west. The canal is still not wide enough for two modern ships to pass (although there is talk of another widening project), so ships must move in convoy and pass only in the Great Bitter Lake. The day was cool and sunny, perfect for appreciating the immense canal project.

We sailed northward at about eight knots for two hours until we reached the Great Bitter Lake. Despite its unattractive name, we noticed beautiful villas along the western edge of the lake—no need for TV in your villa when every day a parade of ships goes past your picture window! The southbound convoy of twenty-odd tankers and container vessels and one passenger ship, which had started well before dawn to reach this spot, was anchored in the lake waiting for us to pass. We threaded between the ships and headed due north again, noticing green car ferries every few miles that darted across the canal with loads of cars, trucks, and workers.

We observed high earth berms on either side of the canal, pierced every few hundred yards by a flat ramp down to the water's edge. Perhaps this was a fording point for additional ferries to carry troops and tanks across the canal, in case the Israelis ever tried to capture the canal again?

We passed a reminder of those dark days from 1967 to 1975, when the canal was closed due to war, with the Israelis entrenched on the east bank and the Egyptian Third Army on the west, and wrecks and rusting ships in the middle. This reminder was an ugly monument, consisting of the giant muzzle of an AK-47 with a huge bayonet, coming up out of the sand like the weapon of a massive buried monster. This was Egypt's way of memorializing the 1973 Yom Kippur war, in which the Third Army was almost destroyed, but the canal and Sinai were negotiated back for Egypt. Perhaps the monument is more symbolic than its

175

makers intended and really represents the tragedy of war that is always ready to emerge from the sands of this region.

The canal, littered with mines and unexploded ordnance, was declared open in 1975 only after British Navy divers had cleared the mines and literally walked the entire length of the canal underwater, checking every square foot for explosives. One can only imagine the underwater curses that must have bubbled up: "Why the bloody 'ell did they bloody choose bloody me—blub blub—for this 'ere bloody job? Can't they bloody clean up their own bloody mess?"

About two thirds of the way up the canal the *Marco Polo* passed the imposing Canal Authority administration building. The authority charges an average ship about $70,000 per transit. In a typical year 16,000 vessels go through, yielding an amazing revenue of more than a billion dollars a year to the Egyptian treasury.

Near the end of the day, with the sun setting over Port Said to our west, the *Marco Polo* dropped the canal pilot and sailed out of one of the two exits at the north end of the canal. We continued out toward the channel marker, passing numerous anchored container vessels, then turned northwest into the Mediterranean for Athens.

In Athens we explored the famous Acropolis, toured the city, and took a tour down the coast to the Temple of Poseidon at Cape Sounion at the tip of the Attic Peninsula. The drive down to the Cape was delightful, with marvelous views of the Saronic Gulf and the dry steep hills marching down to the sea. Cape Sounion is probably the most famous landfall in Greece, since all the ancient galley routes came by here on the way to Athens and the south of Greece. Homer celebrates the sacred Cape in the *Odyssey*, when he describes the death just off the Cape of "the world's best steersman in a gale, Phrontis son of Onetor." He was the helmsman to King Menelaus, and was steering the fleet back from the successful Trojan War. The King stopped to honor and bury

Llewellyn M. Toulmin

Phrontis at Cape Sounion, a very fitting burial place for a great seaman.

The Temple of Poseidon, now in ruins, was built in the fifth century BCE, a thousand years after the Trojan War, at the height of Athens' greatness. The remains of the Temple consist of seventeen dramatic Doric columns, built high on top of the Cape. A more romantic and picturesque spot would be hard to imagine.

From Athens we sailed along one of those old galley routes, down past Cape Sounion, into the main part of the Aegean Sea, headed for the famous ancient city of Ephesus in Turkey on the eastern edge of the Aegean. It is said that Ephesus was founded by the Amazons, and its goddess was Diana (or Artemis), goddess of the hunt. The list of ancient visitors and residents of Ephesus includes Hercules, Alexander the Great, Croesus, St. Paul, St. John, and Mary mother of Jesus. John and Mary both reputedly died and are buried at Ephesus.

We accessed the city from the charming port of Kusadasi, about five miles south of Ephesus. We entered the city through a beautiful columned road, which once had marble colonnades and galleries terraced up the now-green hillsides. The road led down to the fabulous Library of Celsus, built in 135 CE. The library has dramatic marble columns and was built with a very advanced design, with double walls to keep the damp away from the thousands of papyrus scrolls. Ephesus and its surroundings was another area we could spend weeks in, and we made a note to put it on our list of "Must Sees—Again."

From Ephesus we sailed north along the coast of Turkey to the Dardanelles. The Dardanelles is one of those key points that come up over and over in history, due to their strategic location. From the Trojan War to Gallipoli, this twenty-mile-long strait has served as the gateway to the Sea of Marmara, Constantinople, the Black Sea, and Russia beyond. We sailed through the Dardanelles in a dramatic night cruise, passing the site of Troy on our right and a monument to the ill-fated Gallipoli campaign of World War I on the left.

That night we crossed the Sea of Marmara and arrived in the morning at the Golden Horn, the heart of the lively and mysterious city of Istanbul.

Here we left the *Marco Polo* and boarded a small vessel for a cruise up the Bosphorus, the narrow, winding channel that connects the Sea of Marmara with the Black Sea. We passed beautiful historic mansions and fortresses on either side, and marveled at the huge Ukrainian tankers winding their way through the Bosphorus at high speed to keep ahead of the seven-knot current.

We finished our voyage through history with a visit to the fabulous Topkapi Palace, at the tip of the old city where the Golden Horn meets the Bosphorus. The palace was the home of the Sultans and their huge harems from 1478 to the twentieth century. A typical harem, that of Murad III in the 1500s, had over 1,200 women, mostly Circassians, and none of them Turks. Murad had 103 children.

Life in the harem was one of luxurious horror. The rooms are small, cold, and claustrophobic. Many sultans feared assassination by strangulation with the Golden Bowstring, the favorite choice of hit men of the time. They filled their rooms with mirrors, so they could see their killers coming up from behind. The Crown Prince in each regime was in the most danger of all, and he was raised for his entire young life in one room, with small fountains at every windowsill to prevent eavesdropping and spying. Many went mad. The harem was attended by seven hundred black eunuchs. Black men were chosen so that if they ever managed to overcome their castration (this was rare but possible) and impregnate a harem concubine, the result would be immediately obvious. A doctor was allowed into the harem only under close escort by twenty black eunuchs, and he was allowed to see only the hand of the sick concubine before deciding his diagnosis and treatment.

Near the harem is the fabulous Treasury. Here is housed the stunning Spoonmaker Diamond. Pear-shaped, huge, eighty-six carats, it was found by a peasant in Istanbul in the seventeenth century, in a garbage heap. He traded it to a spoonmaker for three spoons. When the spoonmaker realized its value, he took it to a sultan, who made it into a beautiful brooch surrounded by forty-nine smaller diamonds. (Hmmm. Perhaps we should pass up the garage sales for the garbage heaps?)

Other minor trifles housed in the Topkapi Palace include the arm, hand, and skull of John the Baptist, the turban of Joseph, the saucepan of Abraham, and the staff of Moses. (The last is quite handy for parting water obstacles, scaring your boss, and obtaining water in the desert; much better than a Swiss Army knife.) There are also holy relics of the Prophet Mohammed. These include his letters (rather threatening, to the as-yet-unconverted), two swords, dust from his tomb, and the Prophet's bow, banner, seal, mantle, footprint, and broken tooth. Plus sixty-three hairs from his beard!

For us the most lasting memory of the palace and the entire voyage must be the glorious Topkapi Dagger. The Dagger's story began in the eighteenth century, when Nadir Shah of Persia gave Sultan Mahmut I an expensive Indian-made throne. To return the favor, Mahmut sent the shah the beautiful dagger. About to deliver the gift, the sultan's emissary heard that the shah had been assassinated. Thinking quickly, he hid the dagger and returned it to Sultan Mahmut.

The emissary should have been richly rewarded, for the Topkapi Dagger must surely be one of the most beautiful objects on earth. About ten inches long, its handle, pommel, and tip are made from five huge, exquisite emeralds that emit a green fire that pierces your eye and your soul. Below the emeralds of the handle are beautiful diamonds set in gold, followed by a tiny, delicate enamel basket of flowers and fruits, followed by more diamonds. We stared through our binoculars from four feet away for half an hour, studying every square millimeter. Then we studied the room. When we returned home, we immediately rented the caper movie *Topkapi* and began planning our next trip to Istanbul. It'll look lovely over the mantle.

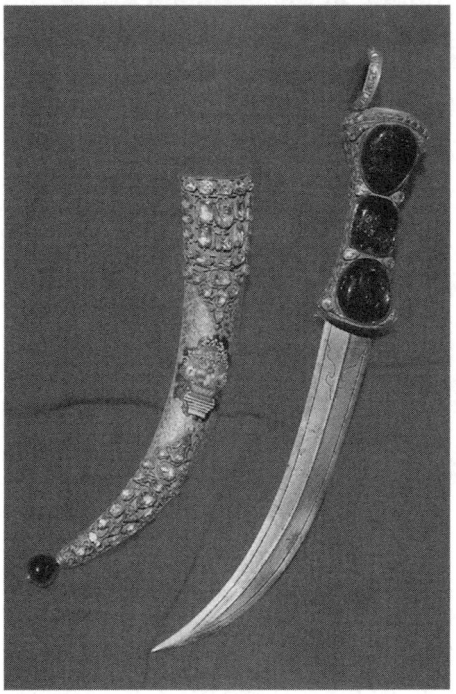

The fabulous Topkapi dagger, worth millions

Llewellyn M. Toulmin

Fifty-seven Voyages in Five Years

Passenger Derek Frost knows the *Marco Polo* better than many of the crew. He has sailed on fifty-seven *Polo* cruises in the last five years, logged over 44,000 sea miles aboard her, been to every single *Polo* destination, and in his own words, "I've circumnavigated, been round, down, and underneath aboard the *Marco Polo*." He is a new type of passenger, the "back-to-backer" or repeater, who is so loyal to his vessel of choice that he often books cruises back-to-back, and only gets off occasionally.

Derek Frost, cruise passenger extraordinaire

Derek started cruising after he retired from the medical supply business. At first he sailed out of Miami, Florida, on several Caribbean cruises with various lines. He didn't cruise for a few years, then wanted something adventurous. He saw an ad for an Antarctic cruise aboard the *Ocean Princess*, and sailed with her in 1992. He loved the Antarctic so much that he wanted to do it again in 1993. But the *Ocean*

Princess was damaged in the Amazon, and Derek's travel agent suggested the new *Marco Polo*, which was about to spend twenty-three days in the Antarctic. Derek says, "I came aboard and found that half the crew had transferred in from the old *Ocean Princess*. The ship, crew, and destinations suited me so well that things just kind of got out of hand!"

Derek Frost was born in Lancashire, England, and now lives in Bournemouth on the south coast of England (to the extent he is ever ashore). He worked for many years in the medical supply industry, selling and developing new bandages and other specialized soft goods. Naturally, everyone wants to know how he affords so much cruising. "I became a director and part owner of my company, and eventually helped take the company public on the London Stock Exchange 'Big Board.' That paid for my hobby."

After he retired at fifty-five he did some consulting back to his old firm for five years, but for the last five years he hasn't worked at all. "That working and consulting interfered with me social life," explains Derek in his Lancashire accent. "To do this much cruising you must have three things," says Derek, "the interest, the time, and the money. I've been very lucky along the way, and have all three. You know, in the Bible it only says how long we have to live, it doesn't say how long we have to work!"

Derek has two children, both grown up. His thirty-eight-year-old daughter comes cruising with him sometimes, but his son is married with a small daughter and can't come cruising yet. Derek is twice divorced and is presently unattached. He likes it that way. "I recently went on a Caribbean cruise—couldn't stand it! The women on board were hunting in packs!"

Derek likes the Antarctic so much that he has logged fourteen cruises there, thirteen aboard the *Marco Polo*. "There is just so much to see there—amazing wildlife, beautiful ice formations, and fascinating scientific bases. It is all so pristine, it is much more beautiful than even Alaska."

Derek doesn't count the countries he has been to, although he is sure he has been to every one of the *Marco Polo*'s more than a hundred destinations. He is not a member of the Travelers' Century Club or other travel clubs. "I also don't keep track of the money I've spent on cruising—it would be too depressing!" he says with a laugh. Derek notes that he "doesn't get any special discounts—just the same breaks that any other repeater would." He says that while working he traveled the world quite extensively, selling medical goods to hospitals on every continent except South America. He researched each destination carefully and saw most of the sights. He is pleased that "Now that I've been to South America and Antarctica while cruising, I've done the Grand Slam of all the continents."

"I do believe in really going somewhere, when I do go," says Derek. "I was once in Antarctica and saw a lady passenger reach out from a Zodiac, touch the land, and say, 'Okay, I've been there; let's go back to the ship now.' I couldn't do that."

Derek is familiar with some of the *Marco Polo*'s competitors. "I know a bit about the *Hanseatic* since her captain comes aboard the *Polo* as ice master in Antarctic waters. And I'm familiar with the *World Explorer* (the old *Lindblad Explorer*). But I like the *Marco Polo* because she is bigger and faster than those two vessels. She can dash across the Drake Passage to Antarctica in thirty-six hours instead of three days, and thus miss some gales. And in a major blow she has wonderful stabilizers, rides very well, and is a larger platform to absorb the force of the waves. She has always made every destination on time, except once in the Tasman Sea when she had to divert to Australia because of very rough weather. Luckily I missed that episode—I just happened to get off in New Zealand and got back on in Australia in time to hear the stories of fifty-foot waves!"

Derek says, "Another reason I like the *Marco Polo* is that it is not *too* large. I've been aboard big vessels with two thousand passengers and have always felt on the periphery of activities. And I like the fact that there are many destinations in a world cruise spread over six to eight months. It's not a ninety-day dash around the world like many other vessels. There are just not that many ships that do real destinational cruising. The beauty of the *Marco Polo* is that it doesn't have a single base it must constantly return to."

Derek pursues an unusual sport for a sailor—he is an avid golfer. "I often play golf ashore with the staff captain or the band leader. We have found many unusual golf courses. The course in Ho Chi Minh City (Saigon) is ironically quite good. It is kept in excellent shape by Japanese managers. The Royal Hong Kong Golf Club is great too. Now that it isn't 'Royal' any more, it is much cheaper and you can actually get in to play."

"I played the most southerly course in the world, at Ushuaia in Tierra del Fuego, Argentina. The wind there doesn't take prisoners. I once chipped a few shots on a beach in Antarctica. Of course I recovered the ball so I wouldn't hurt the ecology. To balance off those southern shots, I am searching for the world's most northerly golf course. I think it's in Sweden near the Arctic Circle. I also get in a lot of golf in the U.K. and U.S. during my summer breaks."

Derek's typical day is relaxing. "I get up at 8:30 A.M., have breakfast, and chat with the captain and my friends. I exercise by walking briskly about two miles on deck. I do this early unless it is humid, in which case I save this for the cool of the evening. I find if I walk early on a humid day then it is just tiring instead of invigorating. Then I read a book; usually just light entertainment. If we are in port, I'll stroll ashore and shop. I've already been on all the tours, so I don't do those any more. Ashore or in port, I enjoy the sunshine and fresh air. I don't use the gym or do aerobics, but I keep trim (Derek is about 6'3" and a well-built 185 pounds) by walking, playing golf, drinking Diet Coke, and not eating every thing available on board."

Derek is very complimentary about the staff and crew. "Captain Eric Bjurstedt is a fantastic professional. He and Staff Captain Roland Andersson are two of the reasons I stay on board. I have met the Chairman of Orient Lines, Gerry Herrod, and he has certainly put together an excellent concept."

While Derek is by far the *Marco Polo's* most loyal passenger, there are many other back-to-backers on a typical voyage. Derek observes that, "Back-to-backers on the *Polo* come from all walks of life and many different countries, including the U.S., U.K., Europe, Mauritius, and all over. I have noticed that many are retired U.S. military officers with good pensions. Many back-to-backers do one cruise as a once-in-a-lifetime jaunt, they like it, do it again, and they're hooked. The fact that the food is very good, the operation is well managed, the crew is very friendly and remembers your name and your drink as soon as you come on board makes it easy to keep coming back."

Fiona Chirrick of the *Marco Polo* cruise staff confirms the loyalty that has been built up in just six years of operation since November 1993. "Of 759 passengers on this India-to-Istanbul cruise, 300 are repeat passengers. Of those 300, 11 are on their eleventh *Polo* cruise, 125 are on their third through tenth cruises, and 163 are on their second cruise. Then there is Derek, on his fifty-seventh cruise. He is special."

Fiona notes that the Polo Club is designed to recognize and encourage back-to-backers and repeaters. "The Club has special pins for repeaters, including a sapphire pin for passengers on their third cruise on the *Marco Polo*, a ruby pin for the sixth cruise, and a diamond pin for ten cruises.

We have a special magazine, special offers, a welcoming bottle of wine, a cocktail party, and a cabin upgrade or an extra night in a hotel, just for Club members. We also have a special reunion cruise each year. This year it is a seven-day cruise in June in the Black Sea."

Derek Frost, the premier *Marco Polo* passenger, cruises about ten to eleven months a year, doing about eleven cruises back-to-back each year. "I don't usually cruise in the summer. I go home to Bournemouth when it's warm. When I get off the ship, the crew lines up, shakes my hand, and wishes me a 'Happy summer vacation!'"

"This year I'll be getting off in Istanbul in May. I'll get home on Monday. On Tuesday I'll probably pop 'round to my travel agent to book my next cruise on the *Marco Polo*."

Llewellyn M. Toulmin

Captain Erik Bjurstedt:
Giant of the Cruise Industry

At six feet four inches, Captain Erik Bjurstedt towers over the cruise industry in both height and experience. He was born in Norway, and always wanted to travel. "My parents thought they would get the wanderlust out of my system by sending me on board a cranky old North Sea tramp steamer at age sixteen as a mess boy. That really backfired, because I came back and said, 'I know what I want to do with my life—I want to spend it at sea.' My parents almost fell over backwards." Captain Erik, as he is universally called, is currently the master of the MV *Discovery* of Discovery World Cruises, which does globe-girdling "soft adventure" travel in almost all the seven seas.

Captain Erik Bjurstedt on the bridge of MV Discovery

Captain Erik finished high school at age seventeen, then shipped out for almost four years as a rating on board cargo vessels. He was then accepted into the Norwegian Mariners Academy in Oslo, where he obtained an officer's license. Later he earned a Master Mariner's ticket. He got his first command as master of a cargo ship, trading between Europe and West Africa.

Bjurstedt's long experience with the cruise industry began in 1970, when he was asked by the company Fearnley and Eger to take command of their first cruise ship, *Sea Venture*. "That was the beginning of the modern cruise industry. Five major American businessmen had approached the Norwegian shipbuilders and asked them to construct and manage the first real cruise ships. The Norwegians agreed, but wanted to supply their own officer corps. I was in the right place at the right time," said the Captain.

"I was in charge of supervising the construction and launching of the *Sea Venture*. I had a team of seventeen overseeing every aspect of the vessel's creation. The most challenging part was the service and business side of the sailing experience. We were told we would have to eat with the passengers and talk with the passengers. 'What!?' we replied. That was unheard of at the time. We even went to dancing school in a nearby town where no one knew us. We went to wine-tasting school and learned English. We wrote down every aspect of our customer-oriented approach in operations manuals that are still the basis of modern cruising—no one had ever done that before."

Captain Bjurstedt has had close ties to the world of entertainment. "This ship, *Discovery*, formerly *Island Princess*, was a backup filming vessel for the famous *Love Boat* TV series that popularized cruising. Her sister ship, *Pacific Princess*, was the primary filming vessel for the series. I got involved with the series later on, when the actors and crew sailed aboard the *Pearl of Scandinavia* on a cruise called

'The Love Boat Goes to the Orient.' I was the master during that cruise, and had great fun interacting with Linda Evans, Joan Collins, John Forsythe, Ursula Andress, and other famous actors in distant Asian ports. The passengers loved it, because they got to be extras or even play bit parts." Later Captain Erik was master for many years of the *Marco Polo* of Orient Lines.

Captain Erik met his wife through show business. "My wife was a singer and dancer on the maiden voyage of the *Sea Venture*. She was English and had been active in the English theater. I kept in touch with her after she left the ship and in 1975 asked her to marry me. Sometimes my wife and family get to accompany me on board the *Discovery*." The nature of the industry has kept them apart somewhat, though. "I recall on our twenty-fifth anniversary my wife counted up how many years I had been at sea alone versus together with her on land. It was nine years together."

One of Captain Bjurstedt's most exciting and scary experiences came early in his career as captain, when he was master of the *Island Princess*, now renamed *Discovery*, his current command. "We think of crime and terrorism as a recent problem, but I encountered it as early as 1972," he said. "We were sailing from Los Angeles to Puerto Vallarta in Mexico. In those days the ship was wide open to visitors, sightseers, and anyone. Even the engine room was open. Early in the cruise we got word from our home office that there was a possible bomb threat against our fleet. We began searching the ship but could find nothing. We would casually look under tables and behind curtains, trying not to alarm the passengers. Then at noon on the second day we got a more specific threat against our ship. We searched vigorously but still found nothing."

"On the evening of the second day I was giving a speech in the evening in the lounge aft, welcoming the passengers. It was 8:25 P.M. Suddenly the staff captain [the second in command] came on the intercom, and said in

Norwegian, 'Erik, I demand your presence in the radio room immediately.' In Norwegian I told the chief engineer to get to the radio room, and wound up my speech very quickly and followed him up."

"On the radio our home office said that they had a tape of the criminal. On the tape the bomber claimed he had planted four bombs aboard the *Island Princess*. There was supposed to be a 'device' in the engine room, on the bridge, in the main dining room, and in an F deck cabin."

The home office had determined that the threat was credible, and had paid the demanded $250,000. "The tape said the bombs were set to go off at 9:00 P.M. The bomber only gave us thirty minutes to find the 'devices,'" said Captain Bjurstedt. "We raced around the ship and found two shoebox-sized objects that looked out of place. We threw them over the side. We closed all the watertight doors and lowered the lifeboats to a boarding position. Then we waited. At 9:00 P.M. there was dead silence on the bridge. We could hear the clock ticking the seconds away. But the deadline passed with no explosions."

"I decided that the threat was over and proceeded on to Puerto Vallarta. A few people later criticized my decision not to turn back to the U.S., but we were as close to Mexico as to Los Angeles, and I felt that the bomber had made up his threat, and I didn't want the cruise to be interrupted. Most passengers were happy to go on. Eventually the bomber was arrested. He turned out to be a major American sports figure, in the Baseball Hall of Fame, with connections to Hollywood, who had gotten into money trouble through gambling. He got his movie star friends to plead his case in court, and he received only six months in jail. Of course, nowadays we have very tight security and excellent systems for preventing that kind of incident," said the Captain.

Captain Erik pioneered cruising to Antarctica aboard the *Marco Polo*. He sailed on four circumnavigations of the continent of Antarctica, and regularly voyages across the Drake Passage from Ushuaia at the tip of South America to the Antarctic peninsula. "When we first started we were alone down there. Now there are many vessels. But it still is beautiful and isolated—not like Alaska. Nowadays you can walk across the Inside Passage of Alaska on the decks of the forty cruise ships there." He has also successfully sailed the Northwest Passage, a rare feat, and he commanded the first vessel to regularly sail the coast of China.

Passengers and crew are crazy about Captain Erik. One passenger aboard the *Marco Polo* liked him so much that he booked fifty-seven cruises with the captain in just five years! "He is a fantastic professional, and is one of the reasons I keep sailing," said this perpetual passenger, who spends about nine months a year at sea.

Captain Erik loves his ship. "It is wonderful to be back aboard the *Discovery*, which I captained before as the *Island Princess*. This kind of traditional-style vessel was built for passenger comfort, safety at sea, grace, and beauty. The recent refurbishment was done very well, and we have all the modern safety systems and conveniences. These bulkheads speak to me."

Captain Erik looks about fifty-nine, so hardly anyone believes the rumor that he is really seventy-two. His secret? "I walk at least an hour on deck every day. And I go hiking in the hills whenever I am home." Although in every bridge announcement he usually mentions his favorite foods, hot dogs and rum raisin ice cream, it is clear from his slim figure that he rarely indulges. Will he ever retire? "Yes, someday. But I want to keep going—it's a fantastic life."

QE2: Royal Treatment at a Pauper's Price

Fifteen years ago I happened to be on a small motorboat in the Solent, just north of England's Isle of Wight, when the *Queen Elizabeth 2* emerged from Southampton Water and began steaming westwards. I was stunned by her beauty, size, and swiftness. I turned the boat and raced alongside the *QE2* at top speed, struggling to keep up. But when *QE2* reached the Channel and put down the hammer, I was left far behind in her wide wake. I vowed that someday I would experience that majesty and speed on board. Recently my dream came true.

I sailed across the Atlantic from New York to Southampton on board the *QE2* on a theme crossing appropriately titled "British Royalty." I thought this would be a great way to celebrate Queen Elizabeth's Golden Jubilee. To honor the special royals in my own family, I naturally took along my wife and mother. (There might have been a regicide, otherwise!)

Our boarding procedure in New York was fast and painless, even though it was clear that security was appropriately tight in the post-9/11 era. Once on board, we explored the ship. She looked so fresh and new, we were quite surprised to learn that she was launched in 1967. We found her large and very tastefully decorated, with twelve decks, 926 cabins holding up to 1,750 passengers, and beautiful public spaces. The displays in these spaces included lovely, large ship models of the *QE2* and other Cunard ships dating back to the *Britannia*, the first passenger steamship to cross the Atlantic, in 1840. Many displays had royal connections, such as plaques listing the visits to the ship by the Queen, Prince Phillip, Prince Charles, and Princess Diana. Some were totally unique—such as the plaque commemorating the ship's service in the Falklands war and the *QE2*'s large brass ship's bell that is sometimes used as a font for christening babies!

Right on time, we backed slowly out into the Hudson and, with the assistance of several tugs, headed south downriver. A large fireboat accompanied us, squirting celebratory sprays of water in all directions. We passed the Statue of Liberty, which seemed to be saluting our voyage with her torch.

Queen Elizabeth 2 with the Statue of Liberty

Approaching the Verrazano Narrows suspension bridge, we held our breath, since the ship's funnel looked so tall that it seemed sure to collide with the bottom of the bridge's deck. But we made it with a few feet to spare, then looked back under the bridge at a glorious sunset and wonderful golden clouds.

When we went below, the purser's office kindly provided us with a brochure listing some of the ship's amazing statistics. Among these were her top speed of 32 knots—over twice as fast as the usual cruise ship; her length of 963 feet—more than three football fields; the size of her two propellers—over 18 feet tall; the weight of her anchors—12.5 tons each; her experience—4.8 million miles steamed in 1,250 voyages; and her gas mileage—50 feet per gallon!

Our cabin was large and attractive, with a substantial closet and very large porthole-style windows. Since the ship is designed for fast ocean crossings where rough weather can occasionally be encountered, no cabins have picture windows.

That night we experienced the ship's famous dining for the first time. We had a lovely meal of prosciutto ham and pears, followed by a truly superb rack of lamb, ending with a delicious vanilla ice cream with mango sauce. The smell was heavenly and the taste even better. The presentation was always surprising and delightful, and the service friendly and helpful, never stuffy.

On this first night our attire at dinner was "informal," which on QE2 means coat and tie for men and cocktail dresses or dressy pantsuits for women. Most of the rest of the nights were "formal," meaning tuxedo or dark business suit for men, and evening gowns for women (although many women used knee-length dressy cocktail dresses). While some ships have gone to a less formal approach, we liked the chance to dress up and to see other passengers looking elegant. On one night when we wanted truly casual dress, we went to the Lido buffet restaurant aft, where casual attire is always accepted, but the food is still excellent.

Later in the voyage I had a chance to speak with the ship's Executive Chef, Karl Winkler. He had worked on the

QE2 for eighteen years and was clearly responsive to passengers' desires. "Our passengers generally like classical dishes such as beef Wellington and duck à l'orange," he said. "Nouvelle cuisine is passé, but we do try to keep our dishes fairly low on fat and starch, and we offer low-calorie and vegetarian alternatives at every meal. And of course we can accommodate any diet or desire. We provide the same high quality of food throughout the ship's five restaurants, but the time spent on cooking to order and elaborate presentation is greater in the Queen's Grill and Princess Grill."

He took me on a tour of the kitchens, which were stunning in their size and complexity. The production kitchen extended across the entire 105-foot beam, and each grill had its own finishing kitchen. Karl estimated the total square footage of the kitchens (not including storage) at over 30,000 square feet, the size of fifteen entire average homes!

On the third day out we passed close aboard rocky Cape Race, Newfoundland, with its hundred-foot-high slate cliffs. We were quite lucky to see the cape and its lighthouse since they are often fogged in. This cape was the first landfall for millions of European immigrants venturing to the New World to begin a new life. Carefully examining a globe, we were quite surprised to find that we were already more than a third of the way to Southampton, although we were just leaving North America.

On the fourth day out, in the noon navigational announcement, the captain said there was some chance of strong winds and twenty- to thirty-foot swells. But luckily these did not materialize, and the ship's amazing stabilizers easily took care of the twelve- to fifteen-foot waves we did encounter. These stabilizers fold up in port. But at sea they extend like wings twelve feet out from the ship, are six feet wide, and use gyroscopes and pumps to actively eliminate 60 percent of the ship's roll.

Every day we went religiously to hear the various world-class lecturers, one of the highlights of the crossing. The most quotable was definitely Robert Lacey, the famous author and commentator on the royals who spoke several times during the voyage. His assessment of the requirement for being a royal: "The essential quality for any Queen is— bravery in the face of other peoples' folk dancing." Lacey's rather racy analysis of the unique attractions of Mrs. Simpson: "She was reputed to have quite a 'grip.' And her lover the Prince of Wales was described as really quite a *little* man. But she had the ability to make a matchstick feel like a Havana cigar...."

The other entertainers on board were also excellent. Harpist Bethany Chattin was so enchanting that my wife Susan asked her to send us her soon-to-be-produced CD. Singer Jacqui Scott brought the best of the West End musicals on board in the evenings. And the other major lecturer, Alastair Bruce, a descendant of Robert the Bruce and a Herald at Arms, brilliantly described the fascinating, little-known titles and offices that still exist throughout Britain. These include the Lord High Admiral of the Wash, Boy Bishop of Hereford, Queen's Champion, Earl Marshall of England, Archdruid of Anglesey, and Cock o' the North, among many others.

We had been a bit concerned that on a long ocean crossing with no port calls, there would not be enough to do. In fact, each day the activities were numerous, interesting, and varied and included movies, health demonstrations, fitness classes, fashion workshops, art auctions, computer training, bridge, crossword, Trivial Pursuit, needlepoint, darts, bingo, French lessons, evening dancing and professional shows, and a passenger talent show.

The other passengers were interesting and varied as well. On this eastbound crossing about 80 percent were American, while most of the rest were British, with a number of other nationalities. Many passengers were older, but many were middle-aged and there were a number of children on board. We had many interesting conversations with other passengers, and were fortunate to make a new friend in a professional photographer who invited us to visit him at his Cape Hatteras retreat.

As we left the dock in Southampton and looked back with fond memories at the graceful *Queen*, I was very glad that I had encountered the *QE2* in the Solent fifteen years before. I knew I couldn't wait fifteen years to board her again.

QM2 = WOW!

We reclined comfortably, looking up at the thousands of brilliant stars overhead. The ship swayed slightly as she drove forward at 25 knots.. Suddenly the stars shifted dramatically, galaxies appeared, and great streaks of color covered the heavens. Harrison Ford whispered in our ear, saying, "And now we will see Earth's place among the stars." For these were not the ordinary stars as seen from an ordinary ship; these were the stars of the only planetarium at sea, on board one of the world's most remarkable ships: the *Queen Mary 2* of Cunard Lines.

The planetarium at sea is just one of many amazing innovations that Cunard has introduced since Sir Samuel Cunard created the first regular trans-Atlantic passenger service in 1840, aboard the paddlewheeler/sail vessel *Brittania*. Cunard inventions over the years have included:

- The system of signal lights now in use on all ships around the world, with green to starboard, red to port, and a white light overhead (1848)
- The first children's playroom at sea (1852)
- The first bathrooms at sea (1870) (before that everyone used a chamber pot or bucket, or went to exposed platforms at the "head" of the ship—hence the term "going to the head")
- The first library at sea (1874)
- The first electric lighting at sea (1881)
- The first iceboxes (1856) and first electric refrigeration at sea (1893)
- The first wireless signals sent at sea (1901)

Llewellyn M. Toulmin

- The first world cruise by a passenger vessel (1922).

Indeed, I think it can be said that without Cunard's new ideas, the cruise industry as we know it today could hardly exist.

Queen Mary 2 is named after the original *Queen Mary*, which was launched in 1936 by the reigning Queen Mary, wife of King George V. Legend has it that Cunard had intended to name the ship after Queen Victoria, who had reigned for sixty-two years and died in 1901. The Cunard representatives asked the king for permission to "name the country's greatest liner after England's greatest queen." The king, perhaps misunderstanding deliberately, said, "My wife will be delighted." And so the name *Queen Mary* was given, and carries on today. The original *Queen Mary* sailed the seas for thirty-three years, crossing the Atlantic 1,001 times, steaming 3.8 million nautical miles, and carrying more than two million passengers. Perhaps her finest moment came during World War II, when she and her sister ship, *Queen Elizabeth*, carried more than 1.6 million troops—mostly Americans and Canadians—more than a million miles across the Atlantic and other oceans. Winston Churchill estimated that the two *Queens* "shortened the war by at least a year." It is this *Queen Mary* that was purchased in 1967 for $3.45 million and converted into a floating hotel in Long Beach, California, which still exists.

The *QM2* keeps up the traditions of her predecessor with remarkable innovations and statistics. Launched in January 2004, she is literally the largest, longest, tallest, widest, and most expensive passenger liner ever built. She boasts:

- A maximum passenger capacity of 3,090

- A price of $780 million, the most expensive passenger ship afloat

- The first Canyon Ranch Spa at sea, with 20,000 square feet on two decks

- The largest library at sea (8500+ volumes and numerous CDs)

- The largest ballroom and dance floor at sea

- The largest jogging track at sea

- The largest wine cellar afloat

- 79 percent of cabins with private balconies

- A cultural academy operated by the University of Oxford

- A displacement of 150,000 gross tons

- An interior volume over twice that of her sister ship QE2

- A length of 1,132 feet (equal to forty-one London buses) and beam of 135 feet (too large for the Panama Canal)

- A height of 236 feet (equivalent to just shy of the Verrazano Narrows Bridge—this was the main design constraint)

- A top speed of 30 knots (34 mph), about twice the usual cruise ship speed

- Gas turbine and diesel engines that develop 118 megawatts of power, about twice the power of the typical large cruise ship

- A drive system of four "pods" that hang below the ship, weigh 250 tons each, produce more power than a jumbo jet, and allow the ship to turn in her own length without assistance from tugs

- The first planetarium at sea, with three shows and narration by Harrison Ford and other famous stars.

Llewellyn M. Toulmin

The enormous bow of the Queen Mary 2

My wife and I took a voyage aboard *QM2* from Quebec to New York in September 2004. We were stunned by the lavish artwork: 565 original works of art and numerous historical artworks and objects. We were impressed with the professionalism of the British and Asian staff, and their extensive experience and attention to detail. We thought that the design team had achieved exactly what they hoped: a vessel that allows for views of the seascapes outside from almost every public space (very difficult to achieve); that is safe in virtually any kind of weather (according to passengers, *QM2* sailed through the 70-knot winds and 21-foot waves of the remains of Hurricane Ivan with no problems at all); and that is beautiful and spacious, yet traditional and thoroughly British.

We felt that the food in the Britannia Restaurant (seating 1,347) and the other restaurants was prepared to a very high standard, though perhaps not quite as good as aboard sister ship *QE2*. In our experience and according to most seagoing chefs, it takes at least eighteen months to really shake down the kitchens and get a totally cohesive team in place. When we sailed, the *QM2* had been cruising for nine months, while the *QE2* has had over thirty years to reach top form. We thought that the conversion of the large breakfast and lunch areas just inside the promenade deck into four very different restaurants in the evening, by using different lighting and pull-down panels, was very clever and worked extremely well.

One of our most delightful eating experiences was watching chef Sean Watier in the Chef's Galley prepare a meal right in front of us. This special, innovative facility has TV monitors and overhead mirrors, and allows an audience of about thirty-five to watch the chef's every move. Chef Watier created a wonderful tropical fruit salad and a Mediterranean tenderloin. Then he finished with a superb Floating Island with orange crisps and marinated raspberries, one of the best dishes we've ever had on a cruise ship.

The shows, lectures, exercise gyms, movies, computer rooms, and other activities were so numerous that we were always busy and engaged. The lectures by Bill Miller on the history of cruise ships were absolutely riveting. We simply cannot understand people who say, "But if I go cruising, what is there to do?" That is certainly not a problem, at least not on the *QM2*.

One of the greatest things about the *QM2* is the tremendous attention she attracts in every port. Over 30,000 people lined the St. Lawrence river and the Quebec docks to welcome the *QM2*. Bands played and the crowd sang their favorite songs, swaying back and forth. In every port we were asked, "What is the *QM2* like?" It was a pleasure to answer, "She's a ship that will take you to the stars!"

Dew from Heaven

Too often we cruise passengers think of our cabin stewards and stewardesses as two dimensional persons, without families, lives or futures. So aboard *Crystal Symphony* on a cruise through the Mediterranean in the summer of 2005, my wife and I decided to have a chat with our energetic, attractive, 24-year-old stewardess, Rasa Janonyte of Klaipeda, Lithuania.

Rasa Janonyte of Klaipeda, Lithuania, stewardess aboard Crystal Symphony

Q: What does your name mean?

A: Rasa means "dew."

Q: Tell us about your family.

A: My father worked as an engineer building ships, but now works in a meat processing firm. My mother is a cook. I have a sister two years younger than I.

Q: Where did you grow up and what do you remember most of that time?

A: I was born and raised in Lithuania. I was only ten in 1991, but I remember that was the time that Soviet tanks killed many of our people. Then later that year the Soviets pulled out of Lithuania, and we had a big party.

Q: Where did you go to school?

A: I graduated from an art-oriented high school. I got a bachelors degree from the Lithuanian Christian Fund College, founded by Canadians and Lithuanians.

Q: What was your major?

A: Theology and sociology. Not too close a tie to cleaning cabins aboard a cruise ship!

Q: Your English is excellent. How did you learn it?

A: I studied English and Russian in high school, and my college was taught entirely in English. So now I write better in English than I do in Lithuanian.

Q: Did you work and travel before joining Crystal Cruises?

A: Yes, I worked in Norway and Ireland as a cook and babysitter. Ireland was hard for me, because as a devout Christian I do not drink. So it was difficult to see many people dangerously drunk.

Q: How did you hear about *Crystal Symphony*?

A: I got an e-mail from our college placement service, saying that Crystal was recruiting for five-month contract stewardesses. They said Crystal paid well but had six star service, so I would have to work hard. English was required but that was no problem for me. Crystal flew me to Florida and I immediately joined the ship for a Caribbean cruise, starting in Key West.

Q: Was the work difficult?

A: The other stewardesses said the work was so hard that I would probably cry for the first two weeks, and it would take two months to get fast at my job. But I am used to hard work and international situations, so in fact my transition was very smooth. No crying for me. I have been here almost two months, and I am pretty efficient now. I tend to feel at home wherever I am, so I am quite content here.

Q: Did the other stewardesses help when you started?

A: Yes, I was surprised and pleased by the close teamwork. The experienced staff all helped me. They said on other cruise lines there is a lot of jealousy and fighting, but here we really are like a happy family.

Q: What is your typical day?

A: I get up at 6:00 am and have breakfast in the crew's mess. We have very good food, almost as good as the passengers. I start work at 6:45, and have 8 to 10 rooms to clean. I usually finish by 1:00 or 1:30 pm. Then I eat lunch and often take a nap. Sometimes if we are at sea, I go up and stand in the prow of the ship to see the ocean and get some fresh air. My friends tease me and call me the *Titanic* girl. If the ship is in port, I will go ashore and walk around for two or three hours, usually alone. I love architecture and nature. At 6:00 pm we have a management meeting, then I do the evening cleaning and turndowns until 10:30 pm. After work I have a midnight lunch and check my e-mail, then go to bed at 1:00 am. Five hours later I start again.

Q: What is the most difficult thing about cleaning a stateroom?

A: To enjoy it. That is a challenge, but I usually succeed.

Q: Do you go to the gym?

A: No, there is no time. And we work so hard that we keep the weight off.

Q: What are your favorite ports?

A: I usually can get ashore in four out of five ports we visit. I loved St. Barts in the Caribbean and Monaco in the Mediterranean. I walked up in the hills above the castle in Monaco, and enjoyed the lemon trees and orange groves.

Q: What are your hobbies?

A: Ashore I love to study art history, read and sing the lead in my church choir. I brought some books aboard, but there's no time to read.

Q: How much do you get paid, and what are the tips?

A: I don't want to go into details, but of course the reason I am here is that I can make a lot more than the $200 per month minimum in Lithuania. Most passengers give the recommended amount for tips. [Toulmin: This is $4 per passenger per day, or about $8 per cabin per day x 30 days x 8 cabins, which equals about $1920 per month. Crystal Cruises stated that all tips are earmarked for each stewardess, and are not "pooled."] And I get free room and board. So I can save some money if I am careful about spending in port.

Q: What is your cabin like?

A: I share a cabin with a girl from Latvia. It is small, with a bunk bed and shower, but it is comfortable.

Q: What do you like about your job?

A: Here I get paid more than I would at home, and I get to see the world and meet interesting people from many countries.

Q: At home do you do any volunteer work?

A: Yes, I have volunteered for five years with "Youth with a Mission," teaching troubled kids in youth camps.

Q: What do you want to do in the future?

A: I will probably leave the ship after one contract. Someday I want to open a youth center in Lithuania for the many kids with drug and alcohol problems. I want to offer them Bible studies, fellowship and an alternative to the streets. I think I need more training before I try this. So I plan to go to the US to obtain a masters degree in youth ministry, with additional studies in music, art and drama.

Toulmin: Thanks, Rasa. I think a little dew from heaven has fallen onto our ship.

Section 5

Clients and Other Disasters

Bustin' the Gamblin'
at the
Sunrise Bar and Pool Hall

My first job in the "real world" involved traveling down to Miami to serve as an intern in the Metro Dade County government. I thought I was going to learn public administration, not how to bust bars. But the main thing I now remember from that job was bustin' the Sunrise Bar and Pool Hall.

My year-long internship with the county government involved rotating through three departments, including the Public Safety Department—the Metro police. But the police thought I was a spy from the County Manager's office, so they buried me in the Management Analysis Bureau, unaffectionately known as the Management Paralysis Bureau because it never did anything.

Police badge of Metro Dade County, Florida

After sitting at my desk for a week with absolutely nothing to do, I was about to go mad with boredom. I hit on the idea of skipping the MAB during the day, and going out each night on a police ride-along—much more exciting, and it actually involved some police work.

Most ride-alongs were actually fairly uneventful. But one night was different. I was riding with Bob, an officer who patrolled south Dade, an area larger than Rhode Island (or even many countries). Bob was aggressive, and didn't seem to have all the wheels on his cruiser. We were riding by the Sunrise Bar and Pool Hall in a black part of the county. Just in front of the hall I noticed a group of black guys crouched in a circle. As we went by I heard a little "click." One hundred yards later Bob said, dramatically, "Did you hear that 'click' ?—they're GAMBLING at the pool hall!" From his tone I thought they were committing mass murder.

Bob got on the radio and called up the other five cars patrolling our huge sector of the county. "They're gamblin' again at the Sunrise—let's get 'em! We'll meet at the Junior High School and take 'em from behind." Most of the other officers agreed, but one thought the idea was "chicken@#$%," so he was left alone to guard the entire south end of the county while we took down the pool hall.

At the Junior High, Bob got out and put on his flak vest, helmet, faceplate, and jackboots, loaded up his shotgun, and got some extra handcuffs. I was trying to look inconspicuous by sinking into the front seat. Bob headed for the bushes with the other officers, then turned, looked at me, and came back. "Get out of the vehicle," he said, "You're coming with us." "Well, actually I am a civilian ride-along *observer*," I said, "and I think I'm supposed to observe—from a distance."

Bob was not interested in listening. He was on broadcast mode. "You're coming with us. And you're going to get at least THREE of them. Or I ain't letting you back in the car."

"How can I get three of them?" I protested. "You've got the pistol, the shotgun, the boots, and the handcuffs. I got nothing. How can I get three of them?"

"One under each arm, and one between the legs," Bob chortled. He grabbed me by the collar and dragged me along on the raid.

We went through some bushes and reached a clearing. The pool hall was about a hundred yards away. In the clearing were some shacks. It was about ten at night, so no one was outside. But Bob and the other cops were making a lot of noise, with all their riot gear. So someone inside one of the shacks called out, "Who's dere?"

Bob said, "Shhhhhh. Police." Bad move, Bob.

The guy in the shack had a dog. Thinking quickly, he kicked it. The dog let out a howl. Every other dog for a mile around began to howl. They all came out of the bushes to investigate. There were at least four million of them. Then they started barking, biting, and chasing us.

We ran through the remaining bushes towards the pool hall, the dogs hot on our heels. But these were no ordinary bushes. This was razor grass, eight feet tall with spines as sharp as a rattler's tooth. We crashed through the razor grass, getting cut, swearing, and sweating.

Finally we arrived at the back of the pool hall. Bob pulled out his gun, kicked open the back door, staggered inside, panted for a moment, then hollered, "Up against the wall, mother#$%#*&s! You're all under arrest for gambling!"

But the guys weren't gambling. They had heard us coming long before. They were playing pool. They looked up, as if surprised, and said, "Oh, my. It's the cops, man." They walked around us, and looked us up and down. "Oh, dear. Y'all look pretty bad, man. You sweatin' bad. Did the dogs bite you? Did the razor grass cut you?"

Bob and the other cops beat a sullen retreat. We made no arrests. But we did stop the gamblin' at the Sunrise Bar and Pool Hall—for an hour at least.

The Wedding Cake
and the Sliding Snake

The smartest thing I ever did was marry my wife Susan. We met on an airplane from Atlanta to Washington, D.C., after visiting our respective parents in Mobile and Daytona. It was fate. Susan was supposed to be on a flight ahead of mine. But her flight was canceled and she ended up sitting in my row, with an empty seat between. I eyed her. She eyed me. I brought out a book—*Even Cowgirls Get the Blues*—to show that I could read. She smiled. But we were both too shy to say anything. The flight was short, and the time remaining was getting shorter. What happened next is in dispute. She claims that she accidentally knocked over her purse. I contend she deliberately turned over her purse, dumping money, including a number of actual quarters (big money in those days), on the floor to attract my attention. Whatever happened, it worked. We started talking. I got her phone number.

Then she passed all the tests I devised. I waited three weeks before calling her. On our first date, she did not object to my car, an ancient Plymouth Valiant (hey, my old employer, the United Farm Workers, said it was the most reliable car made in the U.S.A.). She did not even object to the orange shag carpet that tastefully decorated the car floor and dash. She went out on our first date in a blizzard to a Japanese double feature, including the classic *Throne of Blood*. I realized that this was the girl for me. I proposed to her on a beach in Martinique in the moonlight and have been blissful ever since.

But the way of true love does not always run smooth. Our wedding did have its problems. Think of a wedding as an exercise in project management—there is a contract, a project manager, a goal to be achieved, subcontractors, a venue organizer, supplies, inputs, outputs, etc. As Zorba the Greek would say, "the full catastrophe."

Our major problems involved two subcontractors: the minister and the wedding cake vendor. The minister was supposed to show up forty-five minutes early, hold our hands, and soothe our nerves. In fact, he was twenty minutes late, during which time we were shaking with anxiety. It turned out he has been delayed by a parade through the middle of Alexandria, Virginia, where we were getting married.

The wedding cake vendor had been wonderful when we approached him weeks before the wedding. He showed us numerous elaborate cakes, including some which looked like a fleet of individual flying saucers descending from the sky to attack the guests. He flitted around the cake office, oohing and aahing, saying how "mahvelous" everything would be. But Susan was very firm. She wanted a simple, conservative three-layer cake, with no little plastic figures on top. Just some vanilla icing and some flowers made of icing around the bottom of each layer and on the top, thank you very much. The cakemeister reluctantly agreed.

The great day came. So did the cake. It arrived fifteen minutes before the start of the wedding. A lanky, greasy guy with a ponytail pulled up in a van and brought it in. "Sign here," he said. We opened the box and looked at the cake. And we looked down, and saw—cake. Just cake. The top of the cake had NO ICING. NO FLOWERS made of icing. No nothing. There was icing and flowers on the sides, but absolutely nothing except bare cake on top. We hollered at the delivery guy, "What the #$%#$% is this?" He replied with the classic: "Hey, man, I'm just the delivery guy. You gotta call the office. Which is closed. It opens Monday."

215

Susan was almost in tears. "Don't worry," I said. "I'll take care of it." And I did what any good project manager in a crisis does—I delegated. I called over my Best Man, and explained the situation. "Fix it, please," I begged.

Luckily our Best Man was resourceful. He looked around for materials to hand. Since we were getting married at the Robert E. Lee Boyhood Home, and it was late spring, there were beautiful rose bushes all around. He rushed over to the best roses, yanked out his trusty Swiss Army knife, and prepared to do surgery. But the old battleaxe who ran the Home saw what he was about to do. She came screaming up, and grabbed him by the arm. "Don't you touch Bobby Lee's roses!" she shrieked. He said he wouldn't bother the roses, and started looking around for other flowers. But she followed him around like a bull terrier, and wouldn't let him touch anything.

Finally in desperation, he went over to the dried flower arrangements that we had ordered for the wedding. He grabbed a big double handful of dried flowers, stems and all, and jammed them down into the top of the wedding cake. And you know, it worked. No one noticed. If you look closely at the wedding photos, it does look a little peculiar to see all those dried flowers sticking out. But only we know the secret. Our Best Man was the Best.

Our wedding difficulties paled in comparison to the amazing wedding I heard about from a co-worker, regarding a wedding at Emmitsburg, in northern Maryland, at the popular grotto that replicates the Grotto of Lourdes in France.

Wedding photo of Llewellyn Toulmin and Susan Little. Note the cake with dried flowers inserted in the top.

The grotto wedding began conventionally enough. The bride walked up the aisle, and the happy couple and the minister stood just under the lip of the grotto, with the audience outside and facing the grotto. The top of the grotto was about twenty feet above the heads of the couple. It was lined with thick vines.

Suddenly one of the vines began to move. A few members of the audience noticed and looked up. They gasped. Other members looked up and gasped, too. They pointed. Soon everyone in the audience was looking up at a long, narrow vine directly over the heads of the happy couple. On the vine was a snake. A very big snake. A very big rattlesnake. On a very long, weak vine, that was bending, bending, bending—and suddenly the snake was sliding down the vine, and falling down! He hit the ground between the couple and the minister, with a very big thud. He was quite upset. He darted his head in all directions and rattled viciously.

Incredibly, the minister, bride, and groom stood their ground. They went on with the ceremony. The rattlesnake looked around, saw a nearby bush, and slithered over to the bush. Here he rattled and darted out his tongue, looking like the Devil personified. The minister hurriedly whipped through the rest of the service. Then everyone ran for the cars.

Would I have married Susan if a rattlesnake had slid down the wall of the Lee Boyhood Home and rattled at my feet?

Let's not go there—next story!

Weekend Getaway: East Timor

"Why are you flying to my new country?" asked the friendly young East Timorese man in the airplane seat behind me. He was personable, with a bright smile, and looked part Indonesian and part Portuguese. "Do you work for the U.N.?"

"No," I said, "I'm a tourist."

"What!?" he exclaimed. "We don't have any tourists in East Timor. You must be the first one."

A young woman from the United Nations overheard the exchange and chimed in, "They only opened the country to visitors two months ago. They're going to roll out the red carpet for you—or throw you in the loony bin!"

I had been working on a short e-government assignment in Jakarta, Indonesia. The U.S. ambassador was nervously urging dependents and non-essential personnel to leave, due to anti-American demonstrations. Faced with a boring (and dangerous?) weekend stuck in the hotel, I had decided to fly from the frying pan to the fire. I grabbed a Merpati (the Indonesian domestic airline) daily flight eastwards to Bali and on to Dili, capital of East Timor. This route and a daily flight from Darwin, Australia, are the only ways to get to the world's newest country.

With the passengers—all U.N. workers or locals—staring at me like I was from Mars, I worried a little about my choice for a weekend getaway. But the flight was quite normal, with great views of some of Indonesia's 17,000 islands. Things got a little unusual as we approached Dili, when my new friends pointed out the dry, steep, deforested hills surrounding the large Australian Army compound, and half a dozen white U.N. planes and helicopters on the ground.

The airport was as expected: small, hot, and rather sticky. But my passport stamp was unique: "Arrived East Timor: UNTAET." This was my first introduction to the United Nations Transitional Administration in East Timor. UNTAET was created after a referendum in August 1999 demanded secession from Indonesia. Indonesia had seized the former Portuguese colony back in 1975 and viciously suppressed all dissent since then. Immediately after the 1999 referendum, a short, violent war broke out. UNTAET now runs the country, and will soon hand over the reins of government to the newly elected, democratic East Timorese government. The country is slightly larger than Connecticut, has a population of 800,000, and is located on Timor island northwest of Australia, in eastern Indonesia.

Coming in from the airport I noticed that three quarters of the vehicles on the road were SUVs and pickups painted white with big black "UN" letters on the sides. Many of the other vehicles were from donor agencies. At first the town looked normal, but then I realized that most of the buildings on the main road were recently reconstructed. As the taxi turned onto a side street I began to see the extent of the destruction. Scores of burned-out offices, government buildings, and houses lined the streets. Eerily, almost every one had been cleaned of rubble and debris in preparation for rebuilding—they just looked totally empty, like ghosts. Later I learned that 70 percent of Dili was destroyed by rampaging Indonesian militias, in revenge for the secession. Some other towns in East Timor were 80 to 95 percent destroyed.

Accommodations were definitely out of the ordinary. The Amos "hotel" was a 200-foot-long steel barge, moored just off the main waterfront street. The barge was loaded with a jumble of 100 shipping containers. Each container was converted into a small, rather industrial hotel room with two bunk beds, bathroom and small window. Rates were US$54 per night. The barge hotel had been towed in from Singapore in 2000 to house the numerous U.N. and aid workers, since many of the normal hotels were destroyed.

Just down the street I found another floating hotel, the *Central Maritime*. This 250-foot, upscale cruise vessel was built in Thailand, functioned as a floating hotel in Rangoon for several years, then steamed to Dili in 2000 for a two-year contract. For walk-ins like me, the rate was $130 to $150 per night—rather steep, I thought, for a war zone. My room was a typical cruise ship cabin, but so hot I had to change to a cooler cabin on the shady side of the ship, with better air conditioning.

The Central Maritime cruise ship and floating hotel, Dili, East Timor

The ship was about 80 percent full of Australian Army soldiers in pale green camo, U.S. Marines and U.S. Navy personnel in olive drabs, and civilian aid workers from innumerable countries. I had a late lunch in the ship's dining room. The food was all right but not great, with an emphasis on American-style cuisine and lots of volume.

Small Thai and large Australian policemen packed their pistols in the dining room, despite a large sign ordering "No thong bathing suits, bare feet, or weapons." I wondered if some of the policemen ever broke all three rules simultaneously. That would make a great photo op!

I took a cab—very cheap—to the City Café, the main expat hangout. There I met a French Canadian stewardess with a unique job. "I fly for a two-plane airline," she said. "We fly the De Havilland Dash-7 short-takeoff-and-landing aircraft. We ferry troops, aid workers, and locals around the country, mainly from grass airstrips. We basically serve as a temporary, rented national airline. Our company specializes in this work, which we have done in French Guiana, Cameroon, and here. I have a two-year contract in East Timor. At first I lived in a shipping container on shore. But I've now moved to a more comfortable barracks."

That night I attended a barbecue on the fantail of the *Central Maritime*. It felt very odd to be grilling steaks surrounded by American accents in war-torn East Timor—like a little piece of American suburbia that had floated 11,000 miles away from home.

The next day I hired a hotel staffer, Leandro de Jesus, as a guide. (Since there are no tourists, there are no regular guides.) We drove along the beautiful coast road east out of Dili. I asked him about the war. "I left for West Timor during the problems. When I came back many buildings were destroyed and some people killed." As forgiving as his namesake, de Jesus said, "But I do not hate the Indonesians. They are my brothers. We just had a difference of opinion."

He talked about his new country. "We are very different from Indonesians. We are multi-racial, a mixture of Portuguese, Indonesian, Malay, Chinese, and African. Almost all our people are Roman Catholics, while almost all the 212 million Indonesians are Muslims. We have had elections for Parliament and will have elections for our first

President in a few months. Xanana Gusmão is our national hero and founder of the country, and he will probably be elected. We are drafting our first constitution now. The U.N. will give up power in May 2002. But it will be many years before they leave."

Leandro took me past some very nice beaches and small resorts to a point of land looking back toward Dili. At the top of the point was a benevolent-looking, seventy-foot-tall statue of Christ the King. De Jesus spoke, "With love and tolerance, this war could have been avoided. This statue demonstrates that, since, surprisingly, it was built under the Soeharto regime. He was an Indonesian Muslim, but believed in religious toleration. Unfortunately, the militiamen did not."

Leandro de Jesus with the beautiful Timorese coastline and an upside down bus burnt out during the recent violence in East Timor

Just before my flight back to Indonesia (where things had now quieted down), I talked at the airport with two senior Western policemen. They had volunteered to serve as

UNTAET CIVPOLs (civilian police) on two-year contracts. They said, "The country is very safe and quiet now. There is some petty theft, for which you can hardly blame the locals. They only earn eight dollars a day as laborers, if they can find a job. That amount won't buy two loaves of bread in the ex-pats' supermarket, the 'Hello Mister.'"

They described the odd financial and economic situation. "The entire economy runs on U.S. dollars. It's the official currency here." This was clearly true, despite a lengthy and confusing U.N. notice posted in the airport, ordering residents to use the nonexistent "East Timorese currency."

The policeman continued, "Shortly after the war, the country switched over from the Indonesian rupiah to the U.S. dollar. A plane stuffed with dollars and coins was flown in to jumpstart the dollarization. Some merchants will still reluctantly take rupiah or Australian dollars. These are converted to U.S. dollars in the informal street exchange outside the 'Hello Mister.' The economy is now totally reliant on aid. But there is the possibility of some self-sufficiency based on agriculture, sandalwood and marble exports, and perhaps some oil and gas development."

The officers were critical of the U.N. pay system. "The typical U.N. worker makes a big killing off all the many allowances, extra payments and high base pay here. These rates drive up the cost of the relief effort. They inflate the local economy and that hurts the East Timorese. Worst of all, the system turns altruistic aid workers into leeches. The system should be reformed so CIVPOLs and aid workers break even compared to their pay back home, or even lose a little. Then we'd get a better type of volunteer."

The United Nations was having some law enforcement management problems, according to the officers. "We have forty-one countries who have seconded policemen to the UNTAET CIVPOL force. This shows the broad political support for our work here. But it creates an administrative nightmare. The worst problem is the wildly different standards of officers we get. Some are great, but some are terrible. We have had to repatriate a number of men for being drunk on duty and other infractions. Most were from poor countries with low-quality policing."

"Luckily, the crime situation is now very quiet. The only reason not to come here is the lack of emergency medicine, not any crime or unrest. But that could change once the large number of former militiamen now in West Timor are let back into the East. They may quietly accept the new situation, or they might create real trouble."

So now may be the time for a weekend or even week-long getaway in East Timor, a beautiful country with a dark past and uncertain future. It's a great opportunity to see real nation building, literally from the ground up. If you come, don't bother about a tourist visa. It's not required, the country is so new that there is no embassy in Washington to give you one, and anyway, no one will believe that you're a tourist!

Ballerina, Spy, First Lady: The Story of Kirsty Sword Gusmão

Kirsty Sword Gusmão is the world's newest First Lady, of the world's newest country: Timor Leste. She is probably the youngest First Lady on Earth, also. Her story is so incredible that even Hollywood would boggle at the script.

Kirsty Sword, now thirty-seven, was born and raised in suburban Melbourne, Australia. As a teenager she dreamed of becoming a ballerina and a journalist but never expected that she would be making headlines herself. At Melbourne University she studied Italian and Indonesian and pursued her ballet dreams. But she was too tall for the professional ballet, and she ultimately focused on Indonesian politics and language as her main interest. She joined Australian Volunteers International as a teacher and aid worker in Jakarta, the capital of Indonesia.

Kirsty Sword Gusmão, First Lady of East Timor and former spy for the Timorese Resistance

In 1991 Kirsty was hired as an interpreter on a Yorkshire TV documentary special on East Timor, a part of eastern Indonesia that had been forcibly seized in 1975 by the Indonesian military. An estimated 250,000 East Timorese had been killed or had starved or died of disease under Indonesian military rule over the years in Indonesia's ongoing attempt to suppress the freedom movement.

Shortly after the documentary was made, a massacre took place in East Timor in which many of the people Kirsty had met and filmed were killed. She was profoundly affected, and it was a turning point in her life. "Many thought East Timor was a lost cause," she said in an interview in Bangkok. "But I was so impressed with the courage of the East Timorese and the justice of their cause that I became an undercover agent for their movement. I even had a code name, 'Ruby Blade,' derived from my real name. I became a courier for the cause, and served for four years as the message center for all communications in Jakarta." Observers who later learned of her activities said that if the Indonesian military had learned of her activities, she would have been abducted and killed, without any form of trial.

One of "Ruby Blade's" most dangerous activities was passing messages to East Timorese leaders who were in jail in Jakarta. She posed as a young, naïve woman aid worker whose "Australian uncle was in jail for fraud." She found the prison guards "eminently corruptible" and managed to smuggle in food and messages to the prisoners. The most famous of these was Xanana Gusmão, the legendary poet, pumpkin farmer, and head of the East Timorese resistance. He had successfully hidden in the hills of East Timor for eighteen years before finally being captured and imprisoned for life. Through an intermediary, "Ruby Blade" managed to smuggle a mobile phone to Xanana in his cell. Over the phone and through letters she taught him English, smuggled messages, and helped direct the resistance.

The couple met for the first time in person in an Indonesian jail cell, for only a few minutes, in December 1994. But Kirsty acknowledges she had developed feelings for Xanana even before meeting him. "I had already built up a strong impression of him as a person. I felt he was extremely humble, modest, open, warm, and humane. Meeting him in person confirmed all those impressions." Xanana is also ruggedly handsome, with a salt-and-pepper beard, wide eyes, and an infectious laugh. Kirsty's feelings were returned, and it was clearly love at first sight, in the most difficult of circumstances. There were other difficulties. Xanana was nineteen years older, and he was already married with two children, although his marriage had broken down and his wife had moved to Australia. The most immediate problem was that Xanana's followers were planning a very dangerous jailbreak for him.

President Xanana Gusmão of East Timor, pumpkin farmer, resistance fighter, poet

"The underground leaders outside the jail had concocted a plan in which hired Bosnian mercenaries were going to attack the jail and break out the East Timorese prisoners," said Kirsty. "I brought in word of this plan to him, and he immediately ordered me to stop the effort. He felt that international opinion and the U.N. would eventually lead to his freedom and to independence for East Timor, and that any violent jailbreak could jeopardize all this. So I carried his message out to the underground, and the plan was scrapped." By stopping this dangerous effort, Kirsty probably saved Xanana's life.

Within a few years, Xanana's highly unlikely vision of the future was proved correct. World public opinion and the continued resistance of the East Timorese led to Indonesia granting a referendum, which was overwhelmingly for independence. The United Nations took over East Timor, Xanana was freed, and he was elected president of the new republic, officially named Timor Leste. Xanana divorced his first wife, and in July 2000 he married Kirsty in a quiet ceremony in the hills of East Timor. Their son, Alexandre, was born two months later.

All was not a fairytale ending, however. When it became clear that East Timor would get its independence, hundreds of thousands of Indonesian military and West Timorese "militiamen" had stormed into East Timor. They looted and burned much of the country, so that it is estimated that over 80 percent of the capital, Dili, was destroyed, and many towns were even worse off. Villagers in East Timor say that the militiamen were paid $20 for each East Timorese scalp they brought back to West Timor. Many East Timorese were killed, and many of the women were raped. Some were even abducted and forced to become the "wives"—really the sex slaves—of the militiamen. These poor women were sometimes paraded through the streets as war trophies.

These horrors have given Kirsty one of her major causes in life. She created the Alola Foundation to help women raped by the Indonesian militiamen, and has testified before the U.N. Human Rights Commission in Geneva, attempting to get the abductees returned to their families in East Timor. She launched efforts to help poor East Timorese women sell their crafts overseas. She is the head of the National Reconciliation Commission, where she is trying to bring the country back together again. She serves as one of the key political advisors to her husband, the new head of the country. And she is the First Lady of Timor Leste, with all the ceremonial functions that implies.

Kirsty tries to get away from these official duties by living in the hills above Dili on a modest farm with Xanana. In the morning she takes care of Alexandre, who is now two years old, and her new baby Kay. "I try to give them somewhat of a normal life. And I face the same dilemma as all women all over the world—how to divide my time between my family and the things outside the home that concern me."

Kirsty Sword Gusmão, a.k.a. Ruby Blade, may see her dilemma as typical, but she is surely one of the most remarkable women on the planet.

Llewellyn M. Toulmin

Seeing Guam the Hard Way: Twenty-Eight Years in a Hole

Guam is basically four U.S. military bases and a NASA installation held together by a strip mall. An ugly strip mall. When I visited there, the mall had been stripped of any remaining charm by Super Typhoon Pongsona, which packed winds of 185 mph.

But even though the place looked rather tacky, I had no desire to avoid it all by hiding in a hole in the ground. Yet this is what Guam's most famous tourist did—for twenty-eight years. Here is his story.

Shoichi Yokoi was born in 1915 near Nagoya, Japan. A tailor's apprentice in peacetime, he was drafted and went to fight in Manchuria for three years. He returned to Japan and then received a secret call-up letter from the Imperial Japanese Army. It said, "Leave home as if you were going out for a stroll. Do not pack. Do not say goodbye to your family." He was ordered to report for duty in the Pacific; it was just before Pearl Harbor. He ended up on Guam, serving as a supply sergeant.

When the Americans invaded Guam in July 1944, Yokoi said that "the real fighting lasted for only one day. Then we dispersed all over the island and launched guerilla attacks at night. We fought with swords and rocks against the enemy's guns and planes."

Although it was clear that the battle for Guam was over, many Japanese refused to surrender, fearing shame or execution. "We had been told that the Americans would kill us if we surrendered. So many of us hid in the hills," said Yokoi. For several years he lived in a succession of caves and shelters, with smaller and smaller groups. Eventually he dug a small hole in the ground and lived alone. "I couldn't stand the continuous arguments with my fellow soldiers about who was doing most of the work, and who was finding the most food." It was a *Survivor* episode, for real.

Sergeant Shoichi Yokoi, Imperial Japanese Army

Food was a constant problem, especially since Yokoi rarely ventured outside his hole during the day. He hunted at night, when it was safer. But his catch was slimmer. River shrimp, eels, sago palm nuts, and coconuts were a mainstay of his diet. A real treat was wild rat—"the liver is especially delicious" said the gourmet sergeant. But securing any food was difficult, and "I was always hungry."

Yokoi tried to cook most of his food. He started fires using sunlight and a flashlight lens. After he lost the lens, a major blow, he rubbed sticks together or used gunpowder from his ammunition. To economize, he created a "fire rope" from coconut fiber, which acted like a giant slow fuse, preserving the fire at the end of the rope.

Some food was dangerous. Two of Yokoi's band died in a cave near his, apparently from eating poisonous local toads.

Yokoi's clothes rotted within a few years in the humid weather and frequent downpours. But as a tailor he was able to reconstruct his clothes using fibers from bark of the local pago tree. He would laboriously pound this bark, extract fibers, weave a rough cloth, cut this into the proper shapes, then sew the shapes together.

Medicine, entertainment, reading matter, air conditioning, a mattress with bedclothes—all these were non-existent. What did exist were constant swarms of mosquitos and flies, wasps, snakes and the threat of starvation. His main comfort was his "thousand stitch belt," a wide cloth belt that brought good luck because 1000 individuals had each put in one stitch and a blessing.

The ironies of his situation are amazing. While Yokoi crouched in his cave, planeloads of Japanese tourists arrived every hour, delighted to sun themselves on Guam's beaches just miles from his cave. But their Japan Air Lines planes never flew over Yokoi's cave, otherwise he might have realized that the war was really over. JAL flew to the civilian airport at the center of the island, and never flew the few miles to the south where his cave was located. From his cave, Yokoi saw only US military planes, which were quite numerous. Yokoi's cave was just three miles from a major NASA installation, where high tech dishes monitored the condition of satellites, including ones belonging to the Japanese government. And Yokoi's cave was within sight of a major housing development, where residents watched TV—including a Japanese station—in air-conditioned comfort.

*Diagram of the hiding hole and home for many years of
Sergeant Yokoi in southern Guam*

Yokoi never surrendered. For many years after the war, troops, police and local hunters tracked down Japanese soldiers, left leaflets, and used loudspeakers to broadcast peaceful messages. But even though Guam is only about 10 by 25 miles, there were many good hiding places. And Yokoi said that, "I didn't come out because I was afraid— not afraid of dying, afraid of dying with shame. When I was a kid in Japan I was trained that the spirit of Japan is to die the way the cherry blossoms go—without shame. I was afraid I wouldn't go that way." After 28 years on the run, Yokoi was very hungry one evening and went out at dusk to fish for river shrimp. Unluckily—or luckily—he was spotted and captured by two Guamanian hunters. It was 1972. He had been down in his hole for 28 years.

He became an immediate sensation. Japanese reporters rushed to the island and found the cave. They reported that it was in the southeast, hilly part of the island, ingeniously concealed in a grove of bamboo, beside a stream. The entrance was just two feet square, covered with camouflage, and the entrance hole was nine feet deep. The entrance was lined with wood, with a bamboo ladder leading down. At the bottom was a horizontal living tunnel, 39 inches high and about 10 feet long. This was home. At the end near the stream was a toilet alcove about three feet square. It was designed so that in high rains the water and waste flowed naturally downhill through a drain to the stream.

The Japanese reporters said that, "The odor inside the hole was stifling, a combination of the Frederico nuts and the oily soot from cooking that over the years has seeped into the earthen walls. The stench was so bad that none of us could remain in the cave for long."

Sergeant Yokoi was taken home to huge acclaim. He was welcomed at the Tokyo airport by 5000 well-wishers. His first broadcast words were, "It is with much embarrassment that I have returned alive," which instantly became a popular saying. Within nine months he was married to a younger woman. They took their honeymoon where many Japanese couples do—on Guam.

Yokoi seemed to suffer few after-effects of his trials. He was reunited with his remaining family, wrote a book, starred in a TV show, stayed married, and enjoyed his fame. Yet near the end of his life, in 1997, his fear of a shameful death reappeared. He was stricken with disabilities, and according to his elder brother, Yokoi "chose to starve himself to death, like many of the Japanese soldiers did during the end of the war. He wanted to die like them."

Yokoi is one of the few people who has two tombstones. One gives his correct death date. The earlier one says, "The Late Sergeant Shoichi Yokoi, decorated with the Eighth

Order of Merit. He died at age thirty in 1944 on Guam, when his entire unit fought like heroes to the death."

Sergeant Yokoi's original cave has almost entirely collapsed, and is on inaccessible private land. But his cave has been recreated at the Talofofo Falls Park near the southern end of the island. It is a major attraction for the many Japanese tourists that come to Guam.

I went there on a nice, clear day with typical eighty-degree weather. All the electricity was out, a victim of the super typhoon, so the cable car from the entrance down to the falls and the cave was not working. But I got in the back of a pickup with a group of five young Japanese men with spiky hair and rode down the hill. The falls were beautiful and cool, flowing over smooth rocks to a pool below. The recreated cave was a few hundred yards downstream. Next to it was a Buddhist and Shinto shrine, with markers commemorating Sergeant Yokoi and his two poisoned companions.

We all read the marker that told Yokoi's story. We trooped over and looked down the hole into the cave. We were not supposed to go too near it, or in it, because the earth was so soft from the typhoon's deluge. But we could see the essence: a two-foot-square entrance leading to a large live-in coffin. I asked one of the young men, Katsuto Shi of Takahama, Japan, what he thought of Sergeant Shoichi Yokoi. He rubbed his red, spiky hair and said, "Yokoi was very strong man—but crazy."

Katsuto Shi beside the Yokoi hole

The Most Annoying Country on Earth: I "AS NO VISSA"

I often leaf through the seven passports I have had in my life, looking at the many beautiful stamps and visas from the 121 fascinating countries I have visited. But I am proudest of the simple stamp that says: "Bangladesh: Refused Entry." And therein lies a tale.

It began when I was working as a consultant to a large international development institution. I flew out to Vietnam via the Pacific on a mission and wanted to visit Bangladesh on the westbound return journey, to sightsee and prospect for business, since I had never been there. I was leaving soon, so there was not time to get a visa at the embassy in Washington. They said, "Five business days to get a visa," far more than the usual, an omen of troubles to come. But my highly experienced travel agent looked in his computer, read off the information for Bangladesh, and assured me I could get a business visa on arrival by paying a $50 fee.

Leaving Vietnam and going through Bangkok, I asked the airline staff if there would be any visa problems. "Oh, no," said two charming lady staffers confidently. "There used to be problems, but since you are a U.S. citizen you don't need a visa now."

Arriving in Dhaka, the capital of Bangladesh, I quickly realized that everything I had been told was wrong. "YOU HAVE NO VISA!" shouted the angry immigration official. "YOU MUST HAVE VISA! WHERE IS PAPER?" he yelled.

"I'll sign any paper you want," I said. "Just give me a 'business visa on arrival."

"YOU MUST HAVE PAPER FROM SPONSOR! WHERE IS SPONSOR?" he screeched like a banshee.

"I don't have a local sponsor; I was not told I needed one," I rejoined.

"GO BACK TO BANGKOK!" he bellowed.

There then followed thirty-six almost nonstop hours of negotiations, discussions, numerous trips back and forth through Immigration, and meetings with higher and higher Bangladeshi and airline officials, culminating in a meeting with the Almighty Poobah Himself, the Immigration Officer-in-Charge.

In the course of all this, I learned that several foreigners, mostly Americans, are trapped like this in Dhaka *every day*. The rules had been quietly changed several months earlier, for the umpteenth time, but the government and airlines had not properly informed their employees and the public.

Oddly, no one, not even the Immigration Officer-in-Charge, seemed to want a bribe—which I probably would have paid. "The matter is out of our hands; the government has given us no discretion," he said, and seemed to mean it. All the local officials were trapped in a web of rigidity, ineptitude, and bureaucracy that appeared to be an integral part of the national culture.

The new government was largely to blame. These morons had abolished business and transit visas, changed the days of the work week, and made numerous other silly and disruptive changes that were scaring off visitors and investors.

Naturally I sought help. Airport lounge staff allowed me to use a card phone to call for help—at a 900 percent profit margin over their cost. The hyenas come out to feed when the wildebeest is wounded. I called the local office staff of my client institution, who were quite willing to send a fax to Immigration "sponsoring" me. But no surprise— Immigration didn't have a fax machine. Neither did anyone else in the entire rundown, dirty airport.

Business lounge hyenas were willing to let me call my travel agent in the United States—at $4 per minute for a *collect* call. My only real ally during the ordeal was the manager of my intended hotel in town, who tried valiantly to persuade local officials to let me in. But once they had made up their minds and written the immortal words "AS NO VISSA" on my passport, nothing could shift them.

During a break in the negotiations, I read the local newspapers. The headlines featured a four-hour traffic jam that paralyzed the city—*after* the morning rush hour was over; floodwaters threatening the city; dengue fever and malaria on the rise; a citywide strike; and student unrest. I concluded that I was probably better off at the airport.

The most annoying part of all was being dragged around the airport by a very rude and snotty sergeant, constantly hollering, "FOLLOW! FOLLOW!"

I slept overnight on the floor of the business lounge. For this privilege I was charged $21. While lying on the floor trying to sleep, I reflected on the irony that most of the least desirable countries—the ones everyone is trying to leave— are the toughest to get into. Dangerous countries like Somalia, corrupt countries like Nigeria and Equatorial Guinea, and annoying countries like Bangladesh, often have the most arcane entry rules—and the most beautiful entry visas, with holograms and high-tech security strips. As if anyone would bother to forge them.

Eventually the nightmare ended. I boarded the lousy national carrier (the only airline out that wasn't heavily overbooked) and fled to Dubai and London. On the flight I read the up-to-date airline magazine for the official

Bangladeshi national carrier. It said in five places, in four languages, "Tourist visas: The Officer-in-Charge of Immigration, Dhaka Airport, may issue 15-day visas on arrival."

All in all, I consider being refused entry by a country like Bangladesh to be a touristic badge of honor. And I do think I earned the right to say that I visited and experienced the essence of this most annoying country, even though I never left the airport.

Passport stamp from the world's most annoying country: Bangladesh

World's Worst Traffic Jam?

My wife and I were on a package tour of India and were headed from New Delhi to a castle hotel in Rajasthan by bus. The hotel was about fifty miles away, so, being an experienced Third World traveler, I figured it would take about four hours or so. Wrong!

We trundled along for an hour at about thirty miles an hour, leaving Delhi and its outskirts behind. The countryside was dry and dusty, and it made us thirsty just to look at it. Beside the two-lane road—really more of a lane and a half, when you counted the potholes—were deep ditches on either side. On the edge of the ditches were a few dry, dusty, gray-green trees. Every kilometer or so was an overturned truck deep in the ditch. Our guide called them "dead elephants."

Traffic was heavy but moving. Ninety percent of the traffic consisted of huge, tall, overburdened trucks filled with sacks of rice and other agricultural products. It was easy to see how they could overturn and go into the ditches.

This potholed, narrow, overloaded, dangerous road was one of the four major highways leading out of Delhi, and connecting the capital to the rest of the country.

Suddenly we stopped. There was no town, no traffic light, no intersection, no nothing. Just a line of trucks stretching to the horizon. We sat. We waited. We looked out the window. The air conditioner failed. We sweated. We drank a Coke. We drank all the Coke. We looked out the window some more. We drank some water. We drank all the water. We asked our guide what the trouble was. He shrugged.

This went on for SIX HOURS. We never moved. Finally our guide got out of the bus and walked down the road to find the problem. He came back after an hour. He had not reached the front of the jam. He did not know the cause of the trouble.

After another hour I grabbed the guide and demanded action. We walked up the line of trucks and cars. People were out of their cars, talking, wondering, reading books, cooking meals, setting up camp. Kids were running around the trucks playing tag. We trudged onwards. After about three miles we finally reached the head of the jam. Two trucks were nose-to-nose diagonally across the road, almost touching. Inside, the truck crews were playing cards. Around the trucks an angry crowd had gathered and was screaming epithets at the truck drivers and crews.

I asked the guide to find out what was going on. He questioned people in the crowd and returned with this story.

"Sahib, one of the trucks was traveling along when the driver decided to make a turn into a side road across the oncoming traffic. But he turned too close to an oncoming truck, and there was almost an accident. The two trucks ended up facing each other, blocking traffic in both directions. The drivers got out and began swearing at each other. Then they started fighting. Then their crews started fighting. Then they got tired. So they went back to their truck cabs and ate some chappatis and played some cards. Then they came out and swore and fought some more. Then they went back to their cabs and drank. Then they came out and fought some more. Because of the ditches, there is really no way around the trucks. Two cars tried to get around, and they rolled over upside-down in the ditch. But no one was hurt. The crowd has been begging the truckers to pull back and let one truck go ahead to clear the jam, but they ignore the people. This has been going on for eight hours."

The guide went forward and berated the drivers. He, too, was ignored.

Finally I suggested to the guide that we bribe the drivers to pull back. Twenty dollars and five minutes later, the Mother of All Traffic Jams was broken. We were the heroes of the day, and were cheered by the crowd.

In all it took us thirteen hours and forty-five minutes to go the fifty miles. An average of 3.6 miles per hour. If I hadn't ponied up the money, I'd still be stuck in traffic in India.

A "dead elephant" or overturned truck on an Indian road

Llewellyn M. Toulmin

Uncle KGB Wants Me

This is the true story of how the KGB tried to recruit me as a secret agent.

Ronald Reagan had just taken office, and the small social science consulting firm I was working for was going downhill fast as our federal clients' social science budgets were cut. Looking desperately for alternative sources of income, I decided to write a book about what would happen if Ron pushed the nuclear button. The term "nuclear winter" had not yet been coined, but I was on its track, trying to identify the ecological consequences of a nuclear "exchange."

As part of my research, I wrote letters to the Chinese and Russian embassies, asking if their countries had ever done any research on this topic. I didn't expect an answer, but I thought I should try. The Chinese sent me some glossy magazines called *China Reconstructs,* which I thought had a nice touch of irony, given the topic. I heard nothing from the Russians.

Months passed. My book idea was sidetracked by other projects. One day the office receptionist called and said that a man was waiting to meet me. I had no appointments, so I came out front. I was confronted by a short, dumpy man with an ill-fitting greenish suit and a too-wide orange tie. He presented his card: Boris Davydov, First Secretary at the Soviet Embassy (a few blocks away). In a thick Russian accent he said we should go back to my office to talk. As we approached my office, Boris made sure I was ahead of him. He deftly hooked the door shut with his foot. We were alone.

245

BORIS N. DAVYDOV
FIRST SECRETARY (PRESS)
EMBASSY OF THE UNION OF SOVIET SOCIALIST REPUBLICS

1125 SIXTEENTH STREET, N.W.
WASHINGTON, D. C. 20036

Without any preliminaries, Boris immediately began to pump me about my background—where was I born, who were my parents, what was my nationality, where did I go to school, etc. Within a minute I figured he was KGB or GRU (Soviet military intelligence). But I thought, "Who cares? I have no secrets to hide. Let's see what happens." So I answered all his questions.

Boris spent twenty minutes on me, running through my many jobs chronologically. Then he started on my company. "Does your consulting firm have any contracts with DoD? With the intelligence community?" he asked. I said, truthfully, that we did not. To myself I kinda wished that we *did* have some of those contracts, since that was where the money was.

After forty-five minutes of grilling, Boris established that my firm and I were totally useless to him. We had no security clearances, no clients other than federal or D.C. civilian agencies, and no prospects for secret work. I expected him to laugh and leave.

Instead, he said nothing and stared me in the eyes for two very long minutes. Then out of the blue he said, "Sooo, you like to take nice trips to Caribbean islands?"

Realizing that he was offering to put me on his payroll as a secret agent, I said, "Yes, Boris. I *do* like to take nice trips to Caribbean islands, and I have *paid my own way* to St. Vincent, St. John's, St. Thomas, and lots of other islands."

He looked disappointed, so I said, "You know, Boris, when I wrote that letter, I really was interested in whether your country had done any research on the consequences of a nuclear exchange."

"Oh, no," he said, "in Russia we never think about such terrible subject. No one allowed to do such awful research." I escorted him out the door.

Reflecting later on his approach, it seemed analogous to a lazy police officer with a quota of parking tickets to fill: "Gotta make my quota of spies recruited today, regardless of how useless..."

I told my bosses about the incident and asked if I should call the FBI. But they discouraged me, not wanting any distractions from our feverish marketing. So I did nothing.

Two weeks later in the *Washington Post* there was a front-page article on Boris, naming him as a KGB officer and detailing his techniques. These mainly consisted of going up on Capitol Hill during the lunch hour and rooting through the desks of Congressional aides. Two weeks after that there was a short squib in the *Post* saying that Boris had been declared PNG—persona non grata—and deported to Mother Russia.

Years later, the CIA and NSA came calling, but that is another story...

Gypped in Gypped: Horsewhipping and Bumping Stomachs

Once upon a time there was a mythical Middle Eastern country named Gypped, with no telephone system. Not one that worked, anyway. As recently as the 1960s, businessmen in Gypped who wanted to make international calls would fly to Athens and call from there.

Then Gypped abandoned Socialism and embraced the American taxpayer instead. The U.S. taxpayers, unknowingly generous to a fault, pumped $500 million of aid into Gypped to build a new phone system. And the system worked, after a fashion.

The U.S. aid came with conditions and advisors. The conditions included setting up an independent telecoms regulatory body, turning the state-owned phone company into a private entity, and introducing competition into the telecom sector. The Gypped government pretended to make progress in these areas, and the U.S. aid agency pretended that progress was being made and kept pumping in the dough. Teams of advisors arrived to help implement the supposed reforms, which of course never happened. As one discouraged advisor said, "No one can out-slow a Gypped."

The main reason the reforms never happened was The Minister, known as Pasha Suleiman Suleiman the Magnificent (PSSM). Minister PSSM was an old Socialist who hated Americans and had held power for seventeen years, a record in Gypped. He had no intention of reforming the sector, which he thought was working fine. He was the minister for transport as well as telecoms, and he used the profits from the U.S.-built phone company to create a magnificent monument to himself, a brand-spanking-new subway system in Gypped's capital city. The subway was known as "PSSM's pyramid."

When Minister PSSM wanted to finance a new section of the subway, he would call up the phone company and tell them to cut a huge check and send it over to the subway construction managers the next morning. Over the years hundreds of millions of dollars were siphoned off in this way.

One day a new team of advisors arrived in the capital city. They settled into their hotel and asked for an audience with Minister PSSM, whom they were supposed to closely advise. No reply came from the ministerial palace. The advisors waited, moved into apartments for their two-year contract, and again requested an audience. No reply. This happened every month for six months.

Eventually the advisory team Project Manager, a handsome but naïve young American, became annoyed. He thought it rather rude of The Minister to take $500 million of U.S. money and not even have a meeting with any U.S. advisors. The PM "raised a concern" with the U.S. aid agency, but was told to shut up and not rock the boat.

Seeking counsel, the PM tracked down the PM of the first U.S. advisory team in Gypped. And behold, he was told a wondrous tale.

"When we first arrived in-country," said the first PM, "we sought an audience with Minister PSSM. No reply came from the ministerial palace. We asked again a month later. No reply. We kept asking for eight months—a third of our two-year contract. Finally we were granted an audience. Our team was ushered into the great man's office, and we drank strong coffee and made polite chit-chat. The Minister, a tall, imposing, lugubrious man who never smiled, said, 'Have you been in Gypped long enough to see some cultural sites?'

"I took this opening," said the old PM, "and ran with it: 'Well, your Excellency, we *have* had quite a while to see all of your cultural sites, because we have been here for eight months. And we are a teensy bit concerned about that, since we're meant to be advising you every day on important national policy. Yet this is our first meeting with you.'

"'WHAT?'" bellowed The Minister. "'You've been in Gypped eight months??!!!' The Minister grabbed his telephone and called his male secretary, sitting in the outer office. He began screaming at the secretary down the phone line, then ordered him to come in. The secretary came in, blubbering in fear, and The Minister continued screaming at him.

"The Minister stood up, opened his desk drawer, and pulled out a short horsewhip. In front of our aghast American delegation, he began to whip his secretary, beating him ferociously about the head and shoulders.

"Eventually The Minister's arm got tired. He dismissed his wailing secretary, sat down, and calmly replaced the whip in the desk drawer. 'That will never happen again,' said Minister PSSM. 'Just call me whenever you want an appointment.'

The old PM said, "We left The Minister's office, thunderstruck but confident that we would now become his closest advisors.

"But the joke was on us. Two weeks later we asked for an audience. No reply. And for the rest of our two-year contract we only got one more short meeting with Minister PSSM."

The handsome young Project Manager also was able to secure only two short meetings with Minister PSSM during two and a half years on the project. He later calculated that Minister PSSM had spent about four hours over twelve years being advised by Americans, for which his sector received $500 million. About $125 million per hour. Not bad for a wily old Socialist who supposedly hated capitalism.

* * *

Below Minister PSSM on the org chart was the Gypped telephone company—massive, unchangeable, inscrutable, eternal. It was known as the Arab Republic of Gypped Authority for National Telecommunications: AROGANT.

One of the team members on the latest U.S. advisory team, who had been on the first U.S. advisory team, said of AROGANT, "You know, it's been six years since I was here last. And nothing has changed, except that the huge pile of smelly garbage in the stairwell at the main telephone exchange has tripled in size."

AROGANT Telecom headquarters, somewhere in the Middle East

One day the handsome young U.S. Project Manager went to meet with the Director General of AROGANT. He waited in the DG's outer office, with the other supplicants and petitioners. While he waited he drew designs in the dust on the waiting room coffee table. The dust was quite thick. It blew in from the desert in through the open windows of the AROGANT offices, making it impossible to install computers in the building. This suited the AROGANT management and staff fine. Computers meant change. Change was bad.

Across from the handsome young PM sat a Gypped national. He was obviously upset and was muttering to himself. He stood up and approached the burly male secretary who guarded the door to the DG's office. He began shouting at the secretary in Arabic. The secretary shouted back. The handsome young PM asked another petitioner what was going on. "Oh, it is a very sad story. The petitioner says he is the manager of a boy's soccer team. He wants a telephone installed in his home so that he can arrange an international tour to Europe and America for the team. Without the telephone line he has no chance of arranging the tour, and the dreams of the boys will be crushed. He has been on the waiting list for a phone for seven years, but now he must have it. He has sent letters and telegrams to the phone company, begging for a phone, but he has gotten no reply. So he has traveled all the way here from the south of the country, to beg for a phone in person."

The petitioner shouted even louder and stood over the seated secretary. The secretary, a big muscular man with a large "raisin" on his forehead from bashing his head on the floor during prayer, stood up and shouted back. They screamed epithets at each other and began bumping stomachs, slamming their bodies into each other. The Director General stuck his head out of the office door to see what was going on. This sent the petitioner over the edge. "I WANT MY PHONE!!!" he howled, and tried to break past the secretary to throttle the DG. Just then two AROGANT police showed up. They grabbed the petitioner by the arms and hustled him away, never to be seen again. The DG shrugged and slammed his door. Just another typical day at the great Gypped phone monopoly.

Llewellyn M. Toulmin

The Scrumptious Flying Cows

It is not just U.S. aid projects that can go awry. A Canadian aid expert told me this tale, which he swore was true.

"There was once a country in southern Africa—let's call it Zambezi. The Canadian International Development Agency—CIDA—wanted to help the Zambezis. So they launched an agricultural aid project, which went on for a year. I was hired a year after the project ended, to evaluate it. I was given the project documents, and briefed in Ottawa on what a success the project had been. One of the main project components was interbreeding Canadian with local cattle. The project designers had noticed that the Zambezi cattle were small, thin, and tough to eat. So they came up with the great idea of introducing Canadian cattle, which were large, fat, and great to eat, to improve the local bloodlines."

"In evaluating the project, I first talked to the project manager. He was very enthusiastic about the effort. 'It was great to see the gratitude with which the Zambezis received our cattle. They were so pleased.'"

"Next I went out to interview the Canadian cattle ranchers. They were very enthusiastic about the project. 'We had some excess cattle, and the government bought them off of us at a top dollar price. So we were very pleased.'"

"Then I looked into the project logistics. Air Canada was very enthusiastic about the project. 'Yes, it would have taken months to ship the cattle by sea. So we were asked to fly the cattle to Zambezi. It was rather expensive, but we treated them like first-class passengers. And they all came through fine.'"

"Next I flew to Zambezi. I talked to the local Ministry of Agriculture officials about the project. They thought it was great. 'Canada has done us a great service by introducing these cattle. We are sure that we will soon be able to export strong, healthy cattle to other countries and improve our balance of payments.'"

"Finally I went out to one of the villages where the cattle had been introduced. But I couldn't find any Canadian cattle, or any new mixed-breed cows, either. I asked around but just got blank stares. I went to another village. Same story. At the third village, I couldn't find any evidence of the project, either. I went to the village head man, and asked him what was going on.

At first he looked blank, then he said, 'Oh, yes, I remember now,' he said. 'One day a year ago a lot of ministers and officials and crazy foreigners came to our village in Mercedes-Benzes. They brought along several big trucks full of fat cows and bulls. They said the cattle had flown here from the other side of the earth to mate with our cattle. They said we should feed the cattle and make them welcome. Then the crowd of people went away. We tried to make the new flying cows feel at home. So we let them loose in the village to eat what our cattle eat—dry brush, scrub, and thorns. But I think the new cattle didn't like this food. They must have eaten very rich food at home, maybe even grass and grain. So soon the new cattle all died.' He rubbed his stomach, and smiled. 'We did have some very good steak dinners, though.'"

Llewellyn M. Toulmin

Disasters:
History, Impacts and Myths

Disasters are in the news, due to the 9-11 2001 terrorist attacks in New York, the 2004 Indian Ocean tsunami, the Pakistan quake of 2005, and the 2004 and 2005 hurricane season in the US. It appears likely that disasters will continue to dominate the headlines for some years to come, if global warming experts are right.

Hence it is useful to understand more than the typical TV commentator about the history, impact and myths of disasters. Don't worry, it won't take but a few minutes before you know more about disasters than any newscaster on the planet.

Why am I qualified to talk about this? I have worked on disasters in several foreign countries, including Jamaica, the Caribbean as a whole, and Thailand. I was the Chairman of the Section on Emergency and Crisis Management for the American Society for Public Administration. And I have undertaken a number of projects for all three of the general emergency response organizations at the US Federal level: the Federal Emergency Management Agency, the National Communications System, and the US Agency for International Development's Office of Foreign Disaster Assistance. I wrote or participated in after-action reports on various disasters and incidents, including the 1972 Republican and Democratic conventions, the Hinsdale, Illinois telecoms switch fire, and Hurricanes Iniki and Andrew, and have published on disasters in professional and academic journals. But enough about me, let's talk about disasters.

255

History and Impacts of Disasters

Three charts will illustrate the history and impacts of disasters. First is a chart showing the major world disasters throughout history, listed in approximate order of their deadliness (see exhibit 1 below).

The major messages to be taken from this chart are as follows:

- When Mother Nature decides to kill a lot of people, the weapon of choice is a really big disease. Note that the most terrifying thing about the Black Death and the similar bubonic Plague of Justinian is that they killed 25 to 50 percent of the population. A similar plague today could kills hundreds of millions. No wonder some policymakers are so worried about avian flu.
- Don't live in China. Of the thirteen items listed on the chart (appropriate, eh?), four are in China.
- Only one item was in the US, and that was relatively small.
- Due to their nature, the last four items listed are necessarily small by comparison with the huge disasters listed in the upper part of the table.

Since hurricanes are a particular threat to the US, an analysis of their impact should be useful. See exhibit 2 below.

Here we see the deaths in black columns, and the damage in gray columns, for the selected 10 major hurricanes. The most deaths were caused by the famous 1900 Galveston storm, at about 7000, while the most damage was caused

Exhibit 1
Selected Major Disasters
in World History by Type
and Impact in Deaths

Type	Date	Location	Deaths
Disease: Black Death	1348-50	Europe	75 M; ½ pop.?
Disease: Plague of Justinian	541-2	Europe	25-30M; ¼ pop?
Famine	1959-61	N. China	30 M
Disease: Influenza	1917	Worldwide	22 M
Floods	1931	China, Huang He River	3.7 M
Cyclone/ hurricane	1970	Bangladesh	1 M
Earthquake	1556	China, Shaanxi	830,000
Tsunami	2004	Indian Ocean	180,000
Shipwreck	1945	Baltic, *Wilhelm Gustloff* torpedoed	7,700
Fire	1845	Canton, China theatre	1,670
Explosion	1917	Halifax, Nova Scotia	1,654
Airplane crash	1977	Tenerife, Canaries; two 747s collided	582
Tornados	1936	Mississippi/Georgia	455

Exhibit 2

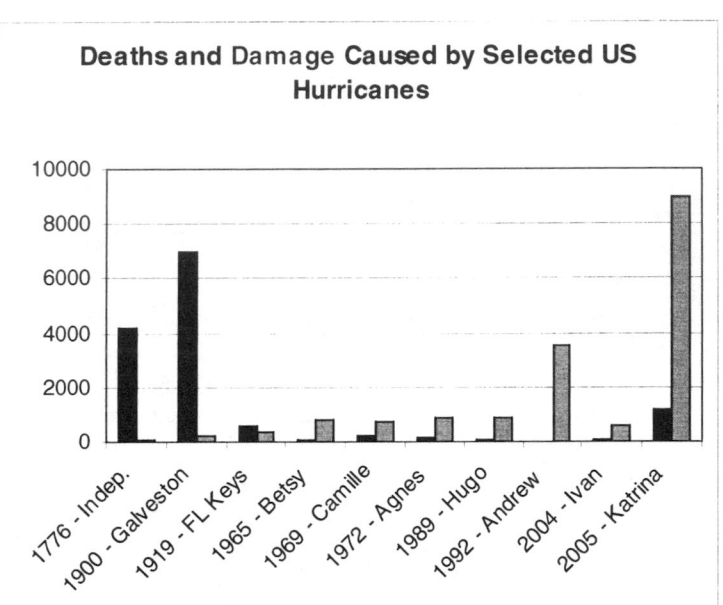

Deaths and Damage Caused by Selected US Hurricanes

by Hurricane Katrina in 2005, with about $90 to 200 billion and counting. (Damage, on the right-hand scale, is measured in units of $10 million, so that Katrina caused roughly 9000 times $10 million, or $90 billion in damage.)

Conclusions to be drawn from exhibit 2 include:

- Deaths from hurricanes are generally declining over time. This is primarily due to better warning and evacuation systems.
- Conversely, damage due to hurricanes in constant dollar terms (which the chart presents) is increasing drastically. This is due to the increasing percentage of the population which is building on the coast, the intensity and height of the construction very near the water, and the lack of strong, enforced, consistent building codes in coastal areas.

Finally, an analysis of the trend in major FEMA disaster declarations should be useful. See exhibit 3 below.

Exhibit 3

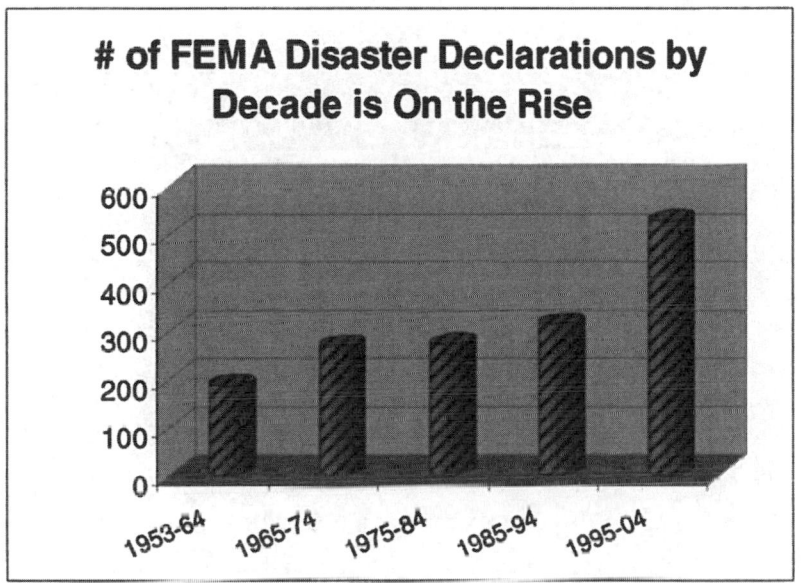

# of FEMA Disaster Declarations by Decade is On the Rise

Here it is obvious that the total number of major FEMA disaster declarations per decade is rising rapidly, after being fairly flat from 1965 to 1994.

Before I discuss the myths of disasters, I should make a point about who actually responds to disasters. Even the smallest disasters can have numerous responders. For example, I studied the sinking of a medium-sized passenger vessel in a lake in the Midwest. Over 55 agencies responded to this one disaster. Major disasters, such as a large hurricane, will have thousands of different agencies and organizations responding. Most responding agencies never make the news, which is a pity, since they are doing good work.

Some types of organizations which respond with little media coverage include:

Religious organizations. Many religious groups have major response units which are vital in providing food, shelter and other services to victims.

Other non-governmental organizations. Many NGOs such as non-religious charities, various associations, ham radio operators, citizens radio groups, etc. respond in a variety of useful ways. Utility companies usually lauch a fantastic response, helping each other and providing assistance in the form of huge caravans of utility trucks, often from hundreds of miles away. Cities and citizens affected by previous disasters are often very generous in providing aid to current victims. For example, the people affected in South Carolina by Hurricane Hugo provided a tremendous amount of aid, including a large caravan of needed goods, to the victims of Hurricane Andrew in south Florida.

State and local governments. Units of governments not affected by disasters will often help those who are hit hard. For example, a substantial contingent of New York City policemen and firefighters dashed to New Orleans after Hurricane Katrina.

Federal organizations other than FEMA. FEMA gets the publicity and the brunt of the criticism. But virtually every Federal (and state) department has an emergency management unit which goes into action during a major disaster, in that department's area of specialization.

And two more general purpose Federal emergency management agencies are never mentioned. First is the National Communications System, a sort of parliament for the telecom systems for all the Federal agencies. NCS answers to the Secretary of Defense, but includes civilian, military and intelligence agencies. NCS has programs which allow Federal (and some state and local) officials to have special telecom access during emergencies, including the ability to "punch through" network congestion, to have calls routed around disaster zones, and to force telecom companies to provide telecom resources to responding agencies if they are not doing so. NCS also obtains private input to disaster planning via the the President's National Security Telecommunications Advisory Council (NSTAC), which includes all the major telecom providers.

The second agency that never receives much credit is the US Agency for International Development's Office of Foreign Disaster Assistance (OFDA). OFDA coordinates the US Government response to all foreign disasters and emergencies. OFDA is small, agile and innovative. For example, it developed the idea and capabilities of the Fairfax County, Virginia and the Metro Dade County, Florida Urban Search and Rescue Teams. These teams can fly out at a moment's notice to any disaster location, anywhere in the world, under OFDA contract. FEMA later borrowed this idea, and also contracted with these same two counties for urban search and rescue skills.

Of course, the Federal agency that responded most heroically to Hurricane Katrina was the US Coast Guard, which reportedly rescued an amazing 33,000 stranded persons along the Gulf Coast, and particularly in New Orleans. As we will find out in the next section, this tremendous rescue effort and success by a Federal government agency is the exception, not the rule.

Myths of Disasters

There are ten major myths of disasters, with several corollaries. These myths occur in both developed and less-developed countries. The myths are as follows:

1. Government officials will rescue the victims of disasters. This myth is believed by all newscasters, and all

261

of the population except those who have actually been in a disaster. The reality is that in most disasters, the vast majority of persons rescued are either self-rescued or are rescued by their neighbors, friends and family. Even heroic local first responders can't rescue that many victims, since there are simply not enough of them. (There is only about one firefighter per 280 population in the US, 1 sworn peace officer per 385 people, and 1 EMT/paramedic per 325 people. And this counts all officials, including administrators. In fact, at any given time in any given area, the ratio of professional rescuers actually on duty to the population may be on the order of 1 to 10,000 or even 100,000.) Most major disasters do not leave thousands stranded in attics or on rooftops, awaiting rescue as in Hurricane Katrina in 2005. Most major earthquakes leave many persons buried in debris, where they are quickly rescued, if alive, by friends and neighbors. And most major hurricanes leave few persons dead and relatively few requiring rescue. Thus Katrina was quite exceptional.

Consider the public policy implications of this—the cost of bringing in FEMA, the National Guard, the Army Reserve, the state governments, etc. to a major disaster is already in the billions. Making this huge, unwieldy system move faster by a day or two may be desirable, but is either impossible or will cost even more billions. But making the self-rescuers and local citizen rescuers more efficient is quite doable and might only cost millions or less. Even in Katrina, if more citizen-rescuers of New Orleans had been trained and prepared for a breaching of the levees, and perhaps provided with inflatable boats in advance of the disaster, rescues could have been safer, swifter and less costly in lives and treasure.

Corollary myths are that the affected population will be so shocked that they will be unable to respond to the disaster, and that "cordons" will be needed for a long time to keep affected victims from re-entering the disaster zone.

(Cordons are barriers around the disaster area enforced by police and the military.) Both myths under-estimate the resilience of disaster victims, who in fact are very motivated to fix their homes and begin normal life again. Local officials almost always overdo the existence of and/or time length imposed for cordons, apparently because it is "something that can be done."

2. Government officials will desert their posts. In fact, this hardly ever happens, even if the officials' families are in danger, the officials are underpaid, or other circumstances tempt the local and state/provincial officials to leave their posts before, during or after the disaster. If New Orleans and Louisiana parish police actually did desert their posts in large numbers during Hurricane Katrina in 2005, then this is doubly shocking and almost unprecedented.

3. Crime rates will spike up during the disaster. In fact, crime rates usually drop before, during and after the disaster. This is apparently due to a feeling of community solidarity, evacuation of some of the population, and the lack of transport after the disaster. The official response, to call out the National Guard or local equivalent to prevent looting, usually results in a lot of bored, expensive guardsmen standing around on every street corner doing nothing, when they could be helping with rebuilding. Of course, lootings, robberies, murders and other crimes do occur during disasters. But often early reports of crimes are found to have been exaggerated by the disaster rumor mill. Officials need to be educated ahead of time to the ferocity and convincing nature of this rumor mill. Usually they don't figure this out until it is too late, then they look foolish.

4. Bodies must be buried as soon as possible after a disaster, to prevent serious epidemics. This myth is replayed over and over by the media after every major disaster. This myth shows how media commentators rarely do their homework, or bother to learn anything about the events they are covering. The fact is that, according to the well-regarded World Health Organization and Pan American Health Organization, "dead bodies do not cause epidemics." If the media would bother to ask the simple question, "So what happened to that epidemic we were warning about?", they would perhaps figure this out.

The effects of spreading this myth are not trivial. Frightened by broadcasters repeating this myth every hour, local officials in developing (and some developed) countries often bury bodies in mass graves, or burn piles of bodies. This prevents identification, prevents the families from experiencing the relief of the grieving process, and can hamper attempts to determine the cause of death if not immediately obvious (as in a chemical or biological attack). Overly quick destruction of bodies, without the proper burial rites, can even make family members in some cultures feel that the victim cannot enter heaven. This can be incredibly traumatic and lead to psychological problems and even violent rebellions against local officials.

5. A good solution to housing the victims is to place them in temporary shelters, such as tent cities, away from the traumatic disaster area. Wrong. Almost all victims usually wish to return quickly to their homes. Tent cities are anathema. Even trailer cities are undesirable. Most victims know instinctively that these "temporary" solutions could go on for years or even generations.

6. Natural disasters cause suffering and death on a random basis. Wrong again. Natural disasters almost always affect the poor and elderly disproportionately. Why? The poor live in the poor parts of town, near the rail yard with the tank car full of chlorine, near the port with the explosives ship, near the levees, or in shacks near the tsunami- and hurricane-prone seashore. Their housing is poorly constructed, and their resources to evacuate and seek shelter elsewhere are minimal. The elderly are weaker and more vulnerable to heat, stress and trauma. None of this is rocket science. All of it needs to be an integral part of any disaster plan in the developed or developing world. Failure to think about the poor and elderly during disaster planning borders on criminal negligence.

7. Any kind of fast disaster assistance is useful. In fact, disaster assistance, if not planned carefully, can easily become a "second disaster." This has occurred in a number of instances, most famously in central America, when so much food was donated after a major hurricane that local populations stopped buying the produce of their local farmers. The farm economy, the mainstay of the country, collapsed. As a result, recovery took years, not months. Disaster assistance needs to be planned to promote self-sufficiency, not dependency.

The corollary of this myth is that "used clothes are needed by disaster victims, and a good way to help is to donate used clothes." In fact this is never a good idea. Used clothes are expensive to store, transport and sort. They are often culturally inappropriate and sometimes are downright insulting. An entire book on this book was titled "No More Left Shoes," and took its title from the shipload of left only shoes once famously sent to Jamaica after a hurricane. The rule should be: NEVER send used clothes.

8. Pets are too unimportant to rescue. Loss of pets can cause major psychological problems for their human masters. And as a society we are big enough and rich enough to save pets as well as humans. Luckily there are specialized organizations such as the Humane Society which launch rescue efforts after major disasters. But *all* rescuers, including police, fire, National Guard, state, Federal and citizen rescuers, need to be trained to rescue pets as well as humans, wherever possible.

9. We cannot prevent or mitigate against natural disasters. Perhaps we cannot prevent natural disasters. But as shown in exhibit 2 earlier, the entire history of disasters in the US is in fact the highly successful mitigation over time of death from disaster. With the proper policies in place, property damage from disasters can also be reduced. Such policies should include: better hurricane, earthquake, tornado and fire building codes; better enforcement of such codes; prevention of building right on the edge of the coast; elimination of Federal and private insurance for new construction on the coast; etc. An innovative idea which could help fund mitigation and response programs would be to levy a (say) three percent Federal tax on all real estate transactions taking place within one mile of the coast. Funds would be earmarked for disaster mitigation, warning systems, disaster education programs, and reconstruction after the next disaster.

10. Individuals and families can do little to help themselves or others to prepare for natural, manmade or terrorist disasters. Wrong, wrong, wrong. FEMA has a free 20 hour training program available for citizens called the Community Emergency Response Team program. The CERT training includes a module on light urban search and rescue. The Red Cross has similar programs. The Mormons (Church of Jesus Christ of Latter Day Saints) have an extensive family preparedness program that is worthy of study by non-Mormons. It includes "72 hour" response packs, a years' (!) worth of food supplies, food storage options, emergency tools, plans, lighting, auto emergency kits, etc.

In summary, many things you heard from the TV during the last major disaster were shallow or just plain wrong. The next major disaster will be the same. It is up to you to educate yourself to the truth—only then will you be on the road to true disaster preparedness.

Section 6

Adventures in Genealogy

The Greatest Hobby on Earth

In 2001 at age 49 I left the large consulting firm where I had labored for 50 to 60 hours a week for 14 years. Semi-retirement was my goal: I would work for 20 to 100 days per year as a free lance consultant in international telecommunications policy and e-government, and have plenty of free time for--what?

About a month after leaving the firm, I was walking through a used book sale at a local high school. I spotted a thick book with an odd title: *The Hereditary Register of the United States, 1972.* Little did I know that that book would change my life.

Curious, I picked it up. The *Register* was written by John Roundtree and Charles Owen Johnson. (I would later have the honor of meeting Charles, one of the great men of genealogy in the US.) It was a listing of all the historical, lineage and genealogical societies in the US. I had only heard of a few of these, such as the Daughters of the American Revolution and the Colonial Dames of America. I was quite surprised to learn that there were over 90 such organizations listed, starting with the Ancient and Honorable Artillery Company of Massachusetts, founded in 1637 and still in existence, and continuing in time up to the Order of the First Families of Mississippi, founded in 1967.

I had never been interested in genealogy, although I loved history. When my parents and grandparents, all avid genealogists, would drone on about their "lines" back to Confederate officers, about their cousins and distant relatives, and (Oh, God!) their visits to local graveyards, I would yawn and my eyes would glaze over. Once when I was a teenager my mother brought out a large chart compiled by her mother, showing our descent from Benjamin Harrison, a signer from Virginia of the Declaration of Independence. I examined the chart and hooted that our earliest ancestor in the middle ages appeared to be "Burger, King of Germany"! I thought that was incredibly funny. Mom was not amused.

But the book intrigued me, somehow. Leafing through it and remembering my mother's charts and notes, I realized that I could join a few of these organizations, maybe even half a dozen or more. At least one sounded rather fun: the "Descendants of the Illegitimate Sons and Daughters of the Kings of Britain." A little switch flipped in my head— suddenly genealogy seemed a bit more interesting. I bought the used book. Best two dollars I ever spent.

I took the *Register* home, studied it, and did some Internet research. It became clear that most of the organizations listed in the book still existed and were flourishing, and indeed many more had been founded since 1972. Genealogy was and is a growth industry, and is perhaps the most popular hobby in America. Most of the lineage-heritage organizations have very strict standards for admission, and require extensive written proofs of every link back to the "propositus," the key ancestor in question.

I recalled that the one organization my mother had joined was the Society of the Lees of Virginia, the proven descendants of Richard Lee "The Immigrant" (1617-1664) and his wife Anna Constable (1621-1663). Mom had urged me to join, too, and when I called her, she said that since she had been accepted, the paperwork to get me in would be minimal. So I made some calls, did a little application typing, and I was in.

I was also hooked. I was suddenly a proven cousin of General Robert E. Lee (fourth cousin five times removed, to be exact), and of his romantic and dashing father "Light Horse" Harry Lee (love that name) of Revolutionary War fame. I was able to attend society meetings at beautiful, private historic houses that were not generally open to the public, and to go on society trips to fascinating places.

One of the first of our Lee Society trips was to the US Military Academy at West Point, New York, where we celebrated the 150th anniversary of Robert E. Lee's Superintendency at the Academy. We attended a church service in his honor, toured the grounds, were invited by the current Superintendent to visit his house, met other Lee descendants, and viewed the Robert E. Lee sword (brought up from Washington, DC by the US National Park Service especially for this occasion). Pretty amazing stuff.

I started seriously investigating other organizations. In quick succession I joined the Sons of the American Revolution (brother organization to the DAR), the Descendants of the Signers of the Declaration of Independence, and Aztec Club of 1847 (the latter based on my relation to a Toulmin who served as an officer in the Mexican War).

I suddenly found that my interest in history had gained a whole new dimension, as I identified actual relatives who had been active in many of the great events of the past. I learned about periods, such as the Mexican War and the War of 1812, of which I knew little. I was amazed to learn that some historians blame or credit one of my gggg-uncles, William Henry Harrison, with actually triggering the War of 1812, by his aggressive tactics as Governor in dealing with the Indians in the Northwest Territory. (William Henry Harrison, a son of Benjamin Harrison "the Signer," later became the ninth US President. I argue that he was our greatest president, since he only held office for a month, and didn't have time to screw anything up! He was the grandfather of Benjamin Harrison, 23rd US President from 1889 to 1893.)

Based on my line to Benjamin Harrison "the Signer" I was able to join the rather fun Descendants of Pirates and Privateers, since Harrison owned several privateering vessels, and even chaired the committee of Congress which in March 1776 authorized privateering against British merchant and naval vessels.

Because I always suspected that one of the reasons my southern grandparents were so keen on genealogy was to prove that all their lines were "pure," I was quite entertained to find a few darker blots on the family register. One ggggg-uncle of French descent married an Indian princess, was accepted by the Indians, and was even elected Chief of the Pushmataha Choctaws in Alabama in the early 1800s. Another ancestor, my ggg-grandfather, in the 1870s reportedly had a black "back yard" family of children, all with exactly the same names and birth-sex order as his "front yard" white children. His son wanted to run for Congress, and approached the father and asked him to "do something" about this potential political problem. So the father disappeared with his black mistress and children for six months, then reappeared alone, apparently having settled the family somewhere far away. The son was duly elected and served for eight years as a Congressman from Marengo County, Alabama. So perhaps somewhere I have some half-cousins of another race....

Delving into the colonial period, I suddenly discovered ancestors who qualified as propositi for societies of ancient Planters, Early Quakers, members of the early Bench and Bar, descendants of Colonial Physicians and Chirurgiens (surgeons), Colonial Clergy, and Colonial Governors. I even qualified for the Flagon and Trencher society, (descendants of colonial tavern-keepers), which holds its annual meetings in colonial taverns in the original thirteen colonies.

271

My grandparents had always said that all, repeat *all*, of our lines were Southern, with no "damn Yankees" hiding in the family tree. So I was stunned to find a line that my folks had ignored that ran to New Orleans and thence up to some distinguished New England families. Suddenly I qualified for the First Families of Rhode Island and of Massachusetts. I even found an ancestor who joined the Ancient and Honorable Artillery Company of Massachusetts in 1638, just one year after it was founded. Through him I became a member by right of descent of this, the third oldest military organization in the world (after the Vatican Swiss Guards and the Honourable Artillery Company of London), and the organizational ancestor of today's US Army National Guard.

Researching my ancestors well before the Revolution, I found that I was very lucky to have several "gateway" ancestors whose proven genealogy jumped the pond back to England and into the British aristocracy. Suddenly an entire new period of history and a new geography opened up. I was able to join the Descendants of the Knights of the Bath and Descendants of the Knights of the Garter, and even the Barons of Magna Charta-- descendants of the barons who stood surety for King John, forcing him to grant and continue to honor one of the most important documents in history.

By this time I was obsessed. I typed applications long into the night. I assembled "proofs" for the various societies of each link between generations and each date for numerous lines—sometimes the proofs were over an inch thick. I studied my parents and grandparents notes and put in hundreds of hours of research to substantiate asserted but undocumented lines. My house filled up with cardboard boxes full of files on family groups and organizations to join. I worked much harder on genealogy than I had on any job. I compiled a database of 2493 ancestors and relatives, with 390 sources and thousands of footnotes. I joined over

40 lineage-heritage organizations. I organized a family reunion of all the numerous descendants of my mother's grandfather and grandmother. I proved that my wife and I are ninth cousins. (Surprisingly, she didn't seem that thrilled by this great news.) I even started to (shudder) visit graveyards, *and liked it!*

And then there were the medals. I was always keen on medals, since I had seen the numerous swimming medals my father had won in Washington, DC in the 1940s, swimming miles up and down the Potomac. Almost all the lineage-heritage societies offer their members medals, either full-sized or miniatures or both. These are worn at formal events, especially during the heritage "social season" in DC in April. I waited impatiently each day for the mailman to come, hoping he would bring another medal for my collection. They looked splendid.

*Lew Toulmin with lineage-heritage medals
and Knights Templar cross*

Forging further back in time, I was able to prove a line from my Harrison clan via a gateway ancestor through the English kings Edward I and Henry III, II and I all the way back to Charlemagne (747-814, King of the Franks and Holy Roman Emperor). Based on this line, I joined the prestigious Crown of Charlemagne society. I learned that many if not most Americans of northern European ancestry are probably descended from Charlemagne, but only 2000 have managed or bothered to prove it.

Finally, the ultimate genealogical prize was within my grasp. In 2005, some of the most reputable genealogists in the US confirmed a link from Charlemagne back to the fabled Merovingian Dynasty, which ruled most of what is now France, Germany, Belgium, Switzerland and northern Italy from 448 to 751 AD. This dynasty has recently become quite famous through the novel *The DaVinci Code*, which claims that the Merovingian kings are descendants of the supposed daughter of Jesus Christ and Mary Magdalene, and that this bloodline is the true Holy Grail. But the genealogists, careful scholars all, only assert that there is a proven link back as far as the first Merovingian, King Merove, King of the Franks. The genealogists founded the most recent heritage-lineage society, the Order of the Merovingian Dynasty[6], 448-751. In October 2005 I was proud to be accepted as the society's 50th member.

I began my genealogical quest wondering how I would fill my time during semi-retirement. Through luck (and a heck of a lot of typing) I found what has to be the greatest hobby of all. Somehow filling up my time has not been a problem!

---

[6] See merovingiandynasty.com

The Search for Brian Boru, High King of All Ireland

Susan wanted to go to Ireland, and I hadn't been there since I was a kid in 1965. So we started planning a major trip, about a month long. Whenever I go anywhere, now that I'm hooked on genealogy, I try to see if there is a family connection. But I didn't recall any Irishmen in my database of ancestors, just Englishmen, Scots, Welshmen of course, and a bunch of continental Europeans. Meanwhile, I was reading up on Irish history, and kept coming across this fellow Brian Boru, the first High King of All Ireland who took his job seriously, and who tried to unite Ireland into a real country in the year 1000. He was felt to be the greatest Irish leader of the middle ages.

Then I recalled that somewhere in my trusty database, way back in time, there perhaps was an Irish chieftain. It was worth a look. So I poked around the database, searching in various ways, until finally I found him and his daughter, my lone Irish folk out of 2493 ancestors and relatives cataloged. He was King Olaf II of Dublin (1005-1034), my 27th great grandfather, and his daughter Ragnihildr (dates unknown). The latter had married Cyan of Wales who was exiled in Ireland; presumably this was how the two met. Cyan was the great-great-grandfather of Llywelyn The Great, Prince of Wales (1173-1240), the most famous of the Welsh princes who resisted English rule. Llywelyn was my 22nd great grandfather via a reliable line with many references. My sources for the Olaf to Llywelyn link were the reputable "Kings and Queens of Britain, Showing Their Descent and Relationships," a huge

275

published chart by Anne Taute and John Brooke-Little, the Richmond Herald of Arms (a chart which graces the entire back wall of our laundry room), and a less reliable Internet site.

I decided to see if Olaf II had any interesting ancestors. I called up various Internet websites and sources, and soon found some sites with good references which stated that Olaf II had a father Sihtric Macamlaib, King of Dublin, who had a wife Slani ingin O'Brian, whose father was Brian Boru, High King of All Ireland! Wow! My 29th great-grandfather. Suddenly I was a descendant of the greatest Irish leader of the middle ages. How cool is that?

Artist's conception of Brian Boru, High King of All Ireland

(Just to confuse things, Slani had married Brian's ex-wife's son (Sihtric) by another marriage. Kinda like marrying your own brother-in-law. Talk about keeping it in the family.)

I started researching Brian Boru more, intent on linking our trip to sites in his life and the life of his descendants. Suddenly our trip had a fascinating theme and a research purpose. Susan's ancestry was included, too, since Olaf II and Brian Boru were ancestors of our (Susan and my) common ancestor, Lt. Col. Thomas Ligon (1623-1675) of Warwickshire and Virginia, a "gateway" ancestor to Magna Charta barons and British, European, and now Irish royalty.

I identified four sites that would help us explore the life, impact and descendants of Brian Boru. These were: Dromoland Castle; sites in and near Killaloe, County Clare; St. Patrick's Cathedral at Armagh, and the Brian Boru Well in Clontarf, Dublin.

Dromoland Castle

We flew to Shannon airport in southwest Ireland, and stayed a night at the Dromoland Castle hotel and resort. This castle is one of the most famous in Ireland, and is the ancestral home of the O'Briens, Barons of Inchiquin, one of the few native Gaelic families of royal blood, and the direct descendants of Brian Boru. Donough O'Brien, son of Brian Boru, owned this site in the 11th century, and had a defensive stronghold here.

It was a resident of this castle, chief of the clan O'Brien, Morrough, known as the Prince of Thomond, who in 1543 was forced to surrender his loyalty to the English King Henry VIII. Morrough was dubbed Baron of Inchiquin and Earl of Thomond (a bit of a comedown from "Prince.") His family lived at Dromoland for more than 1000 years.

The oldest part of the current building was constructed in 1736, and consists of a quadrangle of 29 guest rooms called Queen Anne's court, named after the then Queen of England.

Dromoland Castle, home of the O'Briens for 1000 years

Most of the current structure was built over 15 years, from 1811 to 1826 by Sir Edward O'Brien, Lord of Dromoland, at a fantastic cost. The stone alone cost more than 100,000 pounds, a huge expense at the time.

During the struggles for Irish independence, the castle was targeted, like many other aristocratic homes, for destruction by the IRA. On two occasions the O'Briens learned of gasoline shipments which were sent secretly to County Clare for burning the castle. But local residents pleaded that the O'Briens were fair and benevolent in dealing with their tenants, and the castle was spared at the last minute.

By the 1960s the expense of keeping up the castle was too much, and the castle was sold out of O'Brien hands. However, Conor Myles John O'Brien, *The* O'Brien, Prince of Thomond, Chief of the Name, 18th Baron Inchiquin, 10th Baronet of Leamaneh (whew!) still lives in a grand house beside the castle, and still participates in managing and developing the estate. He is hoping to finance a movie based on Brian Boru's life and the Morgan Llywelyn book called "The Lion of Scotland."

The Dromoland O'Brien family pedigree is kept in a vault at Lloyds of London. It is 36 feet in length!

Our visit to the castle was pleasant and rewarding. The guest rooms were beautifully furnished, and the grounds were gorgeous. The most attractive feature was the lovely garden, protected by a 12 foot high wall, which contained numerous roses, hydrangeas and other beautiful flowers. Perhaps the most amusing feature was a fanciful portrait of Brian Boru showing him in 17th century-style armor.

Sites In and Near Killaloe, County Clare

Traveling north to the town of Killaloe at the south end of Lough Derg, we were able to home in on the life and some remnants of the great man himself. The Brian Boru Heritage Center presents video, text and a painted history of Brian and his life.

Brian Boru was born in Killaloe on the Shannon, into the small, unimportant Dalcassian clan in southern Ireland in 941, in an era of Viking invasions and constant warring among Irish tribes. Brian's tribe claimed descent from Finn MacCool, the legendary giant who built the Giant's Causeway in Northern Ireland, and from other leaders dating back to the year 167 AD. However, it is likely that much of this genealogy was legendary, also, or even manufactured to give the tribe more claim to power.

Brian's father, Cennitig (or Kennedy), was killed by the Vikings when Brian was just ten; Brian's brother Mahon then became King of the Dalcassians. Mahon and Brian fought the Vikings for two decades, defeating them in a battle in 968 at Solohead. This victory allowed Mahon to claim the throne of Munster; he was inaugurated at the famous Rock of Cashel of the Kings, in 970.

But Mahon was treacherously kidnapped and killed by his enemies at the Bloody Pass in county Limerick. This left the door open for Brian, who assumed the throne of Munster and Thomond at the age of 37. He vowed to avenge his brother's death in an elegy he recited at his brother's funeral:

Woe is me! That it was not in battle or combat
He was left for dead, under the cover of his shield.
My heart shall burst within my breast
Unless I avenge this great king.

Brian fulfilled his word by attacking his Viking and Irish enemies on a monastic sanctuary island in the Shannon, and virtually wiping them out.

Brian then temporarily joined forces with his traditional rival Malachy, chief of the O'Neills, who had held the High Kingship of Ireland for many generations. (This title was largely ceremonial at the time, and did not mean that the High King actually controlled the country.) Together Brian and Malachy succeeded in 999 in defeating their common enemies the Vikings at Glen-mama, where 4000 of the enemy were killed. Malachy and Brian marched on Dublin, then a Viking port, and plundered it of gold and jewels, and also took many slaves, captives and hostages.

Brian next began maneuvering to displace Malachy as High King. After some negotiation, Malachy magnanimously yielded the title to the stronger and more popular Brian. They met at the fabulous site of Tara, about 30 miles north of Dublin, the seat of the kings of Ireland. Here 142 kings of Ireland had ruled, and from here half the counties in Ireland could be seen. Brian was inaugurated at Tara as the High King of All Ireland and Imperator Scotorum ("Emperor of the Irish"). He was 61 years old.

(Of course, it was the site of Tara that gave its name to the mythical home of Scarlett O'Hara, of "Gone with the Wind" fame. Scarlett's father was an immigrant Irishman who apparently knew his history.)

Brian at this time was reported to be "a man of fine figure, large stature, and great strength." He was conspicuous for his "mental endowments, sagacity, bravery and piety." He was a musician and harpist, and his harp has become the symbol of Ireland today. It is used on the Irish coat of arms, money (including the Irish Euro), stamps and official buildings.

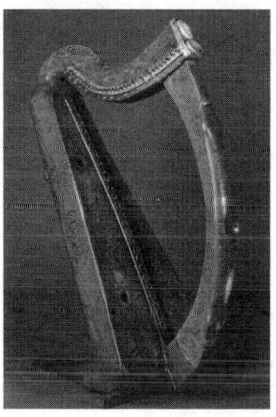

The Brian Boru harp, preserved in the Trinity College library, Dublin. This is probably a 17th century copy of Brian's original harp.

Just a mile north of the Heritage Center we found Brian Boru's fort. This fort probably dates from the Stone Age, well before Brian, and was apparently used by Brian, his brother Mahon, and his father Kennedy. It protected a critical ford across the Shannon, and was used to levy tribute in the form of cattle from traders crossing the river. In fact, "Boru" can be translated as "cattle tribute," and this is likely the origin of his name. The fort in Brian's time was a large wooden stockade built atop a round earthen berm, with a number of circular thatch dwellings inside. Today all that remains is the earth bank and outer ditch.

St. Patrick's Cathedral at Armagh and the the Brian Boru Well in Clontarf, Dublin

After Brian was crowned as High King, he set about showing what he thought the title really meant. He pushed for ecclesiastical reform, restored previously plundered and destroyed churches, united many lesser Irish tribes, encouraged education and learning, consolidated his control over the country by fighting a rebellion instigated by his divorced wife Gormla, and built a large palace at Kincora, just north of Killiloe. (Unfortunately no trace of the palace survives.) He built roads and bridges, and set up trade with Britain and Europe. He kept the kingdom relatively peaceful and prosperous, and presided in 1007 over the great fair and games at Tailteann near Tara, which had been suspended for 80 years due to continuous fighting. He probably began the system of Irish surnames, by which his descendants became known as "O'Brien." He became Ireland's first naval leader, creating a great fleet of ships based at Lough Derg on the Shannon. Some sources call him "the greatest Irishman of all time."

Unfortunately, Brian's Viking enemies still waited in the wings. They supported Brian's ex-wife Gormla and her brother Maelmor in yet another rebellion. The stage was set for the heroic death of Brian Boru.

Brian, knowing that battle was coming, set up camp with his 7,000 warriors, north of Dublin in what is now a suburb, known as Clontarf. The Vikings, also about 7,000 strong, gathered from Scandinavia, the Orkneys, the Isle of Man and the Western Isles of Scotland. The battle took place on Good Friday, April 23, 1014, and every Irish schoolboy knows what happened there.

The battle of Clontarf raged all day, with hand-to-hand fighting in two great lines. Finally the battle began to go Brian's way. At this crucial juncture Brian, now 73, was directing the battle from his tent, praying, and giving instructions to his aides. His guards were distracted and were also looking at the battle, and were not watching in all directions. Suddenly a small party of Vikings led by the warrior Brodir emerged from the woods behind the tent and attacked. Brian unsheathed his sword and cut off Brodir's leg, mortally wounding him. But Brodir managed to kill Brian Boru with the last blow of his war ax.

The Irish under Brian won the day, and the Vikings were ejected from Ireland for all time. But the price was high. The High King was dead. So was his son and many of his chiefs and supporters.

Perhaps most importantly, Brian Boru, still vigorous despite his great age, lost the chance to consolidate his hold over Ireland. It is difficult to say "what if," but it seems likely that if Brian's guards had been more attentive and he had lived, he could have turned Ireland into a real country with a national consciousness, rather than a collection of warring tribes.

Failing that, the next turning point in Irish history was a tragic one. In 1166 a Leinster chief DiarMuid MacMurrogh invited "Strongbow" Richard de Clare, a Norman knight, to come to Ireland to assist him in his inter-tribal squabbles. Henry II of England and France opposed this move, and invaded Ireland to prevent curb Strongbow's new power. Henry II then left Ireland to his landless son John, who became King John of England. Thus England became inextricably entwined in Irish history, as it still is today, almost 900 years later. Perhaps if Brian Boru had been allowed to put a stop to this kind of inter-tribal warfare, England would never have invaded Ireland, and both would have been more peaceful. Perhaps the Scots-Irish, the forced settlers in northern Ireland, would not have existed, perhaps the IRA would not have been founded, and perhaps Northern Ireland, that perpetual thorn in the side of

England and the world, would not exist as we know it today. Perhaps....

Today all that remains of the battle of Clontarf is the "Well of Brian Boru," reputed site of Brian's camp. The well, really a standpipe, is located on a residential street in the suburb of Clontarf. It seems rather a minor monument to such a great man.

Brian was buried at St. Patrick's cathedral in Armagh in what is now Northern Ireland. A large but simple plaque outside the cathedral marks the approximate location of the grave. On the day we visited, a police helicopter hovered continuously overhead, watching out for sectarian violence in the land never quite united by Brian Boru, High King of All Ireland.

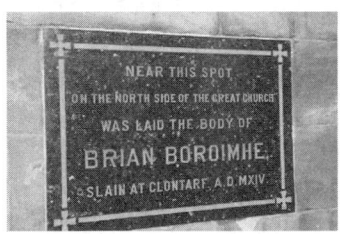

The burial plaque of Brian Boru at St. Patrick's Cathedral, Armagh, Northern Ireland

Crimes Against Genealogy

Do you, like me, pursue America's most popular hobby, genealogy? Do you love the chase through dusty records, libraries and courthouses? The sudden "Aha!" moment? The typing of yet another application to a lineage organization? But are you mad because one of your most promising genealogical research lines has hit the proverbial "brick wall"? Have you tried every library and courthouse in the land without success? Maybe the culprit is not your lack of research ability, but a "crime against genealogy" committed in the past. Here are some crimes I have investigated, ranging from fraud to mass murder.

Fraud, Falsification of Government Documents

I first became aware of crimes against genealogy while traveling in Burma, or Myanmar, as the country's dictators prefer to call it. I mentioned to my guide that I was interested in genealogy, and had done considerable research on my ancestors. I asked if Burmese people were also interested in genealogy. He was an affable, rotund chap, about 50 years old, a professor of history who made about a dollar a day at his job and thirty times that while guiding. He spoke very good English.

"Oh, yes," he said proudly. "We Burmese are all *required* to be interested in genealogy." "Really?" I said. "That's a first. Why is that?" He answered, "When we go to get our adult identification card at age 18, we are required to fill out a genealogical chart that lists all our ancestors back for seven generations. The chart must be complete.

Without that chart we cannot get our ID, and without ID we cannot function in society. In fact we can be arrested and imprisoned for not having our ID."

"Yikes!" I said. "You have to know a lot of ancestors. Let's see how many." I whipped out a pencil and a piece of paper and began muttering. "In the first generation you need to know your two parents, that's two to the first power, and in the next generation two to the second power, then 2^3, and so on, so the total number you need to know is: $2^1+2^2+2^3+2^4+2^5+2^6+2^7$. That's equal to 2+4+8+16+32+64+128, or a total of 254 ancestors! Wow! Very impressive," I said.

"Yes," he said, "We are very good genealogists," looking proud and pleased.

I thought a minute, then heard a little suspicious voice in the back of my head. I asked, "But I know that Burma suffered a lot of damage during World War II, and there have been many troubles since then. How is it that all these records going back seven generations are preserved? What happens if there is a gap, even just a small one? Because you said that the form must be totally complete. Did you have any gaps in *your* form? What did you do?"

My guide tried to change the subject, pointing out a beautiful 11th century temple nearby. But I wouldn't be deterred. Finally he admitted, "When there were gaps, I just made up a bunch of ancestors! I had to." After some more questioning, he said, a little grumpily, "Of course no-one in Burma *really* knows more than two or three generations of their ancestors. We all make up ancestors to fill in the gaps. And anyway, it is the thought that counts. We are creating a beautiful symmetry that is pleasing to the Buddha and to the government. And we are honoring our ancestors, in our own way, even if we don't know their real names."

I sat back, stunned. The concept of truth and accuracy had become so perverted in Burma that even the good guys didn't know what it was. I said, "So suppose all these wonderful records get preserved in a vault somewhere for five thousand years and are discovered by some future archaeologists and genealogists. They will think they have a treasure trove of wonderful records, when what they mostly have is lies!" My guide shrugged and began lecturing on the nearby temple.

I classified this crime against genealogy as "fraud," and began keeping my eyes open for other crimes as I traveled.

Theft of the Courthouse, Theft of Government Records and Property, Brandishing a Weapon

I found my next example right in my own second home town of Daphne, Alabama. Located on the beautiful eastern shore of Mobile Bay, Daphne was the county seat of Baldwin County beginning in 1868. Before that the county seat had been located in several different villages, mostly northwest of Mobile Bay. But as the county was divided and as it moved to the southeast, the courthouse was moved, too. Baldwin is one of the few counties in the country which contains no land that was originally granted to it. It actually crawled southeast like a giant amoeba, until its borders entirely left its original territory. But all those moves were legal.

Illegality began in 1901. The courthouse had been firmly in place for 33 years, since the move in 1868. But citizens in the north of Baldwin were not happy. Baldwin, at about 70 miles long and 35 miles across, was one of the larger counties east of the Mississippi, and is larger than the state of Rhode Island. Citizens in the north end of the county, at Bay Minette, felt that they had to go too far to transact official business. They got together and approached the Alabama Legislature, requesting that the official county seat be transferred from Daphne to Bay Minette. Did some money change hands, such that this crime includes bribery? We will never know. But the legislature rapidly approved the change.

But when the good citizens of Daphne got wind of the plan—they had not been consulted—they were furious. The courthouse meant business, jobs, prosperity and growth. And of course the courthouse records were vital for genealogical, real estate and probate research. They weren't going to let all this go without a fight. They got a local judge to issue an injunction against the move, until the law could be changed back.

There was a legal stalemate until late one dark night, when the Bay Minette gang snuck down to Daphne with guns, a wagon train pulled by oxen, and their own court order. They grabbed the seven foot high court safe, estimated to weigh 9000 pounds, and loaded it on a wagon. They stole the bars off the jail. They scooped up most of the other records, although some were probably lost in the torch lit confusion. They trekked off to Bay Minette, holding off the irate Daphne residents at gunpoint.

The courthouse has remained in Bay Minette ever since. The safe, with its seven inch thick steel doors and construction date of 1871, is still preserved and is on display, commemorating the night that the courthouse was stolen.

Arson, Destruction of Government Property, Obstruction of Justice, Negligence

As genealogists, we have all come across "burned" courthouses and counties. Of course these are incredible tragedies for the communities involved and for the families and researchers active in those counties. Here are some miscellaneous and perhaps surprising facts on burned counties, gleaned from reading and research:

- Half of all Alabama counties have had their courthouses burnt, some as many as four times!

- Two counties in Ohio and two in Texas report that their courthouses were burnt, apparently by indicted criminals who were seeking to destroy the indictments, court records, and potential evidence. Apparently this was a fairly common cause of such arson cases.

- Twenty-two courthouses in Kentucky were burnt during the Civil War. As a Southerner I assumed that this was done by dastardly Yankee generals, but in fact twelve of the arsons were undertaken by Confederate line forces, eight by Confederate guerillas, and two by Union forces, reportedly "by accident." Of the twelve courthouse fires set by Confederate official forces, seven were set by General Hylan B. Lyon, C.S.A., who invaded Kentucky with 800 men in November of 1864 and burned his seven courthouses in just 23 days. Many of the courthouse records were saved from destruction by the pleas of local citizens. Lyon felt he was enforcing the CSA draft law and destroying "Union-contaminated" courthouses.

- Analysis of a list of 99 incidents of major destructions of records in Georgia courthouses, issued by the Georgia Department of Archives and History, reveals that only about ten appear to have been caused by the War Between the States, and of these only three specifically mention General William Tecumseh Sherman. Most of the rest of the incidents were fires during peacetime, with a rare flood, hurricane, tornado or Indian attack thrown in for good measure. A surprising 21 of the 99 incidents occurred during the 20th century.

- A similar list issued by the Library of Virginia showed that approximately 58 incidents of major damage to Virginia county courthouses have occurred over the years, with many counties having multiple incidents. Of these 58, about 21 were attributable to Civil War battles or burnings, with the rest being primarily peacetime fires and Revolutionary battles and burnings. Only three of the 58 incidents occurred during the 20th century. Apparently Virginia officials over the last hundred years were better custodians of their records than their Georgia brethren.

Arson, Destruction of Government Property, Gross Negligence

The destruction of the Royal Library at Alexandria, Egypt, must be one of the greatest losses to history and genealogy ever known in the course of human events.

The library was likely founded at the beginning of the 3rd century BC during the reign of Ptolemy II. The suggestion for its creation, and perhaps the actual founding of the library, can be attributed to Demetrius Phalereus, an Athenian orator, ruler and student of Aristotle who wrote extensively on history, rhetoric and literary criticism.

The library (or libraries, since there may have been several libraries and allied museums) had as its goal building up knowledge on all the peoples of the earth, all the sciences, all the history, and all the trade information available at the time. The library was built up by donations and purchases of the collections of scrolls of individuals; by sending out a letter "to all the sovereigns of the Earth" asking them for copies of all their scrolls and libraries, for copying and return; by searching every ship and visitor that came to Alexandria, and copying all scrolls and parchments found; and by translating numerous foreign works into Greek. The library eventually housed between 40,000 and 700,000 (depending on which source you believe) papyrus scrolls, and numerous additional parchment scrolls (vellum) and later codexes (books). The various famous librarians managed to create a form of early subject catalog, so that works could be retrieved. Major holdings included numerous works on literature, history, geometry, medicine, mechanics, astronomy and philology. In 2004 a Polish/English archaeological team claimed to have found the remains of the library, with 13 lecture halls with a total seating capacity of over 5000. So the library also may well have functioned as the first real university.

Destruction of the library has been blamed on various suspects, and the perpetrator is not certain. The three major suspects are Julius Caesar, Patriarch Theophilus of Alexandria, and Omar, Caliph of Baghdad.

Julius Caesar attacked Alexandria in 47 BC while in pursuit of his arch-rival Pompey. Caesar used fire ships to attack the enemy fleet in Alexandria's harbor. The tactic worked, the fleet was destroyed, and Caesar conquered. This much is clear. What is alleged by most sources is that the fire accidentally jumped ashore, raged through the city, and destroyed the library. Another source alleges that Caesar started a fire ashore to clear a defensive ring around his position, and then the fire got out of control. Ancient defenders of Caesar say that his accidental fires may have burned about 40,000 scrolls or books in a warehouse near the port, but that the main body of the library and museum, housed elsewhere in the city in a stone building, was not harmed.

Patriarch Theophilus of Alexandria lived in 391 AD when Emperor Theodosius the Great in Rome was eagerly converting all his subjects to Christianity. Theodosius ordered the destruction of all pagan temples and Theophilus obtained permission to destroy the library, or what was left of it in the Temple of Serapis, known as the Serapeum.

While it is clear that Theophilus burned the Temple of Serapis, his defenders say that there is little or no evidence that there was a library or any part of the original Royal Library attached to the temple. Defenders also point to other fires, sacks and to the general decline of interest in ancient writings to the decline of the Royal Library or its remains in the period of 47 BC to 391 AD.

Caliph Omar of Baghdah lived in 640 AD and he was an early Muslim leader. The Muslim conqueror of Egypt, named General Amr, reportedly asked Omar for permission to destroy the library at Alexandria, since it contained works which might contradict the Koran. Omar granted permission, and the library materials were used to fuel the city's numerous bath houses. It reportedly took six months to burn all the scrolls and books as fuel for the saunas and steam baths. Defenders of Omar and Amr state that the "six months" story is simply incredible, that key characters allegedly involved in the arson were dead by the time of the crime, that the sources are centuries later and are clearly biased against Muslims, and that contemporary sources do not mention such a massive crime.

Weighing the evidence, it seems most likely that Omar is the victim of slander, that Theophilus did do some damage to the remains of the original library, but that the major part of the destruction of the Royal Library of Alexandria can probably be attributed to the carelessness of Julius Caesar and his troops. The most convincing evidence is the lack of any reference to the Library by independent sources after the time of Caesar. Perhaps his assassination later in Rome was justifiable, after all.

Gender Discrimination, Conspiracy, Bribery, Land Fraud, Interception of Federal Nuclear Compensation Payments

The entire land mass of the Republic of the Marshall Islands in the North Pacific only amounts to 70 square miles, about the size of the District of Columbia. A considerable portion of the land area is reserved for the US Army Kwajalein Atoll Reagan Missile Test Site. The country's population is about 59,000. It follows that land, being so scarce, is quite valuable.

Land is traditionally divided into "wetos," narrow strips that run across an atoll from the seaside to the lagoon. To hold communal possession to a weto once meant that a family could provide for all its needs: housing, food, transport and medicine. But wetos also have religious, tribal and cultural significance. The people felt and still feel that they are part of their land. In the past, disputes over land and wetos were the main causes of tribal wars. Land disputes continue to be the main source of family, clan and tribal difficulties.

Since World War II, land rights have become valuable to some Marshallese as sources of revenue from the US government, which pays compensation to islanders damaged by US nuclear testing. These islanders include residents or former residents of Bikini, Enewetak, Rongelap and Utrik atolls, and islanders who can show health problems caused by nuclear radiation. Despite the fact that this revenue is one of the few sources of hard currency in the islands, it is very doubtful that the payments can ever truly compensate for the health problems, loss of home, trauma, psychological damage, anxiety and numerous other problems caused by the nuclear testing. Because land rights, residency and geneaology are inter-twined, some residents have alleged that their proper payments have been intercepted by crooked land dealings and re-interpretation of residency and family trees.

The paramount tribal chiefs, or "iroij," possess certain rights over each land parcel that are shared with the "alab" or land manager, and with the "drijerbal," the people actually living on the land. This system is further complicated by the fact that the rights can be sold, leased or given away based on handshake agreements. These agreements (and the original land titles, deeds and rights) are virtually never recorded in writing. As can be imagined there is immense room for misunderstandings, changes in recollection, and disputes. Modern investors seeking to purchase land find that they can spend years tracking down all the parties to a parcel—iroij, alab, and the senior representative of the drijerbal--finally get their written agreement to sell, then be successfully challenged years later by a claimant who states that *he* is the correct representative of the drijerbal.

Even more complexity is added by the fact that Marshallese society is matrilineal, and land and chiefly titles are handed down through the female line. This would seem to give women power, but in practice women are usually reserved and quiet, and power is held by the husbands and the iroij. Land disputes are settled in a three member "Traditional Rights Court" which is dominated by male chiefs. Genealogy is female-line oriented and often goes back 15 to 20 generations, so that land and title disputes are usually resolved via genealogical analysis.

It is not just businesses that are frustrated by genealogy-driven land disputes. Currently construction of several schools has been halted due to land disputes, and at least one functioning school has been forced to close.

One of the perverse results of the RMI legal system is that women, who should by custom have considerable control of land, in fact are often cheated out of it. Land disputes taken to the Traditional Rights Court reportedly are often resolved by the chiefs interpreting the genealogy of the case to the advantage of the male claimant, or to whoever pays the highest bribe. The quality of the islands' judiciary is perhaps illustrated by the fact that all three of the top judges in the land, members of the RMI High Court, were recently charged with multiple counts of corruption, libel, cheating and misuse of government funds. The Chief Justice fled the country rather than face prosecution.

Llewellyn M. Toulmin

Arson, Manufacture and Detonation of Explosive Devices, Rebellion, Conspiracy, Destruction of Government Property, Murder and Allied Crimes

The Irish Republican Army has many crimes to answer for in its bloody history. But perhaps the least known is its massive destruction of the genealogical records of Ireland.

The Irish Public Records Office (PRO), modeled on the famous British PRO, was begun in 1862. The location chosen was the Four Courts Building at Dublin on the north bank of the River Liffey near the center of the city. This building housed the major courts in the city.

The first Deputy Keeper of the PRO, Samuel Ferguson, took his job very seriously and created a two part building, with three stories made of cut granite, above a basement. There was a firebreak separating the office building for staff and researchers from the documents repository, the Treasury. Access to the Treasury could be made only via lockable iron doors. The Treasury had 20 vaults in the basement along a central corridor. Above the basement was an area 50 feet high, 140 feet long, and 80 feet wide, filled with five tiers of iron galleries. The basement and the galleries held the priceless records of the Irish people. The Treasury was intentionally made as fireproof and safe as humanly possible.

In 1916 the IRA first damaged the PRO during the Dublin Rebellion of April 24-20. The PRO and Four Courts building were occupied and "furniture, library books and Records used to barricade windows and some of the gates...." After the Rebellion, it was found that luckily the only document which was totally destroyed was the will of one soldier. Much worse was to come, however.

The Four Courts building, Dublin, Ireland, scene of the destruction by the IRA of the genealogies of hundreds of thousands of Irish families

During the "Troubles" of 1922, the IRA was fighting against the separation of Northern Ireland from the southern Irish Free State, as required by the Anglo-Irish Treaty of 1921. The anti-Treaty IRA forces, led by Rory O'Connor, seized the Four Courts building, including the PRO, during the night of April 13, 1922. It is likely that they seized the building precisely because it was so well built that it could be used as an urban fortress to resist the pro-Treaty Irish forces and their British allies. O'Connor stated that "every care would be taken to preserve all documents..." at the PRO.

About 300-400 IRA fighters occupied the building, and it became IRA headquarters for Dublin during the bloody civil war that ensued. Ernie O'Malley became the Director of Organization at the IRA headquarters. After the war O'Malley stated that the PRO was converted into a

296

munitions factory, since it was isolated from the rest of the building. Mines and grenades were manufactured next to ancient Irish wills and documents.

Despite O'Connor's promise to preserve the records, the IRA leadership in fact decided to blow up and burn the entire Four Courts complex, rather than let it fall into British and pro-Treaty Irish hands. In preparation for the expected attack, the IRA compiled its own army records and smuggled them out of the building, for safekeeping elsewhere. To destroy the PRO building, the IRA placed two huge mines below the floor of the building, and also scattered grenades and smaller mines around the area. Each mine contained an entire truckload of gelignite explosive.

British and Irish pro-Treaty forces issued an ultimatum to the IRA to end their illegal occupation of the Four Courts, but the IRA refused, and on June 28 the attack began. Snipers, gunners and light cannon on both sides began firing.

It appears that a shell fired by government forces set off one of the large mines planted by the IRA. At half past noon on June 28, 1922, a huge explosion rocked the city. This was followed four minutes later by a second enormous explosion, undoubtedly the second mine. A huge fire was started, which burned for hours since it was not possible for firefighters to enter the battleground. Numerous smaller explosions also occurred. For hours after the explosions, fragments of documents ranging from Catholic parish registers to twelfth century wills floated over the city and countryside up to seven miles away, and fell like charred rain on the residents below. Incredibly, no IRA men were killed in the explosions. Perhaps justice would have been served if they were.

The explosions and fire destroyed the following:

- At least half of the parish registers of the Church of Ireland (including Northern Ireland, which of course had not yet been separated for records purposes), including marriage records, birth records, baptismal records, and death records
- *All* the tens of thousands of medieval wills of Ireland. Only an index of these still remains
- Almost all 19th century wills of Ireland, with the exception of three counties
- All the estate administrations of Ireland
- The 19th Century Census records still preserved up to that point (although the government had pulped many of these records for use as war materiel during World War I)
- Numerous pension records
- Numerous state, family and legal papers collected by diligent members of the PRO staff.

For most of these records, no backup or second copy existed anywhere.

Rory O'Connor and numerous other IRA leaders were held in Mountjoy Jail in Dublin, and he and three others were executed by firing squad on December 8, 1922. They were shot, without charge or trial, not for their destruction of the Four Courts, but as a reprisal against the IRA for the assassination the previous day of a member of the Irish Free State parliament. The destruction of the genealogy of Ireland was never properly avenged.

Destruction of Private Property, Arson, False Imprisonment, Mass Murder, Torture, Enforced Starvation and Allied Crimes

Undoubtedly one of the greatest criminals of all time was Mao Tse-Tung, now known as Mao Zedong. His life is famous, but his crimes against genealogy are virtually unknown. Yet I would rate him as perhaps the greatest genealogical criminal of all time.

In pre-20th century China the compilation of genealogical records was widespread and even considered obligatory, as part of the worship of family ancestors. The creation of family genealogies can be traced at least as far back as the Zhou Dynasty, 1050 to 221 BC. Under the Chinese system, two types of genealogies were kept, the "Jiapu" and the "Zongpu."

The Jiapu is the family tree of one family, starting with its male progenitor, listing all family members, and including their birth dates and places, death dates and places, major accomplishments, spouses, and geographical movements. These were kept with scrupulous accuracy for many generations, with the exception that a member of the family who committed crimes might be expunged from the record. The Jaipu would be kept in book form, and would usually be entrusted to the oldest son in the family, and handed down from eldest son to eldest son through the generations. Another copy would usually be kept in the village hall. Every generation or two a committee of family members and scholars would convene to update the Jaipu and record the illustrious deeds of the family members.

The Zongpu was similar to the Jaipu, but would cover an entire clan, consisting of many families. Hence Zongpus were much rarer than Jaipus, and were usually commissioned by wealthy merchants, nobles or bureaucrats.

Since the two types of documents focused on accomplishments and geographic location, they were excellent sources for the study of history and of demography and mass migrations, as well as family lines. For example, study of the Zongpus of the huge Hakka clan showed that this group moved in five waves from northern to southern China over a period of 2000 years.

For 5000 years China had no "Dark Ages." Hence millions, perhaps hundreds of millions, of Jaipu, and perhaps hundreds of thousands of Zongpu, were probably in existence in the 1960s. (This was likely still true, despite the fact that the Communists had discouraged the study and compilation of genealogy since seizing power in 1949.) Since each document contained hundreds or even thousands of individual entries, it is probably no exaggeration to say that China had the greatest collection of genealogical materials the world had ever seen, probably with *billions* of total entries.

Enter arch-criminal Mao Zedung. In 1966 he launched what he called the Great Proletarian Cultural Revolution to enshrine Maoism as the dominant cultural and political philosophy of the country, to wipe out his political enemies, and to distract the people from domestic woes.

Mao encouraged the students, Red Guards, military and civil servants of China to destroy any vestige of their old culture. This included libraries, antiques, books, films, phonograph records, paintings, art of any kind, statues, and any other cultural items. China became a cultural desert. Textbooks and teaching materials in schools at all levels were destroyed, and teachers, professionals and learned persons were beaten and killed. Over three million people died violent deaths, and over 100 million suffered significantly.

Importantly for our purposes, Jaipu and Zongpu were specifically targeted for destruction. Within months, millions and possibly billions of priceless genealogical records were destroyed, as Red Guards rampaged through every city, town and village in the country.

The destruction continued at maximum ferocity through 1969, when Mao, perhaps realizing he had created a monster that could destroy even him, declared that the Cultural Revolution was over. Yet destruction and numerous other related abuses continued well into the 1970s, officially ending in 1976 with the arrest of the "Gang of Four." Related abuses of the population included mass imprisonments on baseless charges, dislocations of millions to work camps for "re-education," torture, murder on a mass scale, human rights abuses of all kinds, enforced starvation of various groups or regions, attempted elimination of religious groups, etc. Many of these abuses continue until this day in the world's largest dictatorship.

A Chinese colleague of mine has estimated that only about one percent of Jaipu and Zongpu still exist, either in the possession of the families or in libraries outside of China. As a result of this enormous destruction, members of the largest society on Earth, the mainland, Taiwanese and Straits Chinese, numbering well over one billion, all of whom descend from vigorous ancestor worshippers, in general cannot list any of their ancestors beyond their own grandparents.

Fraud, Lesé Majesté

Roman emperors and aspiring politicians reportedly commissioned genealogists to "prove" that they were descended from Romulus, Remus, other heroes and notables, and even from the gods. Their opponents considered this proof to be fraudulent, and to also to be "an offense against the gods and the emperor" or lesé majesté. But it seemed to get votes, so the practice continued.

Would you like to prove *your* descent from the gods? Many have done so. Here are the steps. First, prove your descent from Charlemagne. This is not too tough if you are lucky enough to have a "gateway ancestor" whose genealogy already links to Charlemagne and is proven and accepted by various reputable genealogists. If you haven't found your gateway ancestor yet, keep looking. Chances are you can find one if you look hard enough.

Second, and this is a bit dicier, obtain a book by Thelma Evans-Reddell called *Americans of Royal Descent*. There is a copy in the Daughters of the American Revolution headquarters genealogical library. This book, unfortunately with no footnotes or sources, purports to show a line from Charlemagne to various distinguished Romans via the rebel Queen of Britain, Boadicea and via Colius--"Old King Cole."

The famous Romans in the direct line allegedly include Claudius, Emperor of Rome; Mark Anthony the Orator; and a line of the Caesar family going back to about 150 BC. (Julius Caesar the Great—and the likely destroyer of the Alexandria Library—is a great-uncle on this line.)

Third, research lines above Mark Anthony. Mark Anthony's father Anton of Rome reportedly claimed descent from Hercules the Great. Hercules was the son of Alcmene and Zeus, the King of the Gods. Zeus was the son of Chronus, the God of Time and one of the Titans, and his sister Rhea. Chronus was the son of Uranus, the god of the sky, Gaia, the god of the Earth. (Just to make it confusing, Gaia was the mother *and* the wife of Uranus.) Gaia was the daughter of Chaos, the great emptiness.

Soooooo, if you can prove descent from Charlemagne, and you are willing to make the leap of accepting Ms. Evans-Reddell and believing in Greek myth, then you, too, can be a lineal descendant of the gods and even of Chaos itself. Whether this is fraud and a crime against genealogy, I leave to your conscience.

Section 7

The Great Race: Classic Cars

Rally Across America

Vroom! Vroom!
The Great Race is Coming

The Great Race – the oldest, richest and most exciting classic car rally in the world -- is coming to the Washington, DC area on Saturday, June 25, 2005. Almost 100 cars going back in time to a 1910 Seldon will start at the US Capitol and rally across the country to Takoma, Washington in a two-week event that will cover 13 states and over 4200 miles. I will be driving my 1968 "Bullitt" Mustang and my wife Susan will be navigating.

Lew Toulmin and the authentic 1968 "Bullitt" Mustang in front of the US Capitol, just before the start of the Great Race

Another team from the DC area will be in a militarized 1941 Buick US Army staff car, driven by Captain Greg Galligan of Alexandria, Virginia, and navigated by Captain Jon Eisberg of Westminster, Maryland. Both are rookies at the Great Race. Their team will represent the US Army National Guard, the principal sponsor of the Great Race.

The rally is not a speed race, but rather is a time-speed-distance (TSD) rally. This means that the cars run over open roads in normal traffic and do not exceed the posted speed limits. Each morning each of the teams are given a list with hundreds of precise written or graphic instructions, such as "at the stop sign, wait ten seconds, then proceed at exactly 30 mph to next instruction," and "at the curve sign, change your average speed to 35 mph for exactly 36 seconds, then to 45 mph until the next instruction." The team that follows the instructions most precisely, does not get lost, and is closest to the pre-set, computer-determined correct time, wins the rally.

TSD rallying is a world wide trend. All of the famous open road speed races of the 1930s to 1950s, such as the Mille Miglia in Italy, the Leige-Rome-Leige race across Europe, and the Rallye des Alpes in Switzerland and Austria, have now been converted to TSD rallies. TSD rallies increase safety for participants and fans. The TSD approach also allows amateur drivers with very old antique cars to compete on a level playing field with more modern classics. TSD rallying tests the navigational and driving skills of team and the reliability of the vehicles.

Over the course of the Great Race TSD rally, teams will follow thousands of instructions that take them along some of the most scenic back roads in America. At each lunch, rest and evening stop, crowds will turn out to meet the cars, bands will play, and car shows and related events will take place. Often the Great Race is the biggest event all year in some of the small towns en route. Each year the route is completely changed, sometimes running roughly east-west in one year and north-south in the next.

Prizes for the rally will total $250,000, thus giving this rally the largest prize fund of any classic car rally in the world. The overall winner usually wins around $55,000. Prizes will be awarded for the overall time/speed/distance winner; to the best of three high school teams competing; to the best in three skill classes; and to the winners of various stages. "Ace" awards will be given to the teams that manage to exactly match the correct required time to the second, an incredible feat. "Ace" awardees get to put a six inch "Ace" sticker, shaped like a wheel with a trailing whoosh on it, on their cars. Amazingly, some experienced rallyists have dozens of these stickers on their vehicles.

Prizes are also given to the cities and towns voted by the teams as the most enthusiastic hosts for the Great Race. Donations are made by the Great Race to the local library or other approved charities in these "Great American Cities."

The oldest car in the rally is a 1910 Selden Raceabout. Like many of the Great Race vehicles, the car has no hardtop or softop, it is simply open to the elements. The car is driven by Frank Currie of Anaheim, California, an 18 year veteran of the Great Race. According to Mike Ewing of the Great Race staff, "Frank's 1910 Selden is so well designed and maintained that it is more reliable than my modern car!"

Many teams are so serious about racing and maintaining their cars that they have full-time support teams, some with mobile workshops, that follow along behind the rally. The support teams and drivers may work all night to fix a car in order to get back in the competition early the next morning.

Other interesting and very valuable cars in the rally include a 1911 Velie Racytype (sic), a 1916 Packard, numerous racers based on Model A Fords, a 1931

Studebaker President convertible, a 1935 Auburn Club sedan, and a 1954 Kaiser Darrin.

Perhaps the most bizarre car in the rally will be car number 87, a 1934 McQuay-Norris Streamliner. This strange car looks like a zeppelin on wheels, is sponsored by the Lane Motor Museum, and is driven by Jeff and Susan Lane of Nashville, Tennessee. They are three year veterans of the event.

One of the most experienced participants in the rally will be Bill Secrest, navigator of car number 79, a Chevrolet two-door sedan. Bill is one of the few people on earth who has literally driven around the entire world, as a participant in the 'Round the World Classic Car Rally in the year 2000. He has also rallied all over South America, Russia and the US, and is planning a rally from Berlin to Shanghai in 2006.

The classic cars will race over fourteen days, making overnight stops at Harrisonburg, VA, Ashland, KY, Louisville, KY, Urbana, IL, Gurnee, IL, Davenport, IA, West Des Moines, IA, Grand Island, NE, Denver, CO, Rock Springs, WY, Twin Falls, ID, Walla Walla, and Puyallup, WA. On July 9, 2005 the rally will finish in Tacoma, Washington.

The Great Race was founded 22 years ago, and has visited over 800 cities and towns in the US, Canada and Mexico. Great Racers have logged nearly 6,000,000 vehicle miles, making stops at some of the continent's best known venues including the White House, The Statue of Liberty Centennial Celebration, the Reforma in Mexico City, the Grand Canyon, the Indianapolis and Daytona Motor Speedways, The St. Louis Arch and in a parade down Broadway in New York City.

1968 "Bullitt" Mustang: The Essence of Cool

Having decided to enter the 2005 Great Race as a journalist-competitor, I reviewed the list of the 96 teams in the demanding rally, looking for the coolest car and the greatest guy to interview. The guy had to be young, handsome, suave and debonair. His car had to be sharp and unforgettable. After a tremendous search, I found him: me.

Me: Please spell your name correctly for me.

Me: Duh!

Me: Oh, right. OK, so tell me about your (my? our?) car.

Me: It's a 1968 Ford Mustang GT fastback, painted Highland Green, with a V-8 "S" code big-block 390 cubic-inch engine, 4-speed, with a black interior.

Me: What is the significance of all that?

Me: That configuration is exactly the same as the car that was used in the 1968 Steve McQueen movie *Bullitt*. There were 317,404 Mustangs built that year, but only 355 with that configuration. Three were used in filming the movie. Only one survived the amazing stunts that the cars were put through. The remaining car is hidden in a hay barn in Alabama or Kentucky, and has been gone since the movie. It's probably worth $250,000 to $500,000. Steve McQueen himself tried to recover the car, but the owner, apparently a recluse, wouldn't sell or even let anyone see the car.

Me: Tell me about the movie *Bullitt*.

Me: The film is about a cop, Lt. Frank Bullitt of the San Francisco Police Department homicide division. He is ordered to protect a Mafia accountant who is going to testify against the mob. It turns out that another guy has been substituted for the real accountant. In the ensuing confusion, there is a fantastic car chase, with Frank Bullitt in his Mustang fastback chasing two assassins in their 1968 Dodge Charger 440 R/T. This is the first really great car chase in movie history. It is the highlight of the movie, and lasts eight minutes. In the script there were no details for the sequence, just one line that said "car chase."

The chase was actually done on the city streets of San Francisco, with the cars roaring over the hills of the city, and with chases on the flat getting up to 130 mph. McQueen did much of his own driving and most of the planning for each stunt, assisted by the assassins/stuntmen in the Charger. Movie chases now are so common now that they are ho-hum, but when this came out it was absolutely electrifying. *Classic Cars* magazine recently rated the *Bullitt* chase as one of the five greatest of all time. The movie is available on video and DVD, and is often shown on TV. It's best on the big movie screen, though, so you can experience the unbelievable car jumps right in your gut.

Me: So the car is famous?

Me: Yes, the Bullitt car is mentioned in almost every automotive, Ford and Mustang history. It has been on the cover of numerous magazines, even recently. In 2005 surveys in the US and Britain confirmed the Bullitt car and chase as the most memorable in movie history. In 2004 *Car* magazine called it "the coolest cop car ever," and rated it as one of the top 10 "coolest cars of all time." In 2001 Ford brought out a special edition "Bullitt" Mustang in Highland Green that had some resemblance the original car. The current Ford Mustang clearly owes a lot of its styling cues to the great 1968 fastback.

Me: What is it about McQueen?

Me: Steve McQueen had more magnetism than all the current male movie stars put together. He had the "X factor" to the tenth power. There is a distance shot in the movie in which he gets out of the Mustang and looks toward the camera, where the assassins are hiding. In a millisecond he projects an intensity from over 150 yards away that is fantastic. His other terrific movies included the *Great Escape, The Sand Pebbles, The Magnificent Seven,* and the original *Thomas Crown Affair,* among 30 others. For about 10 years in the 1960s and '70s he was the biggest star in the world. Just recently Turner Classic Movies made a TV special honoring him called "Steve McQueen—The Essence of Cool."

Me: In the movie does Bullitt get the girl?

Me: Yes and no. Frank Bullitt's girlfriend is played by the beautiful Jacqueline Bisset, and she remains his girlfriend at the end of the film. My theory is that the movie is really about their relationship, which is shown in just a few scenes. Their affair is starting to deteriorate, because of the hard, brutal nature of his police work. So their future is left open to question in the final shots of the movie. Their interaction is brilliantly played by the actors.

Me: How did you acquire the car?

Me: I had a 1968 Mustang fastback previously, but it was a bit of a disaster. There were huge electrical problems created by a major rewiring done by a previous owner. And it was not an authentic Bullitt. So I was looking for a "real" Bullitt when I was visiting my folks down in southern Alabama about two years ago. I got on the Internet and entered "1968 Ford Mustang for sale," just on the chance I would get lucky. I got a hit in central Alabama for an authentic Bullitt, one of the 355 correct cars. I called immediately but was told the car was already sold. I was crushed, since I had been searching for two years. I called

310

back two days later, to tell the private dealer to keep his eyes open for similar cars. He said, "The guy who was supposed to pay didn't come up with the money. As of one hour ago the car is back on the market." I drove up that day, looked at it for 45 minutes, and bought it on the spot for the asking price of $32,900.

Me: What is the car worth now?

Me: That's a good question. Purist Mustang judges and insurance assessors rate it rather low, since the movie car (and my car) are somewhat different than the normal 1968 GT. For example, the movie car's grill was simplified and painted black, and its badges removed, to look more anonymous and ominous. People who appreciate the movie, and Europeans, are willing to pay quite a lot. So I have had insurance estimates and offers to buy ranging from $20,000 up to $50,000. I'm not selling, though.

Me: I'm glad to hear it!

Me: What have you done to the car since you got it?

Me: Lots. Installed a new, larger gas tank for longer range. Made the ignition more authentic and changed out numerous electrical components. Fixed the clutch, parking brakes, vents and various holes in the dash and body. Found and installed a bell under-housing for the clutch/transmission area. Installed sound and heat insulation that was missing. Pulled the engine and installed new exhaust manifolds to gain ground clearance. Redid the steering box. Installed new interior trim.

Me: Sounds expensive.

Me: It only cost ten cents.

Me: What?

Me: Hey, my wife is going to read this, and I don't want her to know I spent another six thou... Let's change the subject.

Me: Right. How did you hear about the Great Race?

Me: I was covering the Around the World Classic Car Rally in England, Pennsylvania and New Jersey in 2000, when I met the legendary Bill Secrest, the great rally navigator. He told me about the Great Race, and highly recommended it. He said, "It is very precise, well run and is the biggest and best time/speed/distance rally in the US." Later I observed the Great Race for two days in Kansas in 2001 when I happened to be there, and was very impressed. Bill will be in the 2005 race, by the way.

Me: Who is your navigator?

Me: My wife Susan. Remember her? You better! You've been married to her for 24 years. She worked for the Library of Congress until she retired a few years ago. She is a wonderful, methodical navigator.

Me: Your car is kind of young for the Great Race, isn't it?

Me: Yes. We are rookies in the Tour class, and are not eligible for the major prizes. The cutoff for fully competitive cars is 45 years old; the Mustang is 37. We do rally every day, get scored, and can get "Ace" awards. We are placed in the middle of the pack so we can stop and do photos and interviews with teams on the rally.

Me: So you're a journalist?

Me: Yes, I write monthly travel columns for *International Travel News* and the *Montgomery Sentinel*. Now I am writing stories about the Great Race teams and the rallying, which is fascinating. I'm also a consultant to the World Bank and the US Agency for International Development in international telecommunications policy and public administration.

Me: Is there anything else interesting about you?

Me: Well, I've traveled to 125 of the 194 countries on Earth. I discovered the real World War II "Bali Hai," and I've been elected to the Explorers' Club, headed by Sir Edmund Hillary. I'm a member of the Descendants of the Signers of the Declaration of Independence. I live in Silver Spring, Maryland and I'm 54 years old. I'm...

Me: Jeez, I thought you were supposed to be "young"! And why are we always talking about you, when what I really want to hear about is that demi-god, Steve McQueen. With you, it's all about "me," isn't it? Just like this interview! Me, me, me, me, me, me, me!

Me: Well, nyeah, nyeah, nyeah! You're all about me, too!

Me: Moron!

Me: Schmuck!

Let's Go Great Racing—Part 1

The Great Race, presented by the US Army National Guard, roared off at noon Saturday, June 25th, with 96 cars ranging in age up to 95 years from a starting grid on Pennsylvania Avenue right in front of the US Capitol. "No other automobile event is known to have started from this historic and august location," said Wayne Stanfield, chief operating officer of the event, which will take the cars for 4250 miles through 13 states over 15 days, to finish in Tacoma, Washington.

The rally route started under a huge Great Race inflatable arch. Each team member, including this lucky reporter, was given a starting medal to wear around his or her neck by two National Guardsman as the cars went under the arch, then each car was waved off every few seconds with the flourish of a green flag.

The "Bullitt" Mustang roars through the Great Race starting gate on Pennsylvania Avenue in front of the US Capitol

My wife Susan and I are driving our classic 1968 Ford "Bullitt" Mustang in this wonderful event, and we are now half way through the amazing competition. Since there are 96 fractious cars and 8 driving days so far, there are probably at least 96 times 8 stories to tell, but let me focus on just a few that illustrate the spirit of the event. These include two near accidents, kindnesses on the road, and the amazing one-good-armed dentist competitor.

KA-BAM: Historic Packard Drops Transmission

"KA-BAM—that's what it sounded like," said Pat Brothers, the female driver of the "Pat 'N Pat" Great Race Team. "We were driving along and suddenly there was this tremendous noise. The steering locked up, I hit the brakes, and our Packard was swerving around the road. I managed to almost keep the car in one lane, however—I 'm real proud of that. I'm still shaking like a leaf. We had to leave the car in the road, because we can't move it an inch."

The near-accident took place on the outskirts of Ashland, Kentucky, as the Great Racers were completing Stage 3 of the rally. Two Ashland police cruisers and a fire truck responded to the scene, but found driver Pat and her husband/navigator, also named Pat Brothers, to be unhurt.

Examination of the underside of the rare 1941 Packard 120 Club Coupe revealed that most of the drivetrain had fallen onto the road, apparently due to the failure of one or more U-joints. Navigator/husband Pat said, "We had heard a whine at lunch time, but thought it was a minor rear end problem, and decided to press on and just baby the car. The whine got bigger, but only when my wife lifted her foot off the gas. As long as she had her foot down on the pedal, things were fine. We tried to keep going to avoid a 'Did Not Finish,' but it's clear we won't make it today. We have a whole extra drive train in our support vehicle, though, so we will try to fix the car overnight and get running tomorrow." Driver Pat added, "This experience was scary, but really exciting!"

All that night and the next day the two Pats worked to rebuild the drivetrain, with the aid of a local hot rod shop in Ashland. "We carry many of the Packard drive shaft parts that were needed in our support vehicle," said husband Pat. "But many of the parts we needed were in the Packard's rear end, for which we didn't have spares. So we fabricated and customized rear end parts from several other local cars and trucks. So now we have a unique car – a Packard/Dodge/Chevy/Toyota. It works great!"

Pat and Pat were able to rejoin the Great Race as it moved through Indiana and Illinois in Stages 4 and 5 of the rally, after having only two dreaded "DNF--did not finish" days. They were so unflustered by their breakdown that they even managed to score two excellent legs of just four and five seconds in penalty points during the Stage 4 rally from Louisville, Kentucky to Urbana, Illinois.

Bomb Squad Almost Becomes Bomb

Guy Mace of the Bomb Squad, Great Race team number 93, was bombing along in his 1932 Ford M-1 Mechanix Special Racer, when it almost turned into the team namesake. "A small temperature switch on our flathead V-8 failed, and that sent engine temperatures soaring on one side of the engine," said Mace, dressed in his characteristic black team uniform. "This created huge back pressure in the engine, and the accelerator suddenly stuck in high. For quite a while I couldn't slow down. Finally we managed to stop and got the hood off. Gasoline was pouring out of the top of the carburetor onto the hot engine. We were lucky we didn't have a fire or explosion. We worked on the engine and restarted it, but it had a very bad knock. So we had to replace the engine with our spare," Guy said casually, as if replacing an engine was as simple as replacing a light bulb. "Unfortunately, the spare has less than five hours running time on it. We've been in first place in the rookie division, but with this new engine we may not be able to hold onto that top spot."

Can Mace and the Bomb Squad "baby" the replacement engine for a while to break it in? "There's no babying equipment during a timed race," said Guy. "We just have to go out and do it."

Kindness on the Road

Kindnesses big and small happened to many of 600 members of the Great Race teams, support crews, and staff as they traveled through the country's heartland. Keith Phillips, support crew to "Focus on the Family" team number 34 was stuck without transportation in Washington, Indiana. Keith needed to buy a bag of ice for his team. He asked a local resident where the nearest ice machine was, and got this amazing answer: "Oh, the nearest place is up this road about a mile away. Here, take the keys to my truck and go get whatever you need. Just leave the keys on the seat when you come back."

Roadside Assistance with a Plasma Cutter

Hugh Hiott, support crew member to team number 9, the "Spirit of America" 1916 Studebaker Racer, reports another inspiring story of roadside assistance. "Our team was passing through Davenport, Iowa when they discovered extensive cracking to the header welds. This was a very serious problem, and could have forced them to withdraw from racing. Through mutual friends, Mike and Doug Garner of Shardo Farms in LeClair, Iowa were contacted.

The Garners agreed to make the necessary repairs at their elaborate workshop on their 15,000 acre soybean farm. They used a plasma cutter, a very expensive and rare tool, to cut out 18 gauge steel to weld onto both sides of the failing parts. The Garners worked for 4 hours, finishing at midnight. The Garners refused any form of compensation for this sterling service." Hugh continued, "The car number 9 team wants to publicly thank the Garner family for their generous, unselfish labor and kindness, which certainly allowed the 89-year-old Studebaker to continue in competition."

The Bravest Dentist of All?

One of the bravest Great Race contestants has to be dentist Rich McKone of Peoria, Illinois, a 20-year veteran of the Great Race and navigator of team number 94, a 1936 Ford two-door. Rich said, "Last Saturday I was cleaning my boat and slipped on some new soap I was using. I fell down onto a dock and shattered the ball socket in my upper arm. I got in the car and drove six hours to find a doctor friend that I trusted to fix it. He operated on the compound fracture, and inserted a big steel pin in my upper arm bone. He put my arm in a sling and told me to take it easy. Tuesday I got in a car and headed for Washington, DC to participate in the Great Race. I wasn't going to miss this great event over some silly soap." As of press time Rich, still with only one working arm, was running fifth in his Grand Championship class, with a score of just 1 minute and 14 seconds in penalty points. Truly a Man of Steel!

Let's Go Great Racing—Part 2

The Great Race of 2005 is now history. It lived up to its name: Great! The rally covered over 4000 miles across 14 states from Washington, DC to Tacoma, Washington, with 96 cars competing, some almost 100 years old. Who won? The race motto is "to finish is to win," so 79 finishing teams won, including this reporter, my wife Susan, and our 1968 "Bullitt" Mustang.

The best score was posted by the amazing team of Greg Cunningham and Sam Goeppinger, in their 1928 Ford Speedster. Their time penalties were an incredibly low one minute and 41 seconds, an average of only about 7 seconds per day in penalties over the 14 days of racing. (In time/speed/distance rallying, the team that follows directions to the second, and has the fewest time penalties, wins.) By contrast, our team score was over 15 times worse. But we won an "Ace" award for a perfect leg, and most important, we finished!

What were the highlights of the race for us? Our best stories involve the memorable people and their cars, our breakdowns, the heat, one daring spectator, and the amazing generosity of the fans.

Most Memorable Car: the McQuay Norris Streamliner

Without a doubt the most memorable of the 96 teams in the rally, both in terms of cars and rallyists, had to be the 1934 McQuay Norris Streamliner and its owners, Jeff and Susan Lane. The car looks like a big silver melon on bright red wheels, with friendly, smiling eyes. According to Jeff, "McQuay-Norris was an auto parts manufacturer based in the mid-west. In 1934 they built just six of these cars as rolling demonstration labs. The McQuay-Norris parts salesmen drove them all over the country, and used them to show off the quality of their auto parts. So the cars were never sold to the public. The car has over 15 special gauges which prove how the McQuay-Norris parts function better than their competitors."

Everything about the car seems odd—the engine compartment, body, windshield wipers—everything. According to Jeff Lane, 44, who owns an auto parts business, "There is no engine compartment separate from the cabin. The driver and navigator have a huge dash in front of them, reaching about four feet towards the curved window in front. The engine is hidden under the dash. The body is wood, skinned in aluminum sheets carefully molded to create a wonderful streamlined shape. There are no windshield wipers. The McQuay-Norris philosophy was that the streamlining would take care of the rain—just drive fast enough and the rain will slide off to the side!"

The bizarre McQuay Norris Streamliner, at the beginning of the Great Race

The Lanes are as memorable as their car. They own and run an auto museum in Nashville, Tennessee, which got started in an interesting way. According to Jeff, "One day I was working on my cars, and my wife Susan said, 'Dear, just how many cars do you have?' I answered, 'Oh, I dunno, maybe 20.' 'Let's count them,' she said. And we counted 75 cars!" So they started a museum and Susan became the curator.

The Museum now has over 125 cars, and specializes in European vehicles, streamlined cars, propeller-driven cars, and micro-cars. The goal of the Museum is to "collect cars that make you smile." The McQuay Norris certainly qualifies.

The Lanes and their bizarre car made it across the country, and scored a respectable 5 minutes and 21 seconds, putting them 33rd in the overall standings, a very good finish. They did have some hairy moments. According to Susan, "You haven't lived until you see your driver reach into the engine and begin working on it while driving. The Streamliner was running rough and my husband Jeff wanted to adjust the carburetor. Since our engine is in the passenger compartment he just opened the dash and started adjusting the fuel flow, while we kept driving down the road. We made our leg with only a one second penalty."

Thunk, Thunk, Thunk: Not a Good Sound

In the Bullitt Mustang, we were driving towards Urbana, Illinois on Stage 4 of the rally, when suddenly there was a faint "thunk" from underneath the car. Then another "thunk," this time a little louder. Then louder, and even louder. This sounded serious. We stopped and examined the tires, thinking we had picked up something that was flailing around, as had happened to us on a regional rally. The tires were fine. The engine was fine when we were not moving. We figured it was the U-joints in the drivetrain, and decided to wait for the sweep truck, known as the "grim reaper," which follows along behind the rally.

But literally within ten seconds a local Good Samaritan stranger appeared, pulling an empty car hauling trailer. "Need a lift for your car into town?" asked Richie Hill of Urbana. Within two minutes the Mustang was loaded on the trailer, and 30 minutes later we arrived at our designated hotel. Richie refused to take any payment, saying, "Next time it might be you picking me up."

Then another guardian angel arrived. John Robertson of Marquette, Michigan, whiz support mechanic to the Kaiser Darrin team, strode up and asked what was wrong with the Mustang. Within 30 seconds he was under the car, poking and prodding. Within four minutes he had a lift lined up at Peter B's, the local Urbana classic car shop, even though it was 9 pm by this time. He and I drove the Mustang very slowly to the shop, lifted it up, and he quickly diagnosed the problem as a simple loose wheel. The aluminum wheel had worked its lug nuts loose, as aluminum wheels are prone to do. Luckily the wheel was not damaged, and we were able to roar back to the hotel in fine style. "I like this car," said angel John, "It's like flying a fighter plane. Just keep the lug nuts tight."

10 Cent Part Lames Mustang

Later in the rally, we were in transit to Twin Falls, Idaho, on an interstate, when suddenly the Mustang just lost power. The battery and starter were fine, but the car just wouldn't start. We were loaded on the dreaded sweep truck, and carried ignominiously into town. Our angels, John Robertson and Walt Anderson of the Kaiser Darrin team, reappeared, and began disassembling the engine. By 11:00 pm they had diagnosed the problem: a 10 cent part, a roller pin, deep in the distributor, had sheared off. But where to find the part at this time of night? We dashed over to the motel of the famous NASCAR Roush Racing Team, which was participating in the rally, and woke up one of the Roush mechanics. Without complaint he got dressed, drove over to his mammoth support truck, unlocked it, and got out an entire tray of roller pins to choose from. We hammered home the part, and all got to bed about 1 a.m.

Heat Doesn't Faze Racers

A heat wave of 90 degree temperatures followed the rallyists from Washington, DC all the way to the Cascade mountains in Washington state. I fought the heat by draping my heads and shoulders in wet towels, so that I looked more like a damp Lawrence of Arabia than a dapper Steve McQueen in the Bullitt Mustang. I also tried a bizarre device which sucked hot air into an ice cooler, and expelled cool air into the Mustang cabin. Perhaps 10 molecules of cool air were detectable. The device is now in a landfill somewhere in Colorado. Other teams used wet bandanas and neck coolers. One ingenious team took off their shoes and put their feet on a seven pound block of ice!

The Mustang dashes across eastern Nebraska in a cloud of hot dust.
Inside, Susan is reaching for a wet towel.

Spectator Races the Racers

We were racing through rolling, green farmland east of Des Moines, Iowa, when we saw a teenaged boy ahead of us. He was astride a dirt bike motorcycle and was positioned in the ditch beside the road, looking back toward us. As we dashed past him he gunned the bike and charged uphill through the ditch. He began racing alongside us, between the road and a high barbed wire fence, using the ditch as a race track. Then in what appeared to be a well-practiced move, he hit a big bump at about 45 mph, and was suddenly looking down at us from 12 feet in the air. He landed safely and stopped, laughing his head off. I said to my wife/navigator Susan, "That crazy kid reminds me of Steve McQueen, doing amazing stunts. But while we are living out the McQueen movie *Bullitt*, he is acting out the great McQueen barbed wire fence jump in *The Great Escape*."

Generosity of the Fans

But the most memorable thing about the Great Race was undoubtedly the interest and kindness of the spectators, entrants, support crews and staff of the rally. The spirit of the rally is to never say die, and to always help out teams in need, and this was certainly the case in every instance we observed or heard of.

A typical story is told by Hugh Hiott, support crew to team number 9, the "Spirit of America" 1916 Studebaker Racer: "Santa Claus is alive and well on the Great Race. He was dressed in a Hawaiian shirt and had a slight paunch. In Twin Falls, Idaho he was looking at our Studebaker when he noticed that the exhaust header was badly cracking at the number 6 pipe-to-collector weld. Santa said, 'Don't worry, I can weld that.' And he did—later that night he appeared at our motel with his welding gear and did a beautiful job of repairing the cracked welds, probably preventing catastrophic damage down the road. With no fanfare he quickly disappeared, leaving a perfect job, requesting no payment, and not even leaving his name. So we dubbed him 'Santa Claus,' and we really believe he exists." On the Great Race, the giving spirit of Santa is alive every day, even though the rally comes through every-town America each year around July 4th.

The Mustang and the 1936 Ford Fordor police car of Jim and Louise Feeney "race" around the Kentucky Speedway track during the Great Race

* * *

Below are profiles of several of the most interesting Great Race teams.

The Daring Darrin Duo and Their Delectable Kaiser Darrin

Loren Ameen, 55, of Marquette, Michigan had never seen a Kaiser Darrin in person or even in pictures until a year ago. But he had heard about the rare car 34 years ago from a co-worker who couldn't stop raving about the amazing fiberglass sports car with the sliding doors. Loren must have been thinking about the unique vehicle for every one of those years, because when he saw one in person in a car museum in May of 2004, he instantly fell in love. Within weeks he bought a 1954 Kaiser Darrin 161 on E-bay.

Unfortunately, as Shakespeare said, "the course of true love ne'er did run smooth." The previous owner described the car as "95% restored." Says Loren, "Now, after buying the car for $38,000, putting in over 1000 hours of work over the last 11 months, purchasing a second Kaiser Darrin as a parts car, bringing in a world class restorer, and laying out over $40,000, *now* it is 95% restored! A big team was required to re-fiberglass the entire body, rebuild the engine, and restore all the systems. I put in many, many hours as part of the team, especially on the body work. I am not a professional body man, but I almost became one on this project."

According to Loren, "There are only a handful of running Kaiser Darrins in the country today. A fully restored one is probably worth about $60,000, and one that is running at all is worth $20,000 to $40,000. If I sold this car I could never recover all I've put into it. But I'd never sell it. It is beautiful."

The Kaiser Darrin was a car ahead of its time. It was manufactured by Kaiser Industries, famous for building thousands of Liberty ships and numerous small aircraft carriers in World War II. After the war, the firm built over 800,000 cars in various models. In 1953 Kaiser acquired Willys-Overland, makers of the well known World War II Jeeps. The Darrin was planned to be the prestige sports car of the Kaiser line, using Kaiser and Willys parts but with a spectacular new body. According to a promotional poster from the 1950s, "the Kaiser Darrin is America's newest, raciest sports car, made with Aeron armor-clad fiberglass, revolutionary spring-assisted sliding doors, disappearing Deauville-styled top, only 36 inches from ground to cowl, three carburetors, dual exhausts, and a high power to weight ratio. There's nothing like it in the world!" The most memorable features are the unforgettable fan nostril nose, swooping sides, and two bizarre doors. And of course that "armor-clad fiberglass"!

The Kaiser Darrin with its amazing sliding doors at the start of the Great Race, US Capitol grounds, Washington, DC

The Darrin was expensive, over $3000 (a huge amount at the time), and the planned clientele was clearly the rich. "As you're driving around Newport, Las Vegas or

Southampton," says the promotional poster, "you can be content that you're driving one car in a million, not one of millions."

That numerical ratio was about right, or maybe even a little low. For Kaiser Industries made only 435 Darrins total, during the two year production run of 1953 to 1954. The high price apparently discouraged buyers, and Kaiser switched its focus to building Jeeps, instead. Loren's car is number 108. "The car was designed by and named for 'Dutch' Darrin, a stylish Parisian designer," says Loren. "He was sort of like Frank Lloyd Wright—he had great ideas but was a bit weak on practical details. Take the famous sliding doors. The doors actually slide forward into the front fenders. They're beautiful. And a great idea. Unfortunately, they don't work very well. And getting Darrin body parts is very difficult. Luckily the mechanical parts are relatively common, since the Darrin uses a standard Kaiser drive train and a Willys six cylinder, 161 cubic inch engine. These components were used on many other Kaiser and Willys vehicles, and so are easy to locate. The car only develops about 90 horsepower, but with its fiberglass body, it only weighs about 2000 pounds, so the pickup is good."

Loren Ameen was born and raised in Marquette, Michigan, a descendant of Swedish immigrants. "My last name means 'trustworthy' in Arabic and sounds Middle Eastern, so everyone is surprised to find that I have blue eyes, blond hair, and my name and family can actually be traced back to 16th century Sweden." Loren worked as a property tax analyst and appraiser for the local mining company. Later he worked as a Certified Financial Planner and served on the Marquette planning and zoning board until he retired.

Loren is proud of his Upper Peninsula town, and is a bit of a town and regional booster. "Our town of Marquette has a lot of history and a gorgeous location right on the southern shore of Lake Superior. The people in down-state Michigan used to make fun of us folks from the U.P. and call us 'Yoopers.' Now we view that as a term of pride. Since the down-staters live below the bridge, we return the favor and call them 'Trolls.'" Over the years there has been a lot of semi-serious talk about the Upper Peninsula seceding from Michigan, and creating a new state, to be called, naturally, "Superior."

Loren had never heard of the Great Race until ten months ago, when his friend Bob Nankervis said to him, "Now that you've got a neat car, you need to think about entering the Great Race." Says Loren, "I kinda got the impression from Bob that he had a lot of rally experience as a navigator. I had never entered a car race or rally of any kind in my life. So Bob became the team navigator. But just recently I discovered that Bob's rally experience consisted of one Sunday afternoon scavenger hunt rally, over 30 years ago!" Both Loren and Bob have been carefully poring over a rally manual and the Great Race rules.

Loren says, "We called our team the Daring Darrin Duo for obvious reasons. We chose the team number of 49 because I was born in 1949."

Loren hoped to do lots of testing on the car before entering the Great Race. Interviewed shortly before the race, Loren said, "We knew we needed to put at least 1000 test miles on the car before beginning the Great Race. Unfortunately, restoring the car has taken so long that we'll be working on it up until the last minute. We are still looking for some rare Darrin parts. The thing we're looking for now is a little plastic cap to cover the license plate light. That part just doesn't exist. We'll probably end up using a piece of Saran Wrap to cover that darn light. And we've only had a chance to drive the car for 150 test miles, instead of 1000! Luckily the car looks great, and our restoration shop Soapy and Sons, led by Craig Sobczek, did a fabulous job on the body and mechanicals. I'm confident the car will do well."

To help ensure their success, the team has a support vehicle and trailer, filled with parts from the second, cannibalized Darrin. "Our support crew of two, Walt Anderson and John Robertson, will be driving a 1994 Chevrolet Suburban. It has over 260,000 miles on it, so we've been working hard on that, too," says Loren. "Luckily Walt is a professor of automobile repair at our local college, so we'll be fine." The team trailered the Kaiser Darrin to Washington, DC, but will likely drive the car back from Washington state to Michigan.

As Loren and Bob rally their unique, stylish Kaiser Darrin across the country and drive it leisurely back, they can be content that their car is not one of millions, but rather is more like one in 100 million.

* * *

Loren and Bob completed the Great Race in great style, without any major mechanical problems. They finished with a score of about 19 minutes, not great, but as rookies, their goal was to finish and they did that with no trouble. And they got one Ace award for completing a perfect leg. They drove the Kaiser part of the way back to the Upper Peninsula, turning heads wherever they went.

The 12-Year-Old Genius
Great Racer

"My goal is to win the Grand Championship of the Great Race this year, as a present for my twelfth birthday," says Sawyer Stone of Hot Springs, Arkansas.

He's not kidding. With ten years of motoring experience, two years of Great Race competition, and his own special technique for navigation, Sawyer and his 68-year-old grandfather-driver David Reeder are a real threat. How does a 12-year-old get 10 years of motoring experience? According to David Reeder, "We have a picture of Sawyer inspecting the underside of a car, *in diapers!* He has always been fascinated by classic cars. He would sit for hours in old cars, looking at the instruments, studying the race instructions, and absorbing the atmosphere. I had been competing in the Great Race for about 16 years, and Sawyer kept studying the course directions and asking if he could participate. So we gave him a shot as navigator. And he did very well, even though at nine going on ten, he was the youngest competitor to ever participate in the Great Race."

Serving as navigator in a Great Race car is arguably more important and difficult than driving, since the navigator reads the complex course instructions and directs the driver. The driver's job is to be "on the needle," keeping exactly on the speedometer reading set by the course instructions and the navigator.

Sawyer Stone and his grandfather in the Great Race

Sawyer has his own special techniques for winning navigation. "We work at being consistent every day," he says. "We take every day and every leg one at a time, and try not to let the pressure affect us. We act as a team, and don't have distracting arguments. Before the race we use a rally computer exactly like the one used by the guys who lay out the course, to test our car and determine how much time we lose or gain under various conditions. This computer hangs on the dash, is plugged in to the speedometer, and has several little red LED screens. It tells you exactly how much time you've lost during acceleration, compared to the ideal of instantaneous acceleration. Of course during the race we can't use that computer. We must rely on our 7-inch analog clock, our Timewise speedometer, which is accurate to ¼ of a mile per hour, and our Great Race digital stopwatch. Since stopwatches were allowed last year, we have switched over, and use the stopwatch for almost everything. It is much easier to read from and it makes calculations easier and more accurate. We are always alert during the rally, because sometimes there are confusing instructions, key road signs hidden behind tree branches, or other obstacles. We have to concentrate all the time."

Sawyer learned a lot of his techniques from videos supplied by the Great Race. "When my grandfather called me up and offered me the chance to navigate, he gave me several two hour videos. They were excellent." But Sawyer developed some of his own techniques, too. "I visualize a little ghost car out ahead of us, which is able to follow the course instructions exactly. So when the instruction says, 'accelerate from zero mph at the stop sign to 40 mph,' my ghost car does that instantly. But we can't accelerate that fast, so we lose time. By visualizing the ghost car ahead of us, I can keep track of how much time we have to make up."

As might be expected, Sawyer does well in math and science in school. He says, "Those are my favorite subjects. English is my least favorite. I am going into the 10th grade in the fall—I skipped kindergarten, the 2nd and the 4th grades. Skipping three grades was pretty easy. I'm not working that hard in school now. My friends are all in my current grade, so I don't have any social problems. The other kids in school think old cars are neat and they keep up with my rally career, but none of them are involved. There was a ten-year-old boy in last year's Great Race from another town. I helped him a lot and he did pretty well. But I'm still the youngest person to have competed. Unfortunately, there are no young girls on any of the teams, yet."

Sawyer has done well in his Great Race rally efforts. "My first year, in 2003, when I had my tenth birthday, we came in 24th overall, which is pretty good for a rookie navigator. Last year we placed 7th overall. We won $5500 total in the 2004 Great Race, and got 13 Ace awards, tying for 3rd in the Ace category. [An Ace award is given for any leg on which the team has a perfect, "zero second" score.] This year we plan to place in the top five for the Great Race, and if we could win the overall championship, that would be awesome. We have also done well in the regional Great Race rallies. In 2003 we came in 2nd in the Cactus Run weekend rally in Arizona. We only missed 1st place by 2 seconds. The top placers were not running for the money, only for pleasure, so we collected the $1350 first place prize. That was great. But the real attraction of Great Racing is being able to compete, see the country, and spend time with my grandfather."

David and Sawyer are driving a 1916 Hudson Four Passenger Speedster. Don't let the age of the car fool you into thinking it's a pussycat. Says David, "In 1916 a Speedster almost identical to mine set a world speed record on Daytona Beach in Florida, by going 102.6 miles per hour. The car produces 90 horsepower, yet was made in an era when most cars had 10 to 20 horsepower. I figure my old Hudson would go 100 mph if I asked it to. But with the precious cargo of my grandson on board, I would never think of doing that. Of course, Sawyer would love to go that fast!"

David Reeder bought his Hudson Speedster ten years ago, sight unseen, over the phone from a family in Hershey, Pennsylvania. "The whole transaction was a pleasure. The car only had about 23,000 miles on it. It had been a one-owner family car, always garaged, with lots of documentation, and was in great shape. I paid about $20,000 for it, and it would probably be worth about $30,000 now. The original 1916 sales price was about $500, considerably more than the $200 to $300 charged for a Model T Ford at the time."

According to David, "To prepare the car for the Great Race, I didn't need to do much. I upgraded the tires, improved the oiling and cooling systems, installed turn signals, stop lights and seat belts, and improved the brakes. You know, in 1916 the average speed on the largely non-existent roads was only 10 to 15 mph and there was no traffic. So brakes were not very important. Now we must drive 60 on the highway, with lots of traffic, so we need much better brakes."

David likes the Hudson but prefers the 1933 Ford Roadster that he and Sawyer used in the 2004 Great Race. "I just love cars from that era. They are so powerful, aerodynamic, and beautiful. I like them so much that I have a collection of about 20 to 25 cars, and many of them are from that period. Some of my favorite possessions are my 1933 Ford Roadster, 1934 Ford Cabriolet, and 1932 Buick Roadster. But this year I wanted to give my grandson a chance to win the overall championship. To do that we needed an older car, to improve our handicap rating factor. So we are using the Hudson."

Sawyer says that the Hudson is harder to compete in. "The Hudson is much slower to accelerate. So we lose a lot of time there. It is an open car, so we will get soaked if a rainstorm comes up quickly. My grandfather has made a soft top, but it takes a long time to put it up, so we can't do that in the middle of the race. Often we don't even have time to put on rain gear. But we have waterproof course instructions, so we don't care if we get wet. And this car will give us a 1.3 second per day advantage over the 1933 Ford. So I am glad we are using the old 1916 Hudson."

Hudsons were ahead of their time almost from the beginning. The company was formed in 1909 in Detroit, Michigan. The car bore the name of its new manufacturer's primary financial backer, J. L. Hudson -- founder of the department store empire that still exists as Dayton-Hudson.

In 1916 Hudson manufactured its first engine, the "Super Six." Previously the firm had out-sourced its engines. The Super Six was the auto industry's first inherently-balanced, modern, high compression L-head motor, and it was much lighter and more powerful than the one previously supplied to Hudson. Throughout the years,

"Super Six" would continue as a familiar Hudson name, even though the engines were continually modernized and redesigned. Hudson emphasized its cars' comfort and carrying capacity, as well as speed. According to David Reeder, "the company would race its cars across the country as a promotion, always carrying four passengers, just to show that the Hudsons had true passenger capacity and practicality."

During World War II all US auto production was halted and every car company produced armaments. Hudson produced aircraft wings and fuselages, Oerlikeon anti-aircraft guns, and landing craft engines. After the war, Hudson introduced its innovative Hornet, a hot new version of the Super Six. This engine and the low-rider Hornet were very successful in racing. From 1951 through 1954 Hornets dominated championships in NASCAR, AAA (later USAC), IMCA, and Pacific West Coast Racing. The period was known as the "Hudson Hornet Hey-Day."

Sales competition led to Hudson merging with its long-time rival Nash in 1954 to form American Motors, which survived until the mid-1980s. The Hudson name passed into history at the end of the 1957 model year.

But the name lives on in the Great Race today, since no less than five of the 2005 entrants, many of them top competitors, are driving Hudsons. At the finish line, in just a few days, everyone will know if a 12-year-old boy, navigating a car 77 years his senior, is the best of those competitors.

* * *

Sawyer Stone and his grandfather did well in the 2005 Great Race, coming in fourth overall with a wonderful score of just 2 minutes and 13 seconds, and winning 8 Ace awards. Sawyer clearly has a great future in Great Racing.

Total Focus
for Fourteen Days Straight

"You gotta put yourself in a two-week trance," says Howard Sharp, 52, successful Great Race driver and co-owner of car number 22, the remarkable 1911 Velie H1 Racytype (sic). "If you want to win, you must get within yourself. You have to forget about your business, your outside life, and your personal problems. You can't allow any distractions to disturb your focus on your car and your race performance."

Howard knows what he is talking about – his 13 year Great Race history has brought many wins and high placements. "I heard about the Great Race on an 'oldies' radio station in Rochester, New York in 1991. I drove down to the overnight stop in my 1946 Chrysler, thinking to show it off. I had no clue about the amazing quality of old cars I would see—I was stunned. At 3 a.m. I was still there, talking to teams and watching them work on their fabulous cars. I thought, 'This is way cool. I'm going to enter the Great Race right away.' I called the Great Race office every day for two weeks straight, but the staff were all on the road with the rally. I finally found out how to enter, and I've been part of the cult ever since. In my first rally in 1992 I placed a dismal 62nd. The learning curve was huge, but the next year I won the Sportsman class. In 1995 I placed 2nd in the World Class, and by 1999 I made it to 3rd in the Expert division. In 2002 I placed 1st in Expert and 1st in the World Class. In 2003 I placed 2nd in the overall championship, missing an overall win by just 3 seconds. I still get sick to my stomach thinking about how close we came. In 2004 we didn't run in the race, my son and navigator Douglas and I took a year off to work on the car and think about our strategy. For 2005 our goal is to win the overall Grand Championship."

Howard is fierce about winning. "The motto of the Great Race is 'To Finish is to Win.' That was fine for my first year, but since then my attitude is that I am in this to *really* win, and to get a paycheck at the end. I am competitive in my business of sportswear sales and in life, and I'm *very* competitive in the Great Race. Some folks socialize on the race, and get to bed late at night. Our goal is to do maintenance on the car as soon as we arrive at the night stop, fix any problems, and get into bed by 9 p.m. We need to be rested in order to win."

Howard is not keen on modern technology to help in winning. "Last year they started allowing digital stop watches. We threw ours out the window. That's just another distracting gadget. My son uses a small, 2-inch analog clock. Those big 7-inch kitchen clocks that a lot of competitors use—they're a mistake. The second hand is real heavy, so it doesn't move as fast on the left side as on the right. They're inaccurate. Headphones? Some competitors spend big bucks on headphones to talk to each other, and end up looking like Kyle Petty. We just use silent hand signals. We have a whole secret code of hand signals worked out between the two of us. No, I won't tell you what they mean—it's a secret."

"We got the 1911 Velie in 1993 after we won the Sportsman class," says Howard. "The Pioneer Auto Museum in South Dakota approached us and said they had a car that would be great for the rally. The Velie was a very fast car in its day, with an incredible top speed of 65 mph out of the box, a huge purchase price of about $1650, and a motto of 'you won't have to eat anyone else's dust—you'll be in front!'"

Howard continued, "The museum staff said the car had been in running condition when they acquired it. We went out to South Dakota and picked up the Velie with a forklift, put it on a truck, and shipped it to New York. I don't see how it could have been running before, because there were no internals in the engine, and the carburetor was in pieces in a bowl. It took three years, until 1996, before we could get the car ready. We rallied it on the Great Race to Mexico City. I could have bought the car from the Museum for about $20,000, but instead we agreed to share ownership. In retrospect I should have bought it, because since 1993 I have poured more than $67,000 and thousands of hours into the car. With its competition history it is probably worth $100,000 now. The car is great, but at 94 years old it is getting tired. It is amazing to me that it continues to do what it has to do every day. I am afraid that this is its last Great Race. The plan is to drop it off back in South Dakota and have them keep it as a museum piece. It's a shame, because this great old car draws the crowds just like a magnet."

Howard says that he has had some wild experiences on the Great Race. "Every day there is another incident. But one stands out in my mind. We were driving along and needed water for the radiator, bad. We stopped at a 7-11 to get some bottled water, since we couldn't find anything else. Of course we were in a terrific hurry since we were losing time. I got six gallons from the clerk and just tossed her a $20 bill without even ringing it up to see the actual cost. Meanwhile, out back my son Douglas had found a farmer's house with a well and a water hose. He started 'borrowing' some water without permission. But he spilled so much that he created a mud hole and the car got stuck in the mud!

Then the farmer came along in his tractor, and we had to persuade him to pull us out of the mudhole we had created next to his house. Eventually we got out of the mud and did fine on the rally stage."

Howard Sharp's 1911 Velie—will it make it for 4250 miles cross country?

Another strange incident occured on the 2003 Great Race. According to Howard, "Our overdrive broke near Dallas. We have three regular gears, but the overdrive is very important, because it reduces gas mileage and vibration by about 33%. Driving the Velie is like driving a bulldozer cross-country, so you need every edge. We pulled out the overdrive and got on the cell phone to the guy in Buffalo, New York who built it. We talked for an hour and a half on the phone trying to figure out the problem. Finally we knew what was needed. Our guy said, 'I'll ship you the parts by FedEx, and you'll get them in two days.' I said, 'That's not good enough. Here is what is going to happen. You are going to get the parts tonight. You will get on the plane first thing tomorrow. You will fly to Dallas/Fort Worth, and I'm going to pick you up at 2:03 p.m. We will fix the overdrive by the end of the afternoon.' Amazingly, he did it and it worked. I was very grateful and offered to pay for him to spend some time in Texas. But he just curled up on the floor for a nap, and flew back that night."

Howard has always been an old car buff. He says, "My very first car was a classic, a 1936 Chevrolet. Once I got interested in the Great Race I became a 'brass car guy' – in love with really early cars. I have a collection of about 25 cars, including a 1909 Hupmobile, 1911 Velie, 1912 Rio, 1912 Hudson, 1912 Rambler, 1913 Overland, 1915 Dodge, 1916 Oldsmobile and 1919 Hudson. I drive them all regularly. Just before this interview I ran the 1916 Oldsmobile into the side of my house—no brakes!"

Howard has some predictions for the 2005 Great Race. "There will be three cars in the overall lead: last year's winners, G.R. Pike and Bobby Hadskey in their 1916 Hudson Speedster; Gary Kuck and Rex Gardner in their 1917 Hudson Indy Racer; and me and my son Douglas in the 1911 Velie. The winner will score inside of one minute of the set time. And the winner will be the team that has some luck, makes the fewest mistakes, minimizes distractions, and maintains total focus for two entire weeks."

* * *

Howard and his son came in eighth overall in the 2005 Great Race, with a score of 2:33, just 20 seconds behind his young rival Sawyer Stone. Howard got two Ace awards. At the end of the race he said, "Maybe I won't retire the car, after all. It's running great and I'm having fun."

Hail to the Chief:
The Studebaker President

Perhaps the most distinguished-looking car in the 2005 Great Race is the magnificent and very rare 1931 Studebaker President 8, Series 80, Four Season Convertible, car number 31. The car has gorgeous lines, dramatic headlights, a rumble seat, golf club compartment, and a lovely tobacco brown and yellow paint scheme. The President is owned by Suzanne Harris of the team "Daughter's Dream," and therein lies a tale.

Suzanne Harris said, "My father and teammate Allen 'Pete' Laughon bought this car in 1951 when he was only 24. He had always wanted a Studebaker President, since the very first car ride he ever took—at age four—was in a brand spanking-new President." Pete continued the story, "I found this President in two pieces. The front half was being used as a flatbed truck. During World War II the previous owner wore out the engine, driving up long hills pulling heavy hay wagons. The back half of the President was rusting away in a barn. I traded my running sedan and a few dollars for both halves and went looking for an engine for the President."

Pete said, "I found a junked President sedan that had been in a riverbed for 10 years. The engine looked tight, so I put in some gas and oil, filled the tires, and fired her up. She started right up and I drove that car home, sitting on rusted springs instead of a seat. I used the engine and other parts off the riverbed car to restore the hay wagon car. It took several years, but by 1955 I won a restoration prize from the Horseless Carriage Club."

"Unfortunately," said Pete, "One of my best friends talked me into selling the President to him. My friend took it apart into about a thousand pieces, then lost interest in the project after a year. He was going to have it crushed, when my brother went out and rescued the car from the junk pile. It took three weekends to haul all the pieces back to our house. So then I entirely restored the car for a second time!"

Suzanne, a real estate broker from Park City, Utah, continued the Presidential odyssey. "Dad held on to the car after that. But he was a bit reluctant to take it on a long rally. So I bought out my uncle's interest and secured Dad's interest, and now the car is officially mine, although of course it really belongs to the entire family. I then persuaded Dad to come along on the Great Race, which I've always been interested in."

For Suzanne this is a family dream come true. She says, "Our team is called 'Daughter's Dream' because that's what this car and the Great Race are. I have always loved this car, which I remember fondly from my childhood. Amazingly, my mother used it as her 'drive-around' car in San Diego when I was a girl. And to have the chance to spend time with Dad and the rest of my family in the President on the Great Race will be wonderful. I am planning to have my daughter and brother rotate in and out as navigator, driver and passenger. So at times we will have three generations in one car."

Pete, now 79, was for many years a car dealership owner in San Diego. He lovingly describes the Studebaker President as a "top of the line vehicle." "The Studebaker President has a 337 cubic inch big-block engine developing about 122 horsepower at low RPMs. The wheelbase is 130 inches, and the dry weight is a hefty 4300 pounds. We get about 12 to 13 miles per gallon if we drive sensibly. There were only about 400 Studebaker Presidents built, and only about 9 are running today. So this is one of the rarest cars around, much rarer than most Packards or other high-end makes. This car has 94,000 miles on the odometer, but that could be 194,000. The President cost about $2000 in 1931, which was enough to buy a good house at the time. An excellent 'condition 2' President like this, which is regularly driven, is worth roughly $80,000 today. A 'condition 1' President, which is virtually never driven and was restored to better than factory condition, recently sold at auction for $192,000."

Pete Laughon of La Mesa, California and the 1931 Studebaker President. He restored the car and was planning to drive and navigate it across the country during the Great Race.

As rookies, Suzanne and Pete are not trying to win the rally. Says Pete, "We are in the Great Race for the fun, and to have a family adventure." Suzanne agrees, and says, "We will trade off roles as driver and navigator, and just go out and have a great time driving this beautiful car across the country."

* * *

During the race, Pete tired of navigating. So his daughter Suzanne drove while his granddaughter navigated from the rumble seat, peering through the small rear window and hollering over an intercom at driver Suzanne. Despite these challenges and a number of major mechanical problems, the Presidential team got two Ace awards and completed 13 of the 14 stages with respectable scores of about 1 to 3 minutes per day.

Band of Teenagers Rally a Ford Four Times Their Age

"Our car drank over a hundred gallons of our blood," jokes Daylan Gibbard, 18, leader of the Walla Walla, Washington Great Race X-cup team. "We skinned our knuckles and cut our hands, while we put in hundreds of hours restoring it. But it's beautiful now." Daylan is proud of Team Walla Walla's 1928 Ford Model A Phaeton, car number 102 in the Great Race. At 77 years old, the Ford is more than four times older than Daylan or any of the other team members. The car was a family car for many years on a farm in Washington state, but then it was cut in half by a previous owner and converted into a pickup. Later a collector bought both halves, but then let the Ford deteriorate even further.

Daylan father Don, adult advisor to the team, takes up the tale. "I bought the car in 1991 for about $3000, after it had been stored in a barn for 13 years and was in hundreds of bits and pieces. I didn't do much with it for another 12 years, until we heard about the Great Race and the X-Cup prize for youth. That got us moving. My son Daylan formed a team of teenagers and we started work. We went from the car being in rusty bits in November 2003 to an almost ready-to-race car by June of 2004."

Why "almost" ready? "In last year's Great Race we were still bolting big pieces of the car on, while we were loading it on the trailer to ship to the start," says Don. "We had done absolutely no test driving or testing. This year we're much better prepared. Our team of six teenagers hopes to cut our previous time in half, and we think we have a shot at winning the $20,000 X-cup prize and college scholarship. Even last year we finished in the middle of the overall pack, which we thought was pretty good for pure rookies. The big team to beat in the X-cup competition is the Explorer Post team in car number 101, a 1930 Ford pickup. They have had the same advisor for eight years and are very experienced." Daylan adds, "Last year our most serious problem was during the practice run just before the start of the Great Race. We had used silicone in sealing part of the fuel system, and the gasoline just ate up the sealant and spread it throughout the system. So we had to pull all the fuel lines, tear down the carburetor, and clean everything out. We managed to do all that in just 15 minutes!"

The Team Walla Walla car, an open style called a Phaeton, sold new in 1928 for just $395. "We put in about $11,000 restoring the Ford Phaeton," says Don, "and it is probably worth about $20,000 now." Daylan adds, "The car has 4 cylinders, 200 cubic inches, and when new developed about 40 horsepower. But we have tuned it so now it gets about 48 to 50 horsepower. We have installed a Great Race-style speedometer and use the digital stopwatch that is now allowed."

Last year Don drove the car during the Great Race. But under the rules, as an adult Don cannot drive this year, and only youth members will take the car all the way across the country from Washington, DC to Tacoma, Washington. The 2005 team consists of four young men and two young women. All except one younger woman are 18-year-olds who have just graduated from high school. The X-cup rules allow youth as old as 21 to compete, and there is no lower age limit for youthful navigators. But most X-cup teams consist of high schoolers. At 77 years old, the 1928 Ford Phaeton is over four times the age of the oldest team members.

Stephanie Klundt, 18, is one of the team's new members who just graduated from high school. "I was always hanging out at the house of the other team members, and

I'm very good at math. There was another boy who wanted to be on the team, but he couldn't go all the way across the country. So Daylan chose me. I was very excited, and I'm really looking forward to being on the team and seeing the whole country." Stephanie is a busy person. In addition to her Great Race duties, she teaches rock climbing at the YMCA, makes pretzels at the Pretzel Twist at the local mall, is active in two religious youth groups, and is a leader at Wyldlife, a religious program for middle schoolers. She is planning to go to Whitworth College in Spokane, Washington in the fall, and will major in either elementary education or engineering. "I love teaching kids," she says, "but I am also interested in math, calculus and engineering."

Stephanie has been studying up on navigational techniques. "I haven't done any practice rallies," she says, "but we have had a number of practice runs here in Washington. We use the navigational tips put together by Bill Secrest, the rally expert. We are building customized performance charts to estimate our time losses."

Stephanie explains the complexities of performance charts. "Every driver is different in his style and how well he knows the car and can move through the gears. So we build different charts for each driver. We have four type of charts—acceleration, deceleration, stop signs (which are a combination), and hill climbs, where we lose time because we are driving such an old car. As we follow the course instructions, we apply the charts to each maneuver. Suppose we go up a hill and the instructions say to go 30 mph. But we know we are not making that speed. So we look at our customized chart, and we can estimate from it that we have lost about 'X' number of seconds, compared to the ideal. Then we apply a 'rule' to make up that time, when we are going down the other side of the hill."

Stephanie says that the rule she uses most is the "rule of 10/10." "This rule says that for every second you're behind, you should drive 10 percent above the assigned speed for 10 seconds. Thus if we lost 4 seconds going up the hill, and the assigned speed coming down the hill is 30 mph, we should drive at 33 mph (10 percent higher than assigned) for 40 seconds (4x10). If we do exactly that, we will have made up all the time, and will be right on the course set time. But to be *really* accurate we should account for the fact that we decelerated from 33 to 30, also." In the Great Race, being precisely on time means winning the prize. Punctuality—sounds like a good lesson for life!

* * *

Team Walla Walla finished second in the X-Cup class, with a score of 7:16, not too far behind the perpetual winners from Ponca City with a score of 5:27, and far ahead of Lawrence High School, who scored 24:45 due to mechanical problems. Walla Walla received two Ace awards and some scholarship funding.

The Walla Walla Washington high school team in the Great Race. Don Gibbard is at far left; Daylan Gibbard is in the center in dark shirt, seated on the running board; Stephanie Klundt is seated on ground, center.

The Most Traveled Man on Earth

Section 8

Pink Belly

Revealed: Beauty Secrets of Exotic Thailand

Win a national beauty contest after just two weeks of coaching? Lose fifty pounds without exercising? Add three inches to your bust and take five inches off your waist with only creams and massage? Fairy tales? Not in exotic Bangkok, Thailand, where all these unlikely tales have come true!

The magic key to the fairy treasure chest is Mrs. Nattavadee Vinsiri, nicknamed "A!" (pronounced "Eh!"). A! is a thirty-nine-year-old human dynamo who is a talent scout, beauty pageant coach and organizer, modeling agent, manager, and trainer all in one. A! is the owner of the P&N family of companies, which includes a modeling agency, beauty salon, acting studio, massage center, and even a restaurant.

A! began working at age nine, selling fish balls in a market near her home in southern Thailand to support her family. Sweet but ambitious, at age eighteen she entered over twenty beauty pageants, winning several Thai city and regional competitions. She then became a sought-after model and manager, and with her husband Pongsonart she set up P&N (after the first letters in their first names).

In 1990, in P&N's first year of operation, A! coached Chanakarn Chaisri, who won the coveted Miss Thailand—World competition (part of the Miss World contest). In her second year, A! took on an unlikely looking girl, Isaraya Apichai, and transformed her in two weeks from a rather plain girl into the winner of the Miss Thailand—World 1991 pageant. Says A! rather bluntly, "My friends said I was crazy to work with Isaraya, that she was ugly and I would lose all the money I invested in her. But she was a very strong and determined girl, she listened to my coaching and my medical and dental advice, and she won the contest."

This remarkable success brought fame and business to P&N, which is now one of the top modeling agencies in Thailand. A! has since managed hundreds of models, and coached the winners of Miss Thailand—Universe 1992, Miss Thailand—World 1994, Miss Thailand 1994, Miss Asia-Pacific 1997 and Miss Thailand—World 2002, as well as many other local and regional contests. She also managed to have three lovely children along the way.

A!'s modest five-story studio complex in a suburb of Bangkok gives no hint of the amazing beauty secrets hidden within. "I try to use all-natural methods to win beauty contests," says A!. "Sometimes cosmetic surgery is necessary, but usually we can achieve the needed results with massage, steam treatments, special creams, and good diet. Thai massage is a big part of our program. We have a wonderful masseur at the school who can totally reshape your body in five to ten sessions spread over two weeks."

A! (left rear) her staff, and her protégé
beauty contestant Jade Naknoi (right rear)

Skeptical, I interviewed the masseur, Natcha Chaochaikong, and got a brief demonstration of her skills. Speaking through an interpreter, Natcha said, "I have been studying and practicing Thai massage since I was fifteen and have a certificate in the art. I can take a girl and add two to three inches to her bust by vigorously massaging her upper arms, upper sides, and lower rib cage. I actually move the fat and cellulite from each nearby area to her chest, so it's good if she has a little extra fat. I can also take up to five inches off a girl's waist, reduce or increase her buttock size, and reduce or firm up her thighs. Removing two inches off the waist is easy. Five inches requires more work but is usually doable. We sometimes do light face massage to subtly change the shape of the face if necessary."

Natcha continued, "I had one client that I reduced from 75 to 50 kilos (165 to 110 pounds) in two months, using hard massage, steam cabinet treatments, and good diet. But to lose *that* much weight you must be strong and brave, because it's a lot of work and can be a bit painful, especially the steam."

I queried, "But surely all this requires lots of exercise and the results disappear quickly?" "Oh, no," said Natcha, "Exercise is helpful but not required. Most of my clients are very lazy! And the results are permanent, unless the client goes on an eating binge."

Jade Naknoi, a lovely twenty-year-old who was living with A! to prepare for the upcoming Miss Thailand contest, confirmed the remarkable massage results. "Natcha's massage added two inches to my bust in seven sessions, so I didn't need cosmetic surgery there. She uses *very* strong massage, so you should be in good health before she starts."

I asked Natcha for a quick sample massage. She began rubbing my arm with her iron thumbs. Within a few minutes the inside of my arm was hot and the skin red from the pressure. "Yikes!" I said. "This is the heavy massage, right?" I asked.

"Oh, no," she said, laughing. "This is the light massage! I can dissolve or move the fat through heavy massage, by using a secret cream, and by having the girl drink lots of water," said Natcha.

I asked, "Are you the best body reshaper in Thailand?"

"Oh, no," she said, giggling modestly. "There are many gurus better than I am. The best one, from northeast Thailand, is now in Hollywood massaging movie stars."

A! described the secret cream: "We use three massage creams: one for firming, one for anti-cellulite, and one for breast enhancement. We can't say what is in the cream, but they smell of peppermint—and they work!"

"We also use a special skin treatment," said A! "We use a little olive oil, then we apply a skin cream made from tamarind, milk, lemon, honey, tomato, potato, saffron, and special Thai herbs. This cream, plus avoiding the sun, gives the skin a soft, supple feel and removes most blemishes and sun damage. For pimples we have our girls avoid chocolate and other fatty foods. We can remove pimples with a steam nozzle and a tiny pinprick. For moles and major blemishes we employ a doctor trained in Japan, who uses a laser removal system. We also have reasonably-priced foreign-trained dentists and cosmetic surgeons available, if necessary. A healthy diet is vital, with low sugars and carbohydrates, lots of vegetables, seafood, and salads, and little fat. Luckily the standard Thai cuisine meets most of these requirements."

At the Miss Thailand—Universe pageant I met one of A!'s proteges. Sayamon Kanjanapangka, known as "Jiffy," was born in Hollywood of Thai parents. She was on an extended visit to Thailand and was persuaded to enter the contest. She confirmed that A!'s methods work. "I lost fifteen pounds and improved my figure and skin by living with A! for two weeks and listening to her advice for six months. Even though I had done commercials, film work, and local beauty pageants in L.A., I learned an enormous amount from A! and her team. I know that A! has been very successful in pageants and modeling with young women like me who are Thai or part Thai, and who live or have been educated in the U.S.A."

At A!'s offices I spoke with "Top" Kornkasem, A!'s senior international booker, about P&N's modeling business. "Thailand is a great place for a model to get started. There is an insatiable demand for new faces here. Unlike Singapore, Hong Kong, the U.S., and the U.K., an attractive model does not need a big 'book' to get started here. We bring in many beautiful girls from Yugoslavia and the Balkans who are just getting started in modeling and who want to build a book. They will work with us for two to three months, and then be ready to crack the bigger markets elsewhere. The most work is for brunettes, since the Thai girls identify more with them. But blondes have opportunities, too. We put up our models near our offices in nice hotels with all the amenities, which only cost $250 to $500 per month. We do all kinds of work—TV, movies, print, catwalks at fashion shows, billboards—you name it. We even book lots of men and children models."

I asked Top about the unsavory aspects of some of the Thai entertainment business. He said, "As one of the top modeling agencies constantly involved in top international beauty pageants, our reputation is and must be spotless. We are very careful with our models and contestants and would never involve them in anything questionable."

Later I spoke with A! about her business operations. A! has an unusual business approach to pageants. "Most of my Thai girls do not have any money. So I usually put up the entire amount for all their coaching, massage, dental work, and other treatments. Then if they win a contest, I keep fifty percent of their after-tax cash winnings. But they get to keep all the cars, gifts, or earnings from commercials. Even though 150 girls enter each contest and we are betting against the odds, we usually make money because we win so often. The only time I've really lost money was recently I coached a girl who won the Miss Thailand—World competition. She won a cash prize of 1 million baht ($23,200) plus a car and a 1 million baht Avon commercial, plus 50,000 baht ($1,162) per month in salary for four years. But then she refused to pay me the $10,000 (a huge sum here) that she owes me from the cash prize. I hope I won't have to take her to court. That would be very sad, since I thought she was my good friend, like all my students."

A! added that "We also sometimes take on Thai or foreign students who can pay fees up front. In that case we charge about 60,000–100,000 baht ($1,390 to $2,325) depending on demand, for two weeks of pageant and modeling coaching, skin treatments, massage and steam treatments. We can also usually find TV, billboard, or print work for photogenic Thai, American, or European novice models who are willing to work here for three to six months to build up their portfolios. Staying in our lovely country that long is no hardship, because Thailand really is the 'Land of Beautiful Smiles.'"

The World's Pinkest Pink Belly

"Pink belly"—a high school or college initiation among boys, in which the victim's stomach is slapped thirty to fifty times until bright pink.

"WHAP! WHAP! WHAP!" The cupped hands of my masseur hit my stomach rapidly with a hollow sound. I did some mental arithmetic: slapped four times per second times sixty seconds times twenty minutes per series times four series per two-hour session times five sessions... Yikes! I had signed up to have my belly slapped forty-eight thousand times! What was I doing?

It has all begun when I was bored in Bangkok and looking for something to do besides temples and markets. I saw an ad for Miss Thailand—Universe tryouts, and decided to check it out. The young ladies were interesting, but the most amazing thing was that many of the contest winners over the years had been coached by just two women. I tracked down one of the women, interestingly named "A!," to learn her beauty secrets. She claimed that she and her staff could transform a girl with potential into a contest winner in just a few weeks.

A!'s secret weapon was her masseur, Natcha. A! said that Natcha, "can add up to three inches to a woman's bust and take up to five inches off her waist, using strong massage."

Through an interpreter I asked if Natcha had ever massaged a man to reshape his body. "Never," she said, looking a little shocked at the idea. I added quickly, "I would want some inches of fat taken off my waist, not added to my chest!"

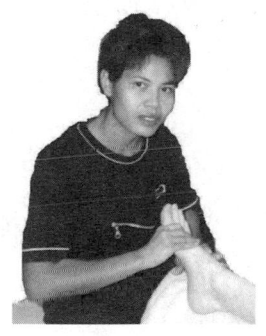

Natcha of the Iron Thumbs

I asked one of A!'s contest protégées if Natcha's methods worked. "Definitely," she said. "I was considering plastic surgery until Natcha added two inches to my bustline and took two inches off my waist. She used hard massage, slapping, a secret crème, and a steam cabinet. Most girls get five to ten sessions over two to four weeks. Natcha's biggest achievement was cutting fifty pounds off a middle-aged lady in four months, with massage and good diet."

I asked Natcha about the need for exercise. "Oh, no," she laughed. "Most of my clients are very lazy! They never exercise. But that isn't necessary under our treatment."

I asked A! for some massage sessions from Natcha. She gave me a 50 percent discount—five sessions for $100.

The first session seemed endless. Natcha's cupped hand slapped the front and side of my stomach, making it bright pink very quickly. But perhaps because her hand was cupped, it didn't hurt as much as a college initiation. What did hurt was Natcha's hard rubbing of my stomach and sides between slapping sessions. She kept asking me, "Jep, ma?" meaning, "Does it hurt?" With broken Thai and sign language I indicated that it did hurt some. With gestures she told me that I must shave my belly hair off before the next session—it was the friction of her hands pulling on the hair that was the real problem.

The worst part came at the fifty-five-minute mark, when I thought the session was almost over. "Only one more hour to go," she said. OHMYGOD! But I stuck it out for the full two hours. At the end I felt sore but not thinner. Disappointingly, the scale the next morning showed no difference.

At five the next morning I got up and covered my belly with shaving cream. I looked in the mirror and thought, "I look totally ridiculous." But I began shaving anyway. It took almost half an hour to cut all the hair off.

Natcha met me at six for my early morning second session, before I went to work. She started the session by measuring my waist with a tape measure. Then she started in slapping and rubbing. But it was much less painful, thanks to the lack of belly hair. And I was less apprehensive, and was even able to relax a bit.

Next morning I still weighed the same, but my stomach felt different somehow. The fat felt thicker—compressed— more like muscle. My internal organs felt fine, and not hot like my arm had felt during the demonstration.

Natcha told me to eat lightly, avoid red meat, and have mostly fruit and vegetables over the weekend. Naturally I ignored her advice, and ate heaps of fatty food at a friend's house in the hills. So it was no surprise that at the beginning of the third session my weight and measurements had not gone down.

But by the end of third session I definitely felt different, harder. And by the end of the fourth session my waist was down an inch.

In the final three of the five sessions Natcha did not slap quite as much, focusing more on kneading and hard massage of my sides. She said she was "moving some of the fat away from the waist, and breaking up some of it." She urged me to drink lots of water, to excrete the broken-up fat.

By the end of my fifth and last session in twelve days I had lost five pounds and an inch and a half off my waist. I had exercised a little but not much. I was impressed but not fully persuaded.

Now it is six months later, and my waist is down by six inches and I have lost thirty-nine pounds. So, did Natcha's bizarre massage techniques work? Well, look at it this way. If your mother caught you with your hand in the cookie jar, and slapped you twenty thousand times, would you eat any more cookies?

The Most Traveled Man on Earth

Section 9

This Sceptred Isle

A Cozy Castle in Cornwall

We sat in the living room of our tiny castle on the north coast of Cornwall. A hundred feet below us the clear waters of the Bristol Channel sparkled in the sunlight. Eight miles to the northeast the ruined fortress of Tintagel, King Arthur's legendary birthplace, was almost visible around the next headland. The unspoiled coast, site of many film and TV shoots, consisted of steep cliffs, beautiful fields, and picturesque villages. We were the lords of all we surveyed—for a week, anyway.

Our three-story, three-room castle was the property of the National Trust, England's nonprofit institution for acquiring and preserving historic sites. The NT owns over 240 locations that are available for week-long rentals, usually at very reasonable prices. NT properties range from modest cottages to converted churches, lighthouses, rooms in large castles, even the engine room of a disused water tower. Our location, Doyden Castle, was probably the premier NT site, due to its gorgeous location. It was booked a year in advance for choice summer weeks.

Doyden Castle was actually a folly, built in 1830 by the local squire as retreat for carousing with his buddies. The structure was about twenty feet square, perched on a cliff surrounded on three sides by water.

Access was by a hair-raising, narrow, cliff-side gravel road, which led back to the mainland and the parent house, a third of a mile away.

Doyden Castle, northern Cornwall

The castle had a kitchen on the ground floor equipped with pots, pans, utensils, sink, stove, and cooktop. There was also a toilet set into the six-foot-thick stone wall, which was ice cold even in summer. On the second floor there was a charming small living room with a fireplace, sofa and chairs, and lovely views up and down the coast. On the top floor was the bedroom, with three single beds and more lovely views.

One of the most entertaining things to do in the castle was to read about the experiences of previous visitors, in the five journals kept in the living room. Winter visitors wrote about "huge storm waves crashing into the cliffs below the castle, shaking the whole hill." Many summer visitors wrote glowingly about tracking down locations from the famous

Poldark TV series, taken from the books by Winston Graham. The series was filmed on this coast by the BBC in the 1960s and presented in the United States as part of PBS's *Masterpiece Theatre* series; it is still available on video. Doyden Castle played a role in the series, as the dramatic residence of the doctor friend of Ross Poldark, the hero of the series.

Not all the journal entries were cheerful, however. One dramatic entry recorded how in 1995 the NT renters were walking south along the coast path a few miles from the Castle, near the mouth of the Camel River. A beautiful tall ship, the *Maria Assumpta*, built in 1858 and one of the oldest ships afloat, came sailing close along the coast making for the river mouth. Although the weather was clear and visibility good, the captain sailed right into the deadly rocks off Rumps Point, just below the shocked walkers. The vessel broke up and sank in nine minutes, killing three of the crew. The captain was convicted of manslaughter and jailed for eighteen months. The *Maria Assumpta* is just one of an estimated 100,000+ vessels that have sunk on British shores over the last 2,500 years of seafaring, many along this still-dangerous coastline.

Outside Doyden Castle there was a wonderful world to explore. The Camel estuary is one of the loveliest in England and is now favored by posh weekenders from London. On the estuary, Padstow boasts several gourmet restaurants and even a TV personality chef. The picturesque village of Port Isaac, just a couple of miles up the coast from Doyden, is famous for its pubs, its Royal National Lifeboat Institution (RNLI) station, and its parking lot. This is one of the few parking lots in the world that is under water twice a day, depending on the state of the tide. So it is good not to tarry too long in the pubs, or you'll be needing the RNLI to rescue your car!

Further up the coast is dramatic Tintagel, where a butte-like peninsula is joined to the mainland by a narrow bridge of stone, perfect for defense. Legend has it that at a castle on this peninsula, Uthur Pendragon and Queen Igerna of Cornwall sired Arthur, the future king of England, and gave him away to Merlin to raise. The famous magician lived in a cave below Tintagel and supposedly still haunts the area. Skeptics scoffed at all these legends, until in the 1990s archaeologists discovered that the site was fortified in the fifth century, and a Latin plaque was found saying, "Artognou father of Coll had this building made." Artognou is translated as Arthur, lending credence to the enduring legend.

While some may doubt the Arthurian legends and castle, there is no doubt that the coziest, most livable castle on the Cornish coast—Doyden Castle—is available to anyone for a week, and is just a phone call away.

Sailing with the Royals

Where can you wake up in your boat to a twenty-one-gun salute, race against some of the world's best yachtsmen, anchor off a castle built by Henry VIII, visit the summer palace of Queen Victoria, attend a nautical evening church service with the Duke of Edinburgh, and pub crawl and party into the night? Only one place—Cowes Week!

For fifty-one weeks of the year, Cowes is a quiet, yachty town of nineteen thousand on the north side of the Isle of Wight, just off the south coast of Britain. But during the eight days of Cowes Week, the town is inundated with a thousand racing yachts, two hundred spectator boats, eight thousand enthusiastic yachtsmen, and hundreds of thousands of spectators. It is the biggest participatory sailing event in the world.

Sailing at Cowes

Cowes Week traces its origins to the early 1800s, when wealthy, aristocratic Londoners began to holiday on the Isle of Wight. At first, they amused themselves by betting on informal races between fast local revenue cutters, smuggling luggers, and pilot boats. By 1815, however, these holidaymakers began building their own vessels and formed a yacht club. In 1817 the Prince Regent joined, and soon the club was given the title of the Royal Yacht Squadron.

The Squadron became a sort of informal reserve for the Royal Navy, and by the mid-1800s it boasted dozens of large vessels mounting in total more than four hundred cannon. Flogging was practiced on many of these vessels—remember that the next time your crew rebels. On one occasion, two RYS yachts collided during a race, and their military-style crews proceeded to board and attack each other's boats with cutlasses and axes!

From this quasi-military background, Cowes Week has evolved into a civilian mega-event sponsored by the Royal Yacht Squadron and nine other local yacht clubs. These clubs are organized into the Cowes Combined Clubs, and the event is sponsored by Scandia (a British financial services firm) and other corporations.

The heart of the event is the racing, which takes place every day in over forty sailboat classes. Races start every five minutes beginning at 10:30 A.M., from a start line extending out from the RYS clubhouse—a modest castle built by Henry VIII in 1538. Most classes finish at the castle three to five hours later, and there is usually a leg that runs right along the shore, so spectators have a great view of the action. Classes can be sent around any of nine hundred pre-designated courses in the historic Solent—the three-mile-wide, protected body of water between the Isle of Wight and England.

Cowes Week often includes allied races, such as the famous Fastnet Race, which involves a dash from Cowes to the Fastnet Light off Ireland and back. As a result, many large ocean racers are often in port alongside the smaller classes.

Related events that take place during Cowes Week usually include:

- Tours of visiting Royal Navy vessels. I saw the HMS *Glamorgan*, a tough destroyer that survived a direct hit by an Exocet missile during the Falklands war.

- Visits by royal yachts and mega-motor yachts of the rich and famous. The Royal Yacht *Britannia* used to come each year before she was retired to Scotland. But the Royals still come, often visiting aboard private megayachts, and sometimes participating in the racing.

- Evening church services, with the lesson read by Prince Phillip, Duke of Edinburgh, Admiral of the Royal Yacht Squadron.

- A huge, thirty-five-minute fireworks display.

- Balls given every night by the ten participating yacht clubs. Some of these balls are open to the public or to visiting yachtsmen with reciprocal club memberships.

- Extensive pub crawling and partying aboard the rafted up yachts.

- Visits to Osbourne House, Queen Victoria's huge palace overlooking the Solent.

- Twenty-one-gun royal salutes fired from the RYS battlements. Twenty-one brass cannons are used for the salutes and for starting the racing classes. The three-foot-long cannons were taken off the "miniature" yacht *Royal Adelaide*, built for the children of William IV.

While chartering or sailing during Cowes Week can be very exciting, the local conditions are very challenging. The four tides per day may rise up to thirteen feet; tidal currents can run up to four or five knots, winds can vary from a flat calm to forty knots in a few hours, temperatures can range from forty-five degrees at night to eighty during the day, and of course the English weather can change from glorious to drizzle to pouring rain back to glorious, in a few minutes.

When we visited, the most amazing event was a hotly contested race of fifty-foot ocean racers. The class started at the RYS castle and dashed out to the Needles at the western end of the Isle of Wight. The leg on the way back took the class right along the waterfront, where we were watching intently. (The water is very deep just offshore, allowing even deep-draft vessels to sail close by.) The racing yachts sailed by only a few yards away, just barely under control in the thirty-knot winds. A wise spectator muttered, "Those lads had better take down their spinnakers, or there'll be trouble soon." Just then a blast of wind split one of the spinnakers, and the yacht rounded up, out of control. She was instantly rammed by another yacht that had been following close behind. Water poured in, and the first yacht sank in about thirty seconds, about a hundred feet from us.

Luckily no one was hurt. But the bank balance of the owner was a bit damaged, since it cost over twenty thousand pounds to raise the boat from the sixty-foot bottom.

Clouds of Glory

Waterloo, Trafalgar, the Charge of the Light Brigade. Almost everyone has heard of these epic British battles, but few are aware that the medals and decorations given for these and many other great events are on display in museums and often for sale in medals houses throughout Britain. So when my wife and I go on our annual Anglophile's pilgrimage to England, we head for the glories of the medals.

We began our most recent trip with a visit to Glendining's, one of the top London auction houses for medals. Founded in 1900, Glendining's is now a division of Bonham's fine art auctioneers. At Glendining's I learned about some of the amazing groups of medals that that firm has auctioned in recent years.

I was particularly impressed by the historic group of awards bestowed on Admiral Sir Thomas Foley, G.C.B., for naval engagements during the Napoleonic Wars. Foley was a close friend of Lord Horatio Nelson, the victor at Trafalgar, and was one of Nelson's famous "Band of Brothers"—captains whose fierce fighting spirit mirrored Nelson's own.

Foley's first major battle was in 1797, when as flag-captain of HMS *Britannia* he helped defeat a Spanish fleet twice the size of the British fleet at the Battle of St. Vincent in the Caribbean.

Foley then served with Nelson at the famous Battle of the Nile in 1798. Here Nelson realized that the French fleet, anchored across Aboukir Bay near the mouth of the Nile, had allowed a small gap between the fleet and the land. He ordered Foley to take his ship HMS *Goliath* into this dangerous gap and lead the van of the British fleet in a surprise attack from the landward side on the French. Foley's success led to a tremendous victory. The destruction of the French fleet secured British naval supremacy in the Mediterranean and helped eliminate the French threat to Egypt and India.

At the Battle of Copenhagen in 1801, Foley commanded HMS *Elephant*, of seventy-four guns, against the Danes. As this battle began going badly for the British, the admiral in charge, Sir Hyde Parker, signaled to Lord Nelson aboard the *Elephant* to break off the engagement. In one of the most famous gestures in military history, Nelson put his telescope up to his blind eye, turned to Foley, and said, "I really do not see the signal." Eventually Nelson prevailed, the victory was won, and the phrase "to turn a blind eye" entered the English language.

Foley's group included the Grand Cross of the Most Honorable Order of the Bath, a breast star for Knight of the Bath, and official gold medals for the Battles of St. Vincent and the Nile. There was also a private gold medal issued by Alexander Davison (Nelson's prize agent) for the Nile victory. (Each senior officer employed a prize agent to sell his shares in the prizes he captured—this was much more lucrative than their "base pay" and was certainly an effective incentive system!) Foley's historic group sold at Glendining's for £40,700.

Glendining's recently sold a lovely group with a strong Asian connection, belonging to Major General William Gairdner, C.B., of the Indian Native Infantry.

The medals of Admiral Sir Thomas Foley, G.C.B.

Gairdner was born in 1789 and was made an ensign in the army in 1808. He served as a lieutenant in the war against Nepal of 1814–16. This conflict ended in a draw, and the two countries learned to respect each other's fighting qualities so much that they have remained allies to this day, and agreed to allow the Ghurkas of Nepal to serve in the British Army! Gairdner also served in the Ava campaign in India, in the one day war against the Maharattas, and in the costly 1845 Ferozeshuhur battle, part of the Sutlej campaign against the Sikhs. He was made a major general in 1854 and died in Scotland in 1861.

Gairdner's group included a Companion of the Bath (C.B.), the Army of India medal, the Maharajahpoor Star and the Sutlej campaign medal. It sold for £2,300.

The medals of Major General William Gairdner, C.B.

One of the most impressive gallantry awards sold by Glendining's in recent years was the posthumous Victoria Cross (V.C.) group of World War 1 medals won by Lieutenant Thomas Wilkinson, V.C. The V.C. is the highest British gallantry award. It is very rarely given, and is made from cannons captured from the Russians during the Crimean War. Wilkinson received his V.C. for bravery at the battle of La Boiselle in France, on July 5, 1916.

Born in England in 1894, Wilkinson emigrated to Canada in 1912 and enlisted in 1914. His citation reads:

For most conspicuous bravery. During an attack, when a party of another unit was retiring without their machine gun, Lt. Wilkinson rushed forward, got the gun into action, and held up the enemy. Later, when the advance was checked, he forced his way forward and found different units stopped by a solid block of earth. With great pluck and promptness he mounted a machine gun on top of the parapet and dispersed the enemy. Subsequently he made two most gallant attempts to bring in a wounded man, but in the second attempt he was shot through the heart just before reaching the man.

Wilkinson's group included (from left to right) the V.C. and a typical World War I trio: the 1914–15 Star, the British War Medal, and the 1914–18 Victory Medal. Wilkinson's group auctioned for £20,900.

The medals of Lieutenant Thomas Wilkinson, V.C.

On an earlier trip to London we visited the well known firm of Spink and Son Ltd. Spink sells antiques, coins and other collectibles, but specializes in medals, orders, and decorations. It is an auction house and a dealer, so buyers can go in and purchase medals on the spot, or send in "want lists." Its medals department is a mini-museum in itself, perhaps not surprising since the firm designs and mints medals for over forty countries and is the medalist to the Royal Household.

While at Spink I learned of the many distinguished orders and medals that the firm has sold in recent years. One of the most beautiful was the Most Eminent Order of the Indian Empire. Founded by Queen Victoria when she assumed the title of Empress of India, it was designed without the usual cross design and patron saint, to avoid offending non-Christians. It was affectionately called "the jam tart" because of the delicious-looking enamel work on the sash badge. It was discontinued with Indian independence in 1947. Full sets with the chain of elephants and peacocks, and the breast star and sash badge, have sold for about £10,000.

My own best purchase at Spink was an interesting medal for the 1867 British punitive expedition to Ethiopia, undertaken in retaliation for Emperor Theodore's holding several British subjects hostage. The medal has an attractive bust of Queen Victoria on one side and the legend "Abyssinia" near the edge. It is named on the reverse to Colour Sergeant Rawlinson of the 33rd Regiment. Most British medals are named, usually on the edge, and thus the recipient's career can be researched and documented. This medal cost me a modest £100.

Our next stop in London was Christie's (which now owns Spink). The oldest auction house in London, Christie's was founded in 1766. It is located on King Street in the St. James's section of London, just a few steps from Spink.

Christie's has had many historic sales in its two hundred-year-plus history, but surely one of the most historic was the sale of the medals of Lieutenant General Sir Henry Pottinger, Bart., G.C.B., P.C., the first British Governor of Hong Kong and Queen's Plenipotentiary to the Emperor of China. Pottinger was born in 1789 in County Down, northern Ireland. He enlisted as a cadet in the Indian

Army and by age sixteen was promoted to ensign. By age twenty-one he was a full lieutenant and was serving on the Northwest Frontier of India. Often he went into hostile territory on secret missions disguised as a native, speaking local dialects, to assess the local political and military situation for his masters in the Raj.

Sir Henry Pottinger, Bt., G.C.B, P.C.

By 1839 Pottinger had been promoted to brevet colonel and was made a baronet for his services to the crown. He was then sent out to China as Her Britannic Majesty's Plenipotentiary to take in hand the deteriorating situation there, which had resulted in the Emperor stopping all trade with England.

Pottinger immediately caused a sensation by refusing to negotiate with any Chinese representatives of lower rank than himself. He next organized military and naval operations against the Emperor's forces on the Ningpo river and captured four Chinese cities, including Shanghai. He was about to capture Nanking (the "southern capital" of China) when the Chinese sued for peace.

The historic Treaty of Nanking of 1842, which Pottinger negotiated and signed, established the terms of the peace. It reopened China to trade and ceded the island of Hong Kong "in perpetuity" to Britain. It was not until 1997 that this historic Pottinger action was reversed!

Pottinger was made first British Governor and Commander-in-Chief of Hong Kong in 1843. He successfully supervised the transformation of the barren, rocky island into a bustling harbor town within two years. Later in life he was made a Privy Councillor (P.C.), was promoted to lieutenant general, and served as Governor of the Cape of Good Hope and Governor of Madras. Sir Henry Pottinger died in 1856 in Malta, heaped with honors from a truly amazing career.

Pottinger's medal pair consisted of the Army of India medal with a clasp for Kirkee and Poona, and the 1840–42 China medal. The latter was named on the edge to "Sir Henry Pottinger H.B.M. Plenipotentiary." The pair, with various mementos, seals, rings, and documents, sold at Christie's for £14,850.

Another fascinating award sold by Christie's was the Imperial Order of the Crown of India. Designed under Queen Victoria in 1878 for ladies only, it was awarded to female members of the Royal Family, Indian princesses, and those connected with the Viceroy of India and the various state governors who distinguished themselves in service to India. It was seldom awarded and was discontinued in 1947 at Indian independence. Only a few have ever been sold. This one sold recently for £5,500.

Later in our trip we spoke with Chris Buckland and Nimrod Dix of the relatively new firm of Buckland, Dix & Wood. Founded as an auction house and valuers, the firm is located in Old Bond Street. It has already established itself as a premier house with such sales as the Upfill-Brown collection of orders and medals, sold for the world record price for a single collection of £260,000.

Nimrod Dix told us about a sale in which the firm planned to auction the terrific Waterloo and Peninsular War group of General Sir Henry Clinton, G.C.B., G.C.H.

Clinton was born in 1771 and served in the Napoleonic Wars. He acted as military commissioner at the battle of Austerlitz and served in Sicily, Ireland, Italy, Switzerland, Portugal, Sweden, India, and the West Indies.

In 1811 Clinton joined Lord Wellington as a major general in Spain in the long and brutal Peninsular War. In this tremendous campaign, Wellington retreated from Napoleon's generals across Spain and Portugal. He lured them into attacking his impregnable position in Portugal, then drove them back across the Iberian peninsula into France. This was a key cause of Napoleon's downfall and made Wellington a national hero. Clinton played a conspicuous part in the Peninsular battle of Salamanca and was made a Knight of the Bath for his services at the battle of Vittoria.

When Napoleon escaped from Elba, Wellington especially asked for Clinton's assistance. Clinton was given command of the third division, which was posted in the right center of Wellington's forces at the world famous battle of Waterloo.

In this campaign of July 1815, the only one where Wellington faced Napoleon directly, Napoleon almost won the battle before it began with a quick, brilliant thrust up through Belgium toward the English Channel, designed to split the British from their German allies. Wellington recovered but almost lost the battle as the French, outnumbering the British effectives by 100,000 to 40,000, wore down the Britons with artillery and repeated cavalry and infantry assaults.

But Napoleon made the mistake of sending up to twenty-six suicidal cavalry charges against Clinton and the other divisions in the British army. These seasoned soldiers quickly formed "squares" bristling with bayonets and muskets, and annihilated the French Hussars, Cuirassiers and Dragoons. Then Napoleon drove massive columns of infantry at the British, but Clinton and the other officers quickly reformed their troops into long, thin lines that poured rapid volley fire into the advancing columns. When the column of Napoleon's vaunted Imperial Guard fell back, the morale of the French was broken, the battle was won, and Napoleon was history.

Sir Henry's contributions toward winning this crucial victory did not go unrewarded. He was made a knight of the orders of Maria Theresa, of St. George of Russia, and of Wilhelm of the Netherlands. He later served in the House of Commons and died in 1829.

Sir Henry Clinton died childless, but who knows— perhaps he has some distant but famous cousins who even today have continued his interest in public service?

Clinton's beautiful group of medals includes the Grand Cross of the Royal Hanoverian Guelphic Order (G.C.H.), the Netherlands Order of Wilhelm, the Russian Order of St. George, the Peninsular Gold Cross, the Waterloo medal, the General Officer's Gold Medal, and the Grand Cross of the Order of the Bath (G.C.B.). The group will probably sell for about £50,000–60,000.

The medals and portrait of Sir Henry Clinton, G.C.B., G.C.H.

A heroic group of medals recently sold by Buckland was awarded to Lieutenant Colonel Tom Lawrence, V.C., for gallantry in the Boer War. Lawrence was born in Worcestershire in 1873 and enlisted in the 17th Lancers as a private in 1894.

By 1900 Lawrence was a sergeant serving in the Transvaal in South Africa, fighting the Boers. In early August Sergeant Lawrence and Private Hayman were scouting three miles in front of the Lancer Brigade when they were attacked by fourteen mounted Boer commandos.

The Boers fired at the two Britons and hit Hayman's horse, and in the fall Hayman was seriously hurt.

At once Lawrence dismounted, dragged Hayman out from under the dying horse, helped him onto his own horse, and tied Hayman to the saddle. Lawrence pointed the horse toward the rear and gave it a vigorous kick. Then, using Hayman's carbine and his own rifle, he kept the Boers in check until the private was out of range. Maintaining a fusillade of fire, Lawrence slowly withdrew two miles on foot, pursued throughout by a dozen of the enemy. Eventually he reached the safety of the Brigade and helped drive off the Boers.

Lawrence received his Victoria Cross from the hands of King Edward VII. Later in life he was severely wounded in France in the Great War, but recovered to serve on General Allenby's staff in Egypt, where he was mentioned in dispatches. Always an avid horseman, he served on Britain's equestrian team at the 1912 Olympic Games in Sweden.

His magnificent group included the V.C., the Queen's South Africa medal with four clasps, the 1901 King's South Africa medal, a World War I trio with a mention-in-despatches leaf, a 1935 Jubilee medal and 1937 Coronation medal, King Feisal of Iraq's War Medal, and a Swedish medal for the Olympic Games. It sold at Buckland, Dix & Wood for £17,000.

At the end of our trip to Britain, in a spectacular exhibit in Edinburgh Castle museum in Scotland, we saw perhaps the finest order or medal of them all.

The medals of Lt. Colonel Tom Lawrence, V.C.

The Order of the Thistle is granted to only sixteen distinguished Scotsmen, making it probably the most exclusive order in the world. On display was a star of the Order, five inches across and made of at least two hundred one-carat diamonds. It glittered in the bright lights and turned the heads of passersby from thirty feet away. It brought to mind a quote from William Wordsworth that summarizes the whole appeal of orders and medals:

"Our life's star...cometh from afar...trailing clouds of glory."

Section 10

It's A Wild Wide World

Running with the Bulls: The Inner Game

Most journalists describe the running of the bulls at Pamplona, Spain, in the Basque country near the French border, as a silly, drunken exercise in idiocy. But they haven't cracked the secret, inner game that goes on right under their noses. Here is the truth, as told to me by Bosun Tom Harding of the Irish tall ship *Jeanie Johnston*, as we raised some pints of Guinness in a bar in northwest D.C.

"I have run with the bulls exactly fifty times, so I know what I am talking about. The festival at Pamplona began in Roman times, when around the year 300 Fermius, the son of a local Christian bishop, was martyred in Amiens, France. The word got back to Pamplona, and the martyred son was eventually transformed into St. Fermin. His festival is held every year from July 6 to July 14.

Tom Harding, boatswain of the Jeanie Johnston, has run with the bulls at Pamplona 50 times

"The running of the bulls always begins at 8 A.M. sharp each day. The real purpose of the run is to get the bulls from their corral at the top of the course to the bullfight ring—the Plaza de Toros—at the end of the course. At the Plaza the bulls will be fought, and killed, later each day. The three major events of each day are the running, a parade down the route, and the bullfights. Drinking goes on 24 by 7.

"In the running of the bulls, there are two groups of animals. In the lead group there are six large steers— geldings—with very wide horns, and six smaller bulls. Oddly, the bulls are much more dangerous, because they are incredibly aggressive. The steers run first and usually faster than the bulls, and the bulls follow the steers. A small group of steers is sent a few seconds after the lead group, to push along any stragglers.

"The running or 'Encierro' is signaled and controlled by four rockets. When the first rocket goes off, you know the gates have opened and the running has started. The second rocket is fired when all the bulls have left the corral. The third rocket is fired when the bulls have reached the Plaza de Toros at the end of the course. The fourth rocket is fired when the bulls are all safe in their pens.

"Most of the several thousand runners position themselves well down the course, near the Plaza de Toros. They just take off at the first rocket, and never get within hundreds of yards of a bull. They are the poseurs, the fakers. The crowd at the Plaza actually boos them when they arrive within seconds of the first rocket.

"The *real* runners, of whom there are only about two hundred, have as their goal literally running amongst the bulls, so close that they can feel their heat, smell their breath, and feel their immense power. Naturally, I am a real runner. You can tell us runners who *really* ran with the bulls—we are totally wired afterwards. We look and feel very different from the fakers who only say they ran with the bulls. It is like no feeling I have ever had before or since—a massive adrenaline rush that doesn't go away for the rest of the day.

"My goal is to get in front of a bull, with his horns on either side of me. That way I avoid getting gored, and also the bull pushes me along so I can go much faster and further than if I were just on my own. Sometimes I run with two bulls on either side of me, and I am just behind their horns. I have to use immense concentration and effort to achieve either of these positions for more than a few yards.

"The horns of the bulls are needle-sharp, and rapidly taper out to the size of a very large human forearm. So you can imagine the impact on your body if this needle gores into you, followed by this huge tapering shape. The hoofs of the bulls are very small and sharp, and have more than eleven hundred pounds of weight behind them. So if they trample you, the hoof usually goes right through your body.

"My tactic is to pick out sections of the nine hundred-yard course and run a section right in the middle of the bulls. They travel at thirty miles an hour, much faster than a man can run, so there is no way to run with them for the entire course. The entire festival lasts eight days a year, so it is possible to run about eight sections of the course, each section about a hundred meters long, in one year. I have run with the bulls fifty times, meaning on fifty different days, and have covered the entire course several times over.

"There are some sections that are even more dangerous than average, because they are longer, so there is no escape, or narrower, so there might be pileups. Once in a long dangerous section I saw a guy running beside a bull. He made the mistake of taunting a bull and attracting its attention. In the blink of an eye the bull hooked his needle-sharp horn around the side of the fellow, neatly removing his kidney. The fellow staggered in shock and almost fell.

But then he looked back and saw more bulls behind him, so he had to keep running to the end of that section, carrying his kidney under his arm. He was grabbed at the exit by the ever-present medicos, who managed to save his life and reattach his kidney.

"The entire running usually only lasts between two and seven minutes, depending on whether any of the bulls get distracted, separated from the herd, or turn back and run alone the other way. This latter is very dangerous, since you can be rammed and pursued to the death by a lone bull that has lost his herd instinct to keep moving down the course.

"Once I saw a friend of mine being gored by a bull, just a few meters ahead of me. I threw caution to the wind and tightly gripped my newspaper roll, which all runners carry as our only protection. I jammed it up the bull's backside, and yelled, 'Toro, toro!' to get his attention. As you can imagine, it worked. The bulls are very intelligent and are bred to kill. When they look at you, you can see if they have designated you as a target. They basically take a picture of you with their eyes, and pursue you until they obliterate that picture.

"This bull chased me for about twenty yards and almost caught me. I jumped up on the eight-foot barricade lining the route, landing there with two young men who were near me in the run. The bull still had my picture in his brain, so he repeatedly rammed the barricade with his horns and head. The barricade uprights are made of six inches of concrete and rebar and would stop a tank. This bull cracked the upright under me with his charges. The three of us on the roost knew that one more charge would dump one or all of us down, and we would die. Luckily, a red bandanna and some loud noise distracted the bull, and he headed away down the course.

"One way to escape an enraged bull who has identified you as a target and gored you is to play dead. I had a friend who forgot this tactic. He was gored but not badly. He fell to the ground but began crawling, trying to get away. The bull pursued him and gored him repeatedly, until he stopped moving. He was injured for life.

"I knew another guy, a very fit U.S. Marine, who wanted to watch the action from very close up, since the high double walls prevent most spectators from having a good view. His plan was to lurk in a doorway on the route, and watch the bulls and runners go by. Unfortunately, a runner was being pursued by a bull and the bull slipped right beside the door, and sliced the Marine's stomach open by mistake. He survived, but barely.

"The bulls and the steers are about the same each day except the last. On this eighth day, the most vicious bulls of all, a small breed called Miura, are let loose. They are not just bred to be killers. They are bred to be totally pathological. Everyone knows that they are saved for the last day because that is the day that the most French tourists participate in the run!

"Hemingway never ran with the bulls. He was too smart for that. He did understand that this was an amazing game of strategy, tactics, skill, experience, adrenaline, life, and death unlike any other. But he just watched from a balcony and wrote about it in *The Sun Also Rises*, and everyone assumed he had had the guts to do it. Everyone was wrong.

"I find it immensely satisfying to have a nice steak dinner each night after the bullfights, and know that I am eating the big SOB that tried to kill me and my friends earlier that morning. The meat is usually kind of tough, although there is a gastronomic club that gives a prize for the juiciest bull, and celebrates his name and the ranch he came from. Each bull has a name, number and ranch of origin. Many bulls are very famous, especially if they kill someone.

"I am fifty-nine years old, much older than the Basque teenagers who make up the majority of the serious runners. There are a few other foreigners who really run with the bulls, but not many. I want to run with the bulls one more time before I die. Of course, the two events might occur simultaneously.

"After the end of the week of the running of the bulls, some enthusiasts don't want to quit. So they have recently started the tradition of the Running of the Buses, where they run in front of the municipal buses that follow the same general route as the bulls. The bus drivers are just as vicious and homicidal as the Miura bulls, so it's a great event!"

The Great Vietnamese Dwarf Hunt

"Would you like a cigarette?" said the small voice of the waiter in the Saigon nightclub. "I don't smoke," I said, turning to look at him. There was no one there. Then I looked down. Way down. He was smiling up at me with a big, friendly face, thick black hair, and a very small body. I glanced around the club and noticed a dozen other tiny men, tending bar and waiting tables, scattered among the many young, normal-sized Vietnamese waitresses. In between bursts of throbbing live music, I was able to learn their story.

"My name is Quynh Nyu Thien Han," he said, "which means 'Beautiful Flower That Hates Forever.' I am thirty-one years old and forty-seven inches high. I was born of normal-sized parents in the Mekong Delta and came to Ho Chi Minh City [Saigon] to earn a living. But I was only able to make a little money selling lottery tickets. Then Mrs. Vo Thi Thu Minh found me two years ago, and hired me as a waiter. I work with the other little people she found, and live with them in a big house she rents for us near the airport. We mainly work at this Live Music Bar Number 1 on Nguyen Minh Khai street in Saigon, but we also work for Mrs. Minh at two other clubs in the city."

Later I spoke with Mrs. Minh about her troupe of little people. "I met Han and some of the other dwarfs in a run-down cafe when they tried to sell me some lottery tickets. I was impressed by their positive attitude and their spirit in overcoming the many difficulties they face. Vietnamese society usually pushes them aside. At first I hired three as waiters, and they were an immediate hit with the bar staff and customers."

Lew Toulmin and his new Vietnamese friend, Quynh Nyu Thien Han, or "Beautiful Flower That Hates Forever"

"Quickly the demand for dwarfs became very great," continued Mrs. Minh, "and I wanted to help more. So I launched a great hunt for dwarfs across all of Vietnam. I used newspaper ads at first, but dwarfs don't usually read papers. So I visited many provinces to find them. I talked to all kinds of people, especially lottery ticket sellers and shoe shiners. I eventually found and hired twenty-four dwarfs, including two women. The little people in my troupe range in age from eighteen to forty-seven and in height from twenty-nine to forty-eight inches tall."

The troupe has written many songs and a series of plays that they occasionally perform at the clubs. These include, naturally, *Snow White and the Seven Dwarfs*. They also perform *Seven Dwarfs Climbing a Mountain*. This latter play is about seven little men fording swollen rivers, climbing a mountain range, and overcoming other difficulties in life, in

393

search of their seven lovers—a sort of Vietnamese *Seven Brides for Seven Brothers.*

Quin Yu Thien Han confirmed Mrs. Minh's generosity. "She pays me $100 a month, a very good salary here. And I have a health plan. I wait tables, sing, play the guitar and harmonica, and really enjoy my work now. I love rock 'n' roll, so working in this live music bar is great."

Life has not been all beautiful flowers, though. Han said, "My wife is normal-sized, almost five feet tall. We have a normal-sized son, Truong Xuan ['Forever Young'], who is six years old. Early last year he was playing with a neighbor's child in the yard on a motor scooter. The scooter started and my son was dragged into the street and hit by a large truck. He lost his leg. So I was very sad all last year. But maybe with my good salary from Mrs. Minh I will be able to save enough for an artificial leg for my son, when he is ready for it. Perhaps our troupe and my family will be able to travel abroad to do our shows in Thailand. Maybe someday we can even visit the United States," he said, looking a little wistful.

Llewellyn M. Toulmin

Mongkut: The King of Fruits You Never Heard Of

Multimillionaire Japanese businessmen go to Thailand for mongkut, golf, and sex, in that priority order. They even schedule their business trips to Bangkok for the hottest, most uncomfortable month of the year—April—because that is the peak of the mongkut season.

What is so fabulous about this fruit? It looks like a small, brown apple, but inside a mongkut are creamy white sections that are beautiful, sweet, refreshing and taste like nothing else. It is a thousand times better than leechees or rambutan, which are commonly served as stylish desserts in Oriental restaurants. And it is much better than mango, to which mongkut is unrelated despite its similar, Western name of "mangosteen."

Mangosteen or Mongkut, king of fruits

Mongkut is rare. It is available only in Thailand and a few other tropical Asian countries between March and June. It is virtually never available in the West. The only place I

395

have seen it outside Asia was at Harrods's in London. There I once saw five semi-rotten mongkut for sale for three pounds (about five dollars) each, thirty times the price in Thailand.

I grew up on mongkut, and I could eat forty of them at one sitting if I let myself. But I didn't really know much about the fruit until I was an adult. I was visiting my father's friend, the great-grandson of King Mongkut, Rama IV (the Yul Brynner character in *The King and I*). We were sitting in the living room of his weekend retreat at the foot of beautiful Kao Yai mountain in northeast Thailand. I asked him if the name of his ancestor King Mongkut was related in some way to the name of the fruit. No, he said, the king got his name from an old Pali word, Pali being an ancient language of India, and the language sometimes used in the Buddhist monkhood. In Pali mongkut means "crown," a fitting name for a king. But the identical word in ordinary Thai only means the fruit. He added some other interesting facts about the fruit:

- The current monarch, King Bhomipol, Rama IX, loves fruit of all kinds, including mongkut. So growers all over Thailand compete to grow the best fruit, to please the royal palate. Queen Victoria reportedly named mongkut as her favorite fruit.

- The best mongkut come from the southeast of Thailand, east of the famous Pattaya Beach.

- There are no varieties, only small (the size of a small lime), medium (the size of a small apple) and large (the size of a large apple).

- Mongkut can be obtained from families in Sri Lanka and India, but not commercially. It is generally unavailable in Cambodia, Burma, Laos, and the Philippines, although it could easily grow there. (I did find some in Vietnam, even cheaper than in Thailand). Oddly, people in these countries (and Japan) love to get gifts of mongkut but don't seem to have the "fruit culture" of Thailand and hence don't usually grow this fruit they adore.

- Mongkut is almost always eaten as a fruit, but in the old days in Thailand mongkut sections would sometimes be used as a condiment on rice, with shallots, chilies, and fish sauce. Even more rarely, it was sometimes eaten with boiled turtle eggs, but this is now, dare I say it, a forbidden fruit.

- Mongkut grow on trees that often take twenty years to mature and bear fruit. So Thais don't plant these trees for themselves, they plant for their children and grandchildren.

- The fruit start out on the tree very small and green, and gradually turn a dark chocolate brown.

- When choosing mongkut in a market, you should look for ones that are small or medium sized, that have green leaves and a shiny brown skin. They should feel slightly squeezable but not mushy. Ideally, they should not have a very hard outer husk, although many do and these are still edible.

After the lecture, my host showed me the right way to eat the fruit.

If the husk is squeezable, then squeeze it around the middle, and tear the top half of the husk off with one sharp twist. (I tried this many times and couldn't master it. Good luck.) Do not use your fingernail to assist in tearing, because the red-purple inner husk is a bit juicy and could stain your fingers and clothes. If the husk is hard, use a knife to cut about three-eighths of an inch into the husk, all the way around the equator of the fruit. Then lift off the top half.

The beautiful inner white sections, looking like a creamy white orange, will now be exposed. If the fruit is medium-sized or large, there will be a section or two that are larger than the others. These have large single seeds inside. Eat these sections first, using a small fork or spoon to lift them out of the husk. Suck the good white meat off the seeds. Spit out the seeds. Do not bite down on the seeds, as they are rather tasteless. Then eat the delicious remaining seedless sections. If some sections are translucent instead of creamy white, or have a little yellow goo, they are a bit past it. Don't eat this part. But enjoy the rest.

If the fruit is very small, with no sections larger than any others, put the white fruit to your mouth and with your teeth lift the sections into your mouth, and yourself into heaven.

All, right, all right, you want to know what it tastes like. Well, imagine a pineapple crossed with a leechee, with pure sweetness, no fibers, and no tartness. Just goodness.

It may not be good Pali, but to me, mongkut is the king of fruits.

Llewellyn M. Toulmin

Knights Templar: Royal Tour with a Noble Purpose

Imagine a tour of a beautiful European town where you hobnob with royals, enjoy personal visits to their private castles, participate in ancient ceremonies of knighthood, and make the world a better place. Impossible? Not really—read on.

Recently I joined an order of charitable knighthood, the Sovereign and Military Order of the Temple of Jerusalem, better known as the Knights Templar. The Order was founded by Crusader knights in 1118 and suppressed by a jealous and greedy French king in 1307. It was reconstituted in 1804 by Napoleon and is a very active body today. Its goals are first response to disasters around the world, building links between East and West, maintaining the religious sites of the Holy Land, and protecting Christians at risk of persecution.

Recently the Order has become rather famous due to the book *The Da Vinci Code*, which postulates that the Knights Templar is a secret society designed to protect the descendants of Jesus and Mary Magdalene, which has the Holy Grail squirreled away in a church basement in Scotland, and which practices ritual sex orgies while clad in white robes with red crosses. Fortunately or unfortunately, the only true assertion is that Knights Templar wear white robes with red crosses.

The royal patron of the Knights Templar is Princess Elisabeth of Ysenburg und Budingen, and she graciously invited knights to visit her for a long weekend meeting at her estate in Germany. There we met her and her amazing family, toured two of her castles, heard reports on Order projects, and invested new knights—all at a very reasonable price.

Princess Elisabeth of Ysenburg und Budingen,
Royal Sponsor of the Knights Templar

The visit began with a tour of the historic town of Budingen, about fifty miles northeast of Frankfurt. The small town was built in 1321 on an island in a river, surrounded by a high city wall, and filled with half-timbered houses, a cathedral, and the schloss (or castle) of Ysenburg und Budingen. All of these elements survive today, making Budingen one of the best preserved and most charming medieval towns in Germany. From our guide we learned that Budingen converted early to Lutheranism and practiced religious toleration, thus attracting religious refugees from all over Europe. But toleration turned to terror from 1560 to 1750, when witch hunts were the order of the day.

The Witches' Tower, a part of the town wall, commemorates the suffering of these hundreds of women, who were imprisoned and tortured in the tower for months or even years. We visited the tower, wandered through the tiny lanes of the Old Town, viewed the small river that has periodically inundated the town, and inspected the dry moat and city walls. We ended the day in an excellent Turkish restaurant, one of the town's many cosmopolitan choices.

The next day we toured the Schloss Budingen, and learned something of the impressive history of the Ysenburg und Budingen family. The Schloss was built during the reign of Emperor Friedrich Barbarossa (1123–1190), predating the town that was later built up around it. The family was given its coat of arms and first land grant by Barbarossa, who was hunting in the forest, got lost, and asked a local woodsman for help. The woodsman was covered in charcoal dust, and drew two black coal dust lines in the snow to show the Emperor the way home. In gratitude the Emperor granted the woodsman a coat of arms with two black lines on a white field. The simple design shows that it is one of the oldest in Europe, a great source of pride for the Ysenburg und Budingen family.

The family later attained autonomous princely status, intermarried with all the major noble and royal families of Europe, and amassed over 75,000 acres of farmland, several castles, and various enterprises near Frankfurt. The family lost its status as independent princely rulers in the early 1800s during the consolidation of Germany, but retained considerable influence, and is the fifth richest noble house in Europe.

HRH Princess Elisabeth Marie Alexandra, the Patron of the Order, was born HRH Princess Schleswig-Holstein-Sonderburg-Gluecksburg in 1945, and married HSH (His Supreme Highness) Karl August Hermann Gotthard, Prinz zu Ysenburg und Budingen in 1975, thus becoming a double princess. Sadly, she was widowed in 1989 when the prince died of a heart attack and car crash.

The Princess's lineage on the Schleswig-Holstein side can be completely traced for more than a dozen generations, with virtually all noble or royal ancestors, and she has many lines back to Charlemagne. Her extended family includes her seventh great-grandfather King George III of England, and she is related to Queen Victoria, the Romanovs, and the current Queen of Denmark, King of Norway, ex-King of Greece, and Prince Philip, the Duke of Edinburgh.

The castle tour highlighted Ysenburg family history and early life in the castle. For example, a complete alchemist's studio, equipped with old instruments, showed how early Ysenburgs sought to convert lead into gold. A huge painting in the dining room showed a wild boar as big as a pony being chased by dogs, demonstrating the family's ongoing love of the hunt. Large Chinese vases were a souvenir of one of the family's service as ambassador to Imperial China. And two small cannons with the family crest were reminders of the time when the Ysenburgs und Budingens had their own army.

That afternoon we heard reports on various Knights Templar projects around the world. Rev. Canon Andrew White, the Archbishop of Canterbury's Legate to the Holy Land, reported on his efforts in Palestine and Iraq, where he is helping to educate street children and orphans, with Templar assistance.

From Ethiopia, HRH Prince Steven Mengesha, a Templar and great grandson of Emperor Haile Selassie, spoke of his efforts to bring medical technology and instruments to his country.

Dame Mary Borum of the United States described her visit to a project in Russia, a four-car train that includes a medical car and a beautiful rolling chapel. The train visits remote villages in northwest Russia and brings medical aid and a place of worship to communities whose churches were destroyed under Soviet rule.

His Grace Bishop Younan, Lutheran Primate of the Holy Land and Jordan, reported on the plight of the 160,000 Palestinian Christians, who are trapped on the West Bank between hostile Muslim Palestinian neighbors and unsympathetic Israeli authorities.

HRH Prince Ali Seraj reviewed how he spent Templar donations to his projects in Afghanistan, where he built the first high school for young women in Kabul and built houses and clinics in remote areas, all at unit prices much lower than typical aid agencies.

Next we moved to the historic Mariankirche church for the impressive Knights Templar investiture ceremony, a highlight of the trip. Knights and dames from around the world were dressed in amazing finery, capped with the white robes and red crosses of the order. New knights were dubbed by Brigadier General Stewart McCarty, the Grand Prior of the U.S. Order, Princess Elisabeth, and Bishop Younan. Squires, ages fourteen to twenty-one, were inducted, promotions made, and special awards and medals given. The processions of the "Lords Temporal and Spiritual" at the beginning and end of the service were pageants of color and ceremony.

That night we were taken by bus to the historic and enormous Ronneburg Castle, another of the Ysenburg family holdings. The 350 knights, dames and guests sat down to a sumptuous three-hour, five-course meal, highlighted by strolling minstrels, huge hunks of pork roast, and a roaring fire.

The Princess began the dinner with a simple greeting in perfect English: "Welcome to our castle. Enjoy yourselves, and eat and drink as much as you can!" As General McCarty said, "That's the kind of royal sponsor you want to have."

At dinner I chatted with nearby knights and guests and was impressed with the quality and noble purpose of the members. Prince Stephen described the needs of Ethiopia. "Starvation is not really the problem in my country today. We need expertise in food production and planning high-impact projects that fit with our way of life. Of course AIDS and AIDS orphans are a desperate need—our country has the second highest infection rate in Africa." During the dinner, knights discussed ways to help Ethiopia, including expanding a charitable institution to sell Ethiopian crafts overseas. A senior U.S. Army officer (of which there are many in the Order) came up to the Prince and said, "I have a charitable foundation and extensive experience in Rwanda, setting up their truth and reconciliation process and Commission. If I can do anything to help Ethiopia heal in a similar way, just let me know."

By the end of the long weekend, I realized I had met dozens of fascinating and giving people, including numerous field-grade military officers, a count, a duchess, an earl, three princesses, and two princes. Not bad for an ordinary Southern boy from Mobile, Alabama.

Section 11

Six Countries in Six Hours

Swimming from Andorra to Zimbabwe

Got museum feet in Moscow and want to do some laps to relax? You'd know where the best pools in town are if you checked out www.swimmersguide.com. This handy website lists over 14,000 facilities with over 15,000 pools in 151 countries worldwide, from Andorra to Zimbabwe. It is the only site of its kind, it's free, and it takes no advertising. For each pool the Web site includes the following information:

- The name and address of the facility

- The phone number to inquire about hours, rates and schedules (which change so often that they are not listed on the site)

- Programs, such as Master Swim teams, clubs, and classes

- A description of the pool—always with length and indoor or outdoor location, often with water temperature and number of lanes or width

- Admission information, including (where available) drop-in prices and discounts for members of affiliated groups and facilities, for senior citizens, and for guests registered at nearby hotels.

The site is the labor of love of Bill Haverland, former VP of a cruise line and now a financial advisor in North Carolina. He has put more than 13,000 hours of unpaid work into the site, looking for pools on the Internet and via mail and phone calls. Says Bill, "I was unemployed and visiting my grandmother. She said, 'What are you going to do now?' Out of the blue, I said, 'I love to swim and I know computers, so maybe I'll combine the two.' The rest is unpaid but happy history!"

Bill says that, "We only list pools that are eighteen meters or longer, so they are good for laps and exercise. We have reviews of some pools, and links to MapQuest for some pools. We have good coverage of most of the world, including the U.S., where we have over 3,500 listings." [According to the Web site, however, Bill has removed listings from any of the states of the United States where citizens of that state have passed a so-called "Defense of Marriage" constitutional amendment by popular vote.] "We list hotels, public facilities, private clubs, indoor, outdoor— anywhere that the public might be able to get into."

Bill continued, "The biggest pool we have found is in the U.S., at Schofield Barracks in Oahu—at 165 yards it's bigger than a double-Olympic. We often get wonderful new listings and reviews from our readers. But we are a little spotty in South America and China. And we have a list, in Japanese, of 1,500 pools in Japan, which we can't read. So if you read Japanese or are traveling to South America or China, get in touch with us on the website. Our goal is to list every pool in the world!"

Lahoree swimming pool, Lahore, India,
probably the world's largest outdoor pool

Classic Car Rally Around the World

Rolls-Royce. Lagonda. Bugatti. Jaguar. Aston-Martin. Ferrari. Do these names make your heart, like mine, beat a little faster? Perhaps you, like me, should include a great race or classic rally in your next foreign vacation.

Recently, for example, I read in my monthly Bible, *Thoroughbred and Classic Cars*, about an upcoming amazing rally, the first-ever "Around the World in 80 Days" road rally. I had to be there for the start. I organized some vacation time, and soon arrived at the Royal Mint near the Tower of London.

For five hours I was awestruck as some of the most beautiful, rare, and valuable classic cars in the world assembled on the Mint grounds. One hundred one cars were there. The oldest was a huge 1912 Locomobile—you'd have to be loco to think of driving around the world in that! There was a 1913 Rolls-Royce Silver Ghost worth half a million. There was a 1964 Facel Vega, the fave ride of 1950s movie stars like Ava Gardner. There was a Citroën Traction Avant (the car of Inspector Maigret), driven by a beautiful Persian refugee lady banker who spoke fourteen languages. There was a 1939 Ford V-8 driven by Ray Carr, a seventy-five-year-old developer who had previously driven across America in a 1909 Stanley Steamer and from Peking to Paris in his Ford. There were two Canadians driving a massive 1938 Packard to raise money for charity. There was a 1935 Chrysler Airflow driven by a beautiful young woman (a Massachusetts State Trooper) and her commercial pilot father. There was a 1954 Aston-Martin DB2/4 driven by the laird of a Scottish castle. And there was a 1964 Mercedes SL driven by the son of Pablo Picasso.

With other members of the public, I peered into the engines, took pictures, talked to the drivers, and watched over the shoulder of the race officials as they "scrutineered" the cars. This involved checking that the cars had not been substantially modified from their original factory specs, and that the required safety equipment was in place. For all this, there was no entry fee for the public.

The next day on Tower Bridge was the great day—the start of the Rally. The clouds parted and the sun shone. All normal traffic was diverted away from the bridge. Sir Stirling Moss, the famous driver, started the cars with a flourish, one pair every minute, in a classic Mille Miglia start. The crowd of six thousand cheered and waved flags from the twenty-two countries in the field, and from the sixteen countries the cars would pass through.

There was one hitch, though. One of the two cars in the front rank, the 1913 Rolls-Royce Silver Ghost, had an owner-driver who was so sick that he couldn't make the start. Under the rules, every car must have two persons on board. The announcer appealed for anyone in the crowd to volunteer to "ride a mile down the road," until the situation could be sorted out. I was at the other end of the line of cars and missed the announcement. Otherwise I could have been aboard! A young blonde woman stepped forward and got in, the crowd cheered, and the Rolls roared off. She rode all the way to Dover. The owner was still sick. She stowed away in the back of the huge Rolls, and snuck into France without a passport or luggage. The owner was still sick. She rode across France and snuck into Italy. The owner was *still* sick, and the young lady, now known as the "flying blonde bombshell" to the press, finally stowed away all the way to Greece, sending back plaintive pleas for her passport and "some extra pairs of knickers"!

Dr. Terry Maxon of Arizona works on the 1913 Rolls Royce Silver Ghost just minutes before the start on Tower Bridge, London of the Around the World road rally. The "flying blonde bombshell" is not yet aboard.

Nine weeks later the Around the World Rally was passing through the United States, after having conquered Europe, Turkey, central Asia and China. I had been following the event every day on the Rally website, keeping up with their adventures. My wife and I rented a car and informally joined the Rally at a beautiful lunch stop in rural Pennsylvania. We talked with the drivers and peered under a 1940 Chevrolet 102 Coupe, affectionately known as the "Jam Tart" because of its bright red color, which was having a major repair done—in fifteen minutes!—by the rally mechanics. We then followed the cars along picturesque roads to their night rest stop.

In the morning we inspected the cars, including Claude Picasso's (yes, the son of *that* Picasso) 1964 Mercedes SL and a 1964 Lancia that had both joined the "Rock 'n' Roll Club"—they had both rolled over at least once. These cars were held together with lashings of duct tape. Luckily no one was hurt. In fact, everyone was remarkably upbeat, considering they had been driving four hundred miles a day for sixty-five days on some of the toughest roads in the world. The drivers' surprising consensus was that Canadian gravel and fire roads are actually worse than most dirt roads in China; all the rollovers had taken place in Canada or the western United States.

We talked with Freddie and Jan Giles of the United Kingdom. She navigated and he drove every mile, often twelve to fourteen hours a day. They were driving a 1968 Hillman Hunter, which they said cost only $3,000 to buy and about $7,000 to prepare for the rally. They led the pack through Morocco, Spain, and France, and eventually won the Rally with a wonderful score of just fifty-two minutes in time penalties. Only two round-the-world cars dropped out before the finish at Tower Bridge, a remarkable record.

To launch your own rally spectator adventures you need to know the lingo. A "race" is naturally an event where the fastest car wins. Races used to be run on open roads until the 1950s when there were many accidents involving spectators. Most races are now confined to closed race tracks with walls and fences protecting the spectators. A "rally" is a timed event (also known as a "regularity") held on open roads. Here it is *not* the fastest car that wins, but the car that most exactly meets the preset time and speed for each road segment. Time penalties are assessed for being late or early at checkpoints. Rallies officially stay below the posted speed limit, although some drivers have been known to put the

411

pedal to the metal to make up lost time. A "tour" or "adventure drive" is a non-competitive drive through beautiful countryside. Some events combine a rally with a tour.

Rallies are organized by many car clubs and groups such as the Classic Rally Association, Trans World Events, and HERO (Historic Endurance Rally Organization). Some events are held under the auspices of the FIA (Fédération Internationale de l'Automobile) or the FIVA (Fédération Internationale des Véhicules Anciens).

As a newbie you might be worried about driving over minor water hazards, like oceans. No worries, mate! Long distance rally cars are often airlifted over oceans or political hot spots. For example, the Around the World Rally was airlifted from Peking to Alaska and from New Jersey to Morocco. Most organizers use huge Russian Antonov cargo planes (much larger than the American C5A), that have been specially modified to carry up to fifty-two cars each!

If you really catch the bug and want to drive in a rally or tour, it may not be as difficult or expensive as you think. Your local car clubs may have events that need co-drivers and navigators. Sometimes car owners on major rallies need co-drivers or navigators and are willing to pay expenses. You can rent classic cars from vendors such as Voditi in France or Classic Car Group in the United Kingdom. You can link up with foreign classic car tour operators such as Continental Car Tours. You can participate in the upcoming Peking-to-Paris rally. Or, like me, you can wait beside a rally start, hoping for an announcement that a co-driver is needed. Just bring your passport and some extra knickers!

The attached chart shows some of the most exotic rallies, races, and tours, so you can plan your own Great Race. Ladies and gentlemen, start your engines!

Event, Month, (Type)	Place	Number And Age of Cars	Notes and Website
Le Jog December (Rally)	Land's End to John O'Groats, (Cornwall to Scotland) UK	120 1920–1975	1650 miles in very tough conditions, only 75% usually finish. www.hero.org.uk
The Winter Challenge to Monte Carlo Jan/Feb (Rally)	6 starts including Brooklands (UK), Ypres, Oslo. Thru the Alps to finish in Cannes, France	250+ 1920–1968	Icy roads and lots of snow; great party at the finish. Remember *A Man and A Woman*? www.classicrally.org.uk
San Marino Grand Prix April (Race)	Near San Marino, n. Italy	Modern Formula 1 race cars	See the Most Serene Republic of San Marino. www.formula1.sm
Mille Miglia May (Rally)	Brescia, Italy	500+ 1927–1957	1000 miles around Italy, recreating historic race; lots of Bugattis. www.millemiglia.it

Event, Month, (Type)	Place	Number And Age of Cars	Notes and Website
Scottish Malts May (Rally)	Through the Scottish Highlands	170+ 1920–1974	Visit six single-malt whiskey distilleries from the Firth of Forth to the Isle of Skye. www.hero.org.uk
Monaco Historic Grand Prix May (Race)	Monaco	180 historic race cars 1924–1965	Six classes streak through the streets of Monaco. www.visitmonaco.com
Monaco Grand Prix May (Race)	Monaco	Modern Formula 1 race cars + 3 other classes	The most glamorous Grand Prix. The Tao of Steve McQueen lives! www.visitmonaco.com
Leige-Rome-Leige June (Rally)	Belgium to Rome or other Italian destination	Pre-1960	Recreates a famous 1931-1960 race. www.motorclassic.com

Event, Month, (Type)	Place	Number And Age of Cars	Notes and Website
Le Mans June (Race)	Le Mans (closed road race track 100 mi. SW of Paris)	80+ Modern Formula 1 race cars	Twenty-four hours; camp out with 200,000 spectators; world's greatest auto race? www.lemans.org
Rallye des Alpes July (Rally)	Geneva thru Swiss & Austrian Alps	60+ 1919-1971	1500 miles; a million hairpins. www.rallyedesalpes.com
Peking to Paris 2007 (Rally)	Peking to Paris, via Russia	80+ cars Pre-1968 classics	Another stunner from CRA; re-creates 1907 Peking to Paris race. www.endurorally.co.uk/

Breaking the Hundred-Country Barrier: If It's Two O'Clock, This Must Be Sharjah

Some of my coworkers say I'm obsessed with visiting new countries. They think I'm on some sort of Mad Quest to visit every country on Earth. Horsepucky! I can prove they're wrong. If I were obsessed, would I jump on a plane to a conference in Abu Dhabi without checking whether it's considered a "country"? Would I fail to notice that my routing from Washington includes a brief stopover in Bahrain, a country I hadn't visited? Would I fail to check on the surrounding area, to see if I can up my total of countries? See? Told 'em so. QED.

In my rush to the plane I don't even bring along the official list of Travelers' Century Club (TCC) countries. Just in case you don't know, TCC is a club for people who have visited 100 or more of the 315 TCC authorized "countries or separate territories." They determine what qualifies as a "country," using the Amateur Radio Relay League definitions and their own research and rules.

During the flight to Bahrain, I pick up the Gulf Air airline magazine and study a map of the region. Suddenly the names begin jumping off the page. I realize that each of the seven United Arab Emirates has a name vaguely familiar from the TCC list. Abu Dhabi is just one of the UAE emirates, and I think EACH ONE of the emirates is counted as a SEPARATE COUNTRY on the list! OMIGOD! That means that, counting Bahrain, the magic number of 100 countries, which once seemed so distant, is possibly within my grasp. My current total is 96. If I break 100 I can join the TCC! I'll be recognized as a modern Knight of Travel, having gone on a long and arduous Quest, honored by the Fellowship of the Round World. (Okay, okay, so most of the Quest was in Business Class and I've got more frequent-flyer miles than God, but it was LONG, anyway.)

When I get to Bahrain I call my wife, wake her up, and have her go to the file cabinet to look up the TCC list and confirm my suspicions. I am right. (Me, obsessed? She seems to think so—but what does she know? Just 'cause it's 4 A.M. her time.) Bahrain is my number 97—only three more to go!

Bahrain in the third millennium BCE was a lush sacred paradise with lots of greenery, heroic figures, and wise men enjoying eternal life, according to the *Epic of Gilgamesh,* the world's oldest poetic saga. (At least according to the *Lonely Planet* guidebook. What, you thought I actually READ the *Epic of Gilgamesh*? Right. Don't be daft. I just threw that in for the culture vultures. I'll bet even the *Lonely Planet*eers didn't read the *Epic of Gilgamesh*. They probably swiped that reference from some earlier guidebooker who swiped it from some Victorian writer—heck, the *Epic* may not even EXIST anymore. Maybe it NEVER existed. I mean, have you ever even MET anybody named "Gilgamesh"?)

Bahrain today is a hot, sandy island whose main products are overpriced duty-free items imported from elsewhere, sold by underpaid young Filipinas. Bahrain has another really useful product to boost its GDP: lottery tickets for $130 each for tourists, for a one-in-a-thousand chance at a Mercedes or BMW. Needless to say, I don't buy any.

One unexpected Bahraini product seems to be hordes of young Ukrainian and Russian women waiting at the airport. I ask a Filipina clerk, and she sniffs, "These are ladies on their way to Dubai to sell themselves." I think she is exaggerating, but later learn from media reports that she is right—the biggest export to the Gulf from the fallen Soviet Union is fallen women. Trotsky and Dzerzhinski must be spinning in their graves.

Arriving in Abu Dhabi (number 98—getting close), I expect to see remnants of the sleepy, inefficient, and rather squalid pearl diving and fishing village I had heard about years ago. Not! The first hint of change comes with my visa. The hotel obtains an expedited visa for me and even sends an efficient young Bangladeshi man to ensure I get the visa at the airport. Of course this modern and efficient service costs a pretty penny—$100, no less. Oh, well, Uncle Boss will pay.

On the way into town I am awed by the infrastructure—six-lane highways with little traffic, a huge concrete sports complex, modern bridges, large new hotels, manicured plantings in median strips, large villa-style houses, and a grid system of paved roads, each one with beautiful curbs and gutters and clear signs in Arabic and English. According to the *Lonely Planet,* as recently as 1958 Abu Dhabi consisted of a rundown fort and a few beach huts. Shows what forty years of Western petrodollars can do.

The next morning is a rest day, Sunday, before the conference starts on Monday. I have one short day to achieve my goal. (Of course, I could always skip some of the conference—hmmm.) I call the Hertz desk and request a car for 9 A.M. No problem. Comes 9 A.M.—no car. I jump up and down. Time passes. White foam drips onto my shirt. Frantic calls to the garage. The car has a broken right front wheel. No other cars available. Can I drive 300 miles on three wheels? Why not? For a wild moment I consider it. After all, a Knight on a Quest can use any steed—look at Sancho Panza. Instead, I calmly begin strangling the Hertz clerk. (Who, me? Obsessed?) A Honda two-door miraculously appears. I depart quickly before the police are called.

Heading northeast up the coast toward Dubai, I am again struck by the infrastructure. The highways are nicer and much less crowded than the United States. The only difference is the British-style roundabouts at every major intersection, even on the "interstates." The gas stations look the same. The countryside looks like Arizona without the saguaros but with a sea twinkling off to the left.

I blast along at high speed until I come to a construction zone that slows me down some. Off again at seventy miles an hour when I come to some high bumps in the highway—"sleeping policemen" apparently attempting to slow me down. Really great view of the Gulf from six feet in the air. Praise Allah: Honda makes extremely good shocks. In two hours I come to the fabled city-state of Dubai.

Dubai is the commercial center of the UAE and relies mainly on re-exporting (unkindly called "smuggling" in some quarters), trade, banking, and a portion of the UAE oil revenues (and, of course, on those poor Ukrainian and Russian girls). Interestingly, these oil revenues are doled out by Abu Dhabi, which controls about 70 percent of the land and oil in the UAE, to the other emirates as a sort of welfare for the wealthy.

Since I am in a hurry to hit the other countries in my personal Century Quest, I decide to drive through Dubai (number 99!) as fast as I can on the beltway, vowing to stop in town on the way back. (No, I don't need to get out and touch the ground to count the country. I drove through the darn place, didn't I? Hey, I don't make the rules. Complain to the TCC, if you're peeved.)

Naturally as soon as I make this decision I hit a mammoth traffic jam. The traffic jam looks remarkably similar to the jams in the 98 previous countries. Time passes. Traffic crawls. The Traffic Monster wraps around me like a giant anaconda. Will Our Hero ever make it out of number 99 to number 100? I stare at the office building beside me, which looks like every other office building in the world, and contemplate the exotic nature of international travel.

What seems like hours later I finally cut my way through the Laocoön of traffic (these Hondas have really great horns). My depression lifts as ahead I see the Promised Land—a huge highway sign over the beltway saying in English and Arabic: "Sharjah." (No, I'd never heard of it before, either. But it is on The List.) It seems like just an extension of Dubai: concrete highway, tall buildings in the distance, fast-food outlets in the foreground, sand in the middle.

BUT THIS IS IT—COUNTRY NUMBER 100!

THE HOLY GRAIL OF TRAVEL IS MINE!

To celebrate the great epiphany, I decide to sample a bit of the local Sharjahese (Sharjac? Sharjahoise?) culture. I stop for lunch at the most typical, popular local eating establishment: Kentucky Fried Chicken. I am pleased to report that the Sharjahtick Kentucky Fried Chicken is almost indistinguishable from the Colonel's Original Recipe, the only difference being a dollop of sand in the Extra Crispy. I ask about the best local dessert in the desert, and am directed next door to Baskin-Robbins. Sharjahnos clearly will not suffer from a lack of the Three Basic Food Groups: fat, salt, and sugar.

Later I learn from a friend stationed in the Gulf that Sharjah has a wonderful, huge rug market-cum-warehouse. He has spent every weekend for months viewing thousands of Persian rugs smuggled in from Iran, and has bought over fifty at what he claims are the lowest prices anywhere. He has them stored in Europe as an investment.

Llewellyn M. Toulmin

The Sharjah KFC serves typical Shajahese cuisine

But even if I knew that I wouldn't have stopped. I have the bit between my teeth. Today is not for shopping, it is for ADVENTURE (twenty-first century style, of course). I still have a few hours of daylight left to conquer new realms. Pedal hits metal. I roar out of Sharjah on my Quest for the next country: Ajman.

Unfortunately, I have turned onto the coast road, and there are no large highway signs to announce Ajman. So I am more than half way through the country before I see the "Ajman Beach Hotel" and realize I'm already there. (Hey! It's only a mile wide, for Allahsake. It doesn't even have a tourist office.) I drive slowly past the palace, the harbor with some motorized dhows (no one sails anymore), and the big attraction, the Al-Bahar Restaurant and Petrol Station. (Hope they keep their functions straight.) Right. Number 101. Been there. Done that. Would have "Got the T-shirt" but the T-shirt shops are closed. How many minutes for that country? Fifteen? Twenty? Am I efficient or what? Next!

The six-lane highway deteriorates to a two-lane asphalt road. I feel like Lewis and Clark as I explore this uncharted region. My speed slows to a deliberate pace as I carefully scout for hidden dangers ahead. I can barely break sixty-five. On the left the Gulf ("Arabian" to the Arabians and "Persian" to the Iranians and oddly to the U.S. Navy) sparkles in the sunshine. On the right are the first signs of a line of ridges and mountains paralleling the road and coming ever closer to the sea. It is hot, but my mighty Honda and its AC successfully do battle with the vicious elements. I muse on the rough and rugged nature of serious adventure travel.

Whoops! While pondering my philosophy of travel I miss the turnoff for Umm al-Qaiwain (don't they know that *u* always follows *q*?) and can't find a turnaround for a mile. Oh, well, what the hell: let's keep going to the end of the line, Ras Al-Khaimah (Al must have been an early explorer here; his name is everywhere). I'll hit UQ on the way back.

Ras al-Khaimah (number 102), known as RaK, 200 kilometers northeast of Abu Dhabi, is very quiet and seems more like a 1950s style Arab town. There are no curbs and gutters in RaK, few villas, no tall buildings, and not many paved streets. There are some mangy dogs. Very atmospheric.

I drive through the small old town to the gravelly beach at the tip of the RaK peninsula. The cliffs loom not far away. They will march down to the sea just a few miles up the coast and block access to the little isolated, strategic bit of Oman that sticks out into the Strait of Hormuz—one of the most critical choke points on Earth.

Next to a working gravel pit I climb down onto the narrow beach and pick up a few small shells for my wife. I spend a few minutes wishing she were here, as Damsel to my Knight.

The Gulf is surprisingly clear and inviting. Recalling a co-worker who is trying to swim in every major body of water on earth (now he IS obsessed), I dip my hand in and taste the Holy Water at the outer limit of my Quest. I recall the Meaning of Life and recite the Vow of the Knight of Travel: *Vigilum meum mortum maximandi wingae mille miglia* ("I promise to die with more frequent-flyer miles than anybody").

Twenty klicks later, driving back toward Abu Dhabi, I find the turnoff for Umm al Qaiwain. UQ (pronounced as it looks) is on a long peninsula lined with undistinguished shops, mostly closed as I pass, with the old town at the tip. I drive through the town, find the harbor with no boats, and look for the fort and old watchtowers listed in the *Lonely Planet*. The book says that "most of the streets are not signposted, but it is hard to get lost in a place this small." I get lost and can't find the watchtowers. The guide also says that UQ is "definitely worth an hour of your time," but that "once here you are unlikely to see any compelling reason to stay much longer." Hmmm. This, from the most PC guidebook on earth (barring *Rough Guide*, which doesn't count). Okay, I'm OUTTAHERE. Number 103: twenty-five minutes, tops.

I head southwest toward Dubai. Big decision time. I can drive back down the coast road, or turn inland and try to find a bizarre isolated piece of Oman—a circle of land about five kilometers across called the Madha Omani Enclave—that has broken off from the main part of Oman and is floating in a sea of UAE. Or I can head for my only unvisited emirate, Fujairah, on the east coast of the UAE. Or I can try to reach Oman via the Al-Ain (that Al guy again) oasis. Any of these would be number 104.

Since the sun is setting and all the 104s are 200 klicks out of the way, I decide to head straight back to Dubai and Abu Dhabi. Six countries in six hours is probably enough, even for me.

In Dubai (rightly called "Do Buy" by some), I stop at the gold souk in the middle of town. Every possible type of gold chain, necklace, bracelet, anklet, ring, earring, nosering, eyebrowring, navelring, unmentionablering, etc. is on display in a huge ten-block souk. I am overwhelmed and enormously tempted by this show of materialism. I sense evil sorcerers trying to get Our Hero (yes, I mean me) to leave the high spiritual plane I have obtained (I'm sure, gentle reader, you've noticed my spirituality), and forcing me to stoop to base bargaining and commerce. To defend against these evil djinns I begin to chant my anti-shopping mantra:

THEREISTOODARNMUCHSTUFFINTHEWORLD

STOPMAKINGSTUFF

STOPBUYINGSTUFF

THEREISTOODARNMUCHSTUFFINTHEWORLD

The mantra works. The newly minted Knight of Travel leaves the Souk of Temptation without succumbing.

By 9 P.M. I am in my bed in the Abu Dhabi Hilton. Jet lag, country lag, a Knight-sized bed, and my success give me a good night's rest. My Quest is complete. The Holy Grail of Travel is mine. (But I am NOT obsessed.)

Time passes. Months later, having visited eight more countries [Togo, some "Stans," "Turkey in Asia" (stupidly missed it on my first trip to Istanbul; spent twenty minutes there this time), Macedonia, Serbia (talked my way ten meters in without a visa by soft-soaping a Border Nazi), Ecuador, and Iceland (hey, I saved Uncle Boss $1,000 by taking Icelandic across the Pond)], I have a thought as I am finishing this article. Suppose I take a common-sense approach to what constitutes a "country"? Instead of counting Wales and Alaska and Hawaii and Midway and Java as "countries," I wonder how many REAL countries I have that everyone could agree on. I am sure of course that I have more than 100, since I have hit 112 TCC "countries." I recount. As the count gets higher and the remainder of the list shortens, an icy feeling grips my heart. OMIGOD! I've only visited 88 or 89 countries! (89 if you include The Sovereign and Military Order of the Knights of St. John the Hospitaller of Jerusalem, Rhodes, and Malta— TSaMOotKoSJtHoJ,RaM for short. SaMOotKoSJtHoJ,RaM is recognized by the Guinness Book of Records but not by TCC. C'mon, TCC! TSaMOotKoSJtHoJ,RaM issues passports to its three citizens and has its own air force—whaddaya want from a country?) GETBACKTOTHEPOINT! I DON'T HAVE MY CENTURY! I'VE LOST MY HOLY GRAIL! Sorry to run, but I gotta catch a...

* * *

EDITOR'S NOTE: Dr. Toulmin was last seen driving a mobile lounge at Washington's Dulles Airport down runway 01 Left in pursuit of a departing Air Albania Airbus. His wife Susan has started a support group, "Travelers' Century Countries Anonymous," with a 100-step recovery program.

Travelers' Century Club

"World Travel... the passport to peace through understanding"

This is to certify

Llewellyn M. Toulmin

having visited 100 or more countries and island groups of the world,
has qualified for membership in the Travelers' Century Club.

Klaus Billep

Chairman August 7, 1997

Appendix:
The *International Travel News*, Travelers' Century Club, and Charles Veley Lists of Countries

International Travel News (*ITN*) is a monthly newspaper/magazine for high-volume but budget-minded international travelers. (I am the cruise editor for *ITN* and write a monthly column called "The Cruising World.") *ITN* has compiled a list of "actual" countries that does *not* include territories, islands, provinces, states, enclaves, and other non-sovereign geographic entities. This list has 195 countries on it (including Timor Leste or East Timor, the most recent addition). The *ITN* list is presented below. More information can be obtained from *ITN* at

> *International Travel News*
> 2120 29th Street
> Sacramento, CA 95818
> 800-486-4968 (subscriptions)
> 916-457-3643 (editorial)
> www.intltravelnews.com.[7]

---

[7] *Note that the list of United Nations members is slightly different, at 191 member states, as of 2005. Other lists which are not presented here include the ham radio DXCC list, which includes uninhabited territories, and the Guinness list, which has only 265 "countries" but which includes 14 "secret" locations (such as Bouvet Island) which are apparently chosen just to be difficult.*

427

The Travelers' Century Club was founded in 1954. Its goal is to promote peace through international travel. Persons who have traveled to 100 or more countries and territories are eligible to join as full members; persons with 75 or more may join as aspirant members. There are chapters with regular meetings in Los Angeles, New York, Dallas, Colorado, and Florida. A committee of the Club decides which countries are sovereign and which dependencies are separate enough due to geography, culture, or history to warrant being considered separate territories. Interestingly, when the club was founded, no one dreamed than any person could possibly reach all the countries on the list. By 1960 the qualifying membership was only 43 persons, compared to 1,700 today.

The TCC list is updated regularly to reflect changing political conditions; the latest was updated in January 2005. The current TCC list of 315 countries and territories is provided below, for readers who wish to tot up their "score." About nine living persons have reached all the 315 countries and territories on the TCC list. The TCC address is

Travelers' Century Club
P.O. Box 7050
Santa Monica, CA 90406-7050
310-458-3454
www.travelerscenturyclub.org

Charles Veley, who claims to be the current most traveled man on earth, has compiled an "extreme" list of countries, territories, enclaves, and islands that is designed for extreme travelers and persons who have run out of TCC and other countries. Charles uses the TCC list, the Amateur Radio Relay League "DXCC" list, and other sources to compile his list. He is also open to suggestions for modifying his list of 570 entities. His list is presented last below. His Web site is www.mosttraveledman.com.

Llewellyn M. Toulmin

The *ITN* list of "actual" or "common-sense" countries is as follows:

NORTH AMERICA
Canada
Mexico
United States

MIDDLE AMERICA
Antigua & Barbuda
Bahamas
Barbados
Belize
Costa Rica
Cuba
Dominica
Dominican Republic
El Salvador
Grenada
Guatemala
Haiti
Honduras
Jamaica
Nicaragua
Panama
Saint Kitts & Nevis
Saint Lucia
Saint Vincent & the Grenadines
Trinidad & Tobago

SOUTH AMERICA
Argentina
Bolivia
Brazil
Chile
Colombia
Ecuador
Guyana
Paraguay
Peru
Suriname
Uruguay
Venezuela

EUROPE
Albania
Andorra
Austria
Belarus
Belgium
Bosnia & Herzegovina
Bulgaria
Croatia
Czech Republic
Denmark
Estonia
Finland
France
Germany
Greece
Hungary
Iceland
Ireland
Italy
Latvia
Liechtenstein
Lithuania
Luxembourg
Macedonia (FYR)
Malta
Moldova
Monaco
Netherlands
Norway
Poland
Portugal
Romania
Russia
San Marino
Serbia and Montenegro (formerly Yugoslavia)
Slovakia
Slovenia
Spain
Sweden
Switzerland
Ukraine
United Kingdom
Vatican City

ASIA/MIDDLE EAST
Afghanistan
Armenia
Azerbaijan
Bahrain
Bangladesh
Bhutan
Brunei
Burma (Myanmar)
Cambodia
China
Cyprus
East Timor
Georgia
India
Indonesia
Iran
Iraq
Israel
Japan
Jordan
Kazakhstan
North Korea
South Korea
Kuwait
Kyrgyzstan
Laos
Lebanon
Malaysia
Maldives
Mongolia
Nepal
Oman
Pakistan
Philippines
Qatar
Saudi Arabia
Singapore
Sri Lanka
Syria

429

Taiwan
Tajikistan
Thailand
Turkey
Turkmenistan
United Arab
  Emirates
Uzbekistan
Viet-Nam
Yemen

AFRICA
Algeria
Angola
Benin
Botswana
Burkina Faso
Burundi
Cameroon
Cape Verde
Central
  African
  Republic
Chad

Comoros
Congo,
  Democratic
  Republic of
Congo,
  Republic of
Côte d'Ivoire
Djibouti
Egypt
Equatorial
  Guinea
Eritrea
Ethiopia
Gabon
Gambia
Ghana
Guinea
Guinea-
  Bissau
Kenya
Lesotho
Liberia
Libya
Madagascar

Malawi
Mali
Mauritania
Mauritius
Morocco
Mozambique
Namibia
Niger
Nigeria
Rwanda
São Tomé
  and
  Príncipe
Senegal
Seychelles
Sierra Leone
Somalia
South Africa
Sudan
Swaziland
Tanzania
Togo
Tunisia
Uganda

Zambia
Zimbabwe

OCEANIA
Australia
Fiji
Kiribati
Marshall
  Islands
Micronesia
Nauru
New Zealand
Palau (Belau)
Papua New
  Guinea
Samoa
Solomon
  Islands
Tonga
Tuvalu
Vanuatu

The TCC list of countries and (semi-) sovereign territories is as follows:

PACIFIC OCEAN (40)

Australia
Bismark Archipelago (New Ireland, New Britain, Bougainville, Admiralty Islands)
Chatham Islands
Cook Islands (Rarotonga, Aitutaki, Penrhyn)
Easter Island
Fiji Islands
French Polynesia (Tahiti,Tuamotu, Austral, Gambier)
Galapagos Islands
Guam
Hawaiian Islands
Johnston Island
Juan Fernandez Islands (Robinson Crusoe Island)
Kiribati (Gilberts, Tarawa, Ocean Island)
Line/Phoenix Islands (Palmyra, Fanning, Christmas, Canton, Enderbury, Howland)
Lord Howe Island
Marquesas Islands
Marshall Islands, Republic of (Majuro, Kwajalein, Eniwetok)
Micronesia, Federated States of (Pohnpei, Kosrae, Chuuk,Yap,Caroline Islands)

Midway Island
Nauru
New Caledonia & Deps. (Noumea, Loyalty Islands)
New Zealand
Niue
Norfolk Island
Northern Marianas (Saipan, Tinian)
Ogasawara (Bonin, Volcano Island, Iwo Jima)
Palau, Republic of
Papua New Guinea
Pitcairn Island
Ryukyu Islands (Okinawa)
Samoa, American (Pago Pago)
Samoa, Western (Apia)
Solomon Islands (Guadalcanal, New Georgia, Tulagi)
Tasmania
Tokelau Islands (Fakaofu, Atafu, Union)
Tonga (Nukualofa)
Tuvalu (Ellice Island, Funafuti, Vaitapu)
Vanuatu (New Hebrides Islands)
Wake Island
Wallis & Futuna Islands

NORTH AMERICA (6)

Alaska
Canada
Mexico
Prince Edward Island
St. Pierre and Miquelon
United States (continental)

CENTRAL AMERICA (7)

Belize (British Honduras)
Costa Rica
El Salvador
Guatemala
Honduras
Nicaragua
Panama

SOUTH AMERICA (13)

Argentina
Bolivia
Brazil
Chile
Colombia
Ecuador
French Guiana
Guyana (British Guiana)
Paraguay
Peru
Suriname (Netherlands
   Guiana)
Uruguay
Venezuela

CARIBBEAN (27)

Anguilla
Antigua and Deps. (Barbuda,
   Redonda)
Aruba
Bahamas
Barbados
Cayman Islands
Cuba
Dominica
Dominican Republic
Grenada and Deps.
   (Carriacou, Grenadines)
Guadeloupe and Deps.(Marie
   Galante)
Haiti
Jamaica
Leeward Islands, French (St.
   Martin, St. Barts)
Leeward Islands, Netherlands
   (Saba, St. Eustatius, St.
   Maarten)
Martinique
Montserrat
Netherlands Antilles (Curacao,
   Bonaire)
Puerto Rico
San Andres & Providencia
St. Kitts and Nevis
St. Lucia
St. Vincent & Deps. (Bequia,
   Canouan Grenadines)
Trinidad and Tobago
Turks and Caicos Islands

Virgin Islands, U.S. (St. Croix, St. John, St. Thomas)

Virgin Islands, British (Tortola, etc.)

ATLANTIC OCEAN (13)

Ascension
Azores Islands
Bermuda
Canary Islands
Cape Verde Islands
Falkland Islands
Fernando do Noronha
Faroe Islands
Greenland (Kalaallit Nunaat)
Iceland
Madeira
St. Helena
Tristan de Cunha

EUROPE & MEDITERRANEAN (67)

Aland Islands (Mariehamn)
Albania
Andorra
Austria
Balearic Islands (Mallorca, Minorca)
Belarus
Belgium
Bosnia and Herzegovina (Sarajevo)
Bulgaria
Corsica
Crete
Croatia
Cyprus, Republic
Cyprus, Turkish Federated State
Czech Federated Republic
Denmark
Dodecanese Islands (Rhodes)
England
Estonia
Finland
France
Germany
Gibraltar
Greece
Guernsey and Deps (Alderney, Herm, Sark, Channel Islands)
Hungary
Ionian Islands (Corfu, etc.)
Ireland (Eire)
Ireland, Northern (Ulster)
Isle of Man
Italy
Jersey (Channel Islands)
Kaliningrad
Kosovo
Lampedusa
Latvia
Liechtenstein
Lithuania
Luxembourg
Macedonia
Malta
Moldova
Monaco
Montenegro
Netherlands
Norway
Poland
Portugal
Romania
Russia
San Marino

Sardinia
Scotland
Serbia
Sicily
Slovakia
Slovenia
Spain
Spitsbergen (Svalbard, Bear
    Island)

Srpska
Sweden
Switzerland
Trans Dniester
Turkey in Europe (Istanbul)
Ukraine
Vatican City
Wales

ANTARCTICA (7)
Argentine South Pole
Australian Antarctic Territory
    South Pole (Mawson, Davis,
    Macquarie, Heard)
Chilean South Pole
Falkland Islands
    Dependencies (British
    Antarctica, Graham Land,
    South Shetland, South

Sandwich, South Georgia,
    South Orkney)
French Southern and Antarctic
    Territory South Pole
    (Kerguelen, Crozet,
    Amsterdam, St. Paul)
Norwegian (Bouvet)
New Zealand South Pole
    (Ross Dependency)

AFRICA (52)
Algeria
Angola
Benin (Dahomey)
Botswana (Bechuanaland)
Burkina Faso (Upper Volta)
Burundi (Urundi)
Cameroon
Central African Rep.
Chad
Republic of Congo
Democratic Republic of Congo
Djibouti
Egypt
Equatorial Guinea (Rio Muni,
    Fernando Poo)
Eritrea
Ethiopia
Gabon
Gambia

Ghana (Gold Coast, British
    Togoland)
Guinea (French)
Guinea-Bissau
Ivory Coast
Kenya
Lesotho (Basutoland)
Liberia
Libya
Malawi (Nyasaland)
Mali
Mauritania
Morocco
Morocco,Spanish (Ceuta,
    Melilla)
Mozambique
Namibia
Niger
Nigeria
Rwanda

São Tomé and Príncipe
Senegal
Sierra Leone
Somalia (Italian Somaliland)
Somaliland (British)
South Africa
Sudan
Swaziland
Tanzania (Tanganyika)

Togo
Tunisia
Uganda
Western Sahara (Spanish
  Sahara)
Zambia (Northern Rhodesia)
Zanzibar
Zimbabwe (Southern
  Rhodesia)

MIDDLE EAST (20)
Abu Dhabi
Ajman
Bahrain
Dubai
Fujeirah
Iran
Iraq
Israel
Jordan
Kuwait

Lebanon
Oman
Palestine
Qatar
Ras Al-Khaimah
Saudi Arabia
Sharjah
Syria
Umm Al-Qaiwain
Yemen

INDIAN OCEAN (14)
Andaman-Nicobar Islands
British Indian Ocean Territory
  (Chagos, Arch, Diego
  Garcia)
Christmas Island
Cocos Islands (Keeling)
Comoro Islands (Anjouan
  Moheli, Grand Comoro)
Lakshadweep,Union Territory
  of (Laccadive Is.)
Madagascar

Maldive Islands
Mauritius and Deps. (Agalega,
  St. Brandon)
Mayotte (Dzaoudzi)
Reunion & Deps. (Tromelin,
  Glorioso)
Rodriguez Island
Seychelles
Zil Elwannyen Sesel (Aldabra,
  Farquhar, Amirante Islands)

ASIA (49)
Afghanistan
Armenia (Yerevan)
Azerbaijan (Baku)
Bangladesh
Bhutan
Brunei

Cambodia
China, People's Republic of
East Timor
Georgia
Hainan Island
Hong Kong

India
Indonesia (Java)
Irian Jaya (Dutch New Guinea)
Japan
Kalimantan (Indonesian Borneo)
Kashmir
Kazakhstan
Kyrgyzstan
Korea, North
Korea, South
Laos
Lesser Sunda Islands (Bali, Timor, Indonesia)
Macau
Malaysia
Moluka
Mongolia, Rep.
Myanmar (Burma)
Nakhichevan

Nepal
Pakistan
Philippines
Sabah (No. Borneo)
Sarawak
Siberia (Russia in Asia)
Sikkim
Singapore
Sri Lanka (Ceylon)
Sulawesi (Celebes, Indonesia)
Sumatra (Indonesia)
Taiwan. R.O.C.
Tajikistan
Thailand
Tibet
Turkey in Asia (Anatolia, Ankara, Izmir)
Turkmenistan
Uzbekistan
Vietnam

The "extreme" Charles Veley list of countries, enclaves, territories, states, provinces, amateur radio locations, etc., is as follows:

PACIFIC OCEAN (82)

Admiralty Islands (Manus)
Austral Islands
Australian Capital Territory
Baker & Howland Islands
Banaba (Ocean Island)
Bougainville (Buka)
Chatham Islands
Chesterfield Islands
Chuuk, State of
Clipperton Island
Conway Reef (Cevu-i-Ra)
Cook Islands (Southern)
Coral Sea Islands Territory
Daito Islands
Ducie Island
Easter Island
Fiji Islands
Galapagos Islands
Gambier Islands
Guam
Hawaiian Islands (including Northwest Hawaiian Islands)
Henderson Island
Jarvis Island
Johnston Island

Kermadec Islands
Kingman Reef
Kiribati (Gilberts Chain)
Kosrae, State of
Kure Island
Line Islands, Northern (Christmas, Fanning, Washington)
Line Islands, Southern (Caroline, Flint, Malden, Starbuck, Vostok)
Lord Howe Island
Loyalty Islands
Marquesas Islands
Marshall Islands, Republic of
Mellish Reef
Midway Island
Minami Torishima
Nauru
New Britain
New Caledonia (mainland)
New Ireland
New South Wales
New Zealand
Niue
Norfolk Island
Northern Cook Islands (Manihiki, Penrhyn)
Northern Marianas

Northern Territory (Australia)
Oeno Island
Ogasawara (Bonin, Volcano Island, Iwo Jima)
Palau, Republic of
Palmyra Atoll
Papua New Guinea (mainland)
Parece Vela (Okino Torishima)
Phoenix Islands
Pitcairn Island
Pohnpei, State of
Pukapuka (Northern Cooks)
Queensland
Revillagigedo Islands
Rotuma
Ryukyu Islands
Samoa, American
Samoa, Western
Society Islands
Solomon Islands
South Australia
Tasmania
Temotu Province (Santa Cruz Islands)
Tokelau Islands
Tonga
Torres Straits Islands
Trobriand Islands
Tuamotu Islands

437

Tuvalu
Vanuatu
Victoria
Wake Island
Wallis & Futuna
  Islands
Western Australia
Yap, State of

NORTH AMERICA (72)
Alabama
Alaska
Alberta
Arizona
Arkansas
Baja California
  (Norte & Sur)
British Columbia
California
Chiapas
Colorado
Connecticut
Delaware
District of Columbia
Florida
Georgia
Idaho
Illinois
Indiana
Iowa
Kansas
Kentucky
Labrador
Louisiana
Maine
Manitoba
Maryland
Massachusetts
Mexico
  (North/Central)
Michigan

Minnesota
Mississippi
Missouri
Montana
Nebraska
Nevada
New Brunswick
New Hampshire
New Jersey
New Mexico
New York
Newfoundland
North Carolina
North Dakota
Northwest
  Territories
Nova Scotia
Nunavut
Ohio
Oklahoma
Ontario
Oregon
Pennsylvania
Prince Edward
  Island
Quebec
Rhode Island
Sable Island
Saskatchewan
South Carolina
South Dakota
St. Paul Island
  (Canada)
St. Pierre &
  Miquelon
Tennessee
Texas
United Nations HQ
  (New York)
Utah
Vermont
Virginia

Washington
West Virginia
Wisconsin
Wyoming
Yucatan Peninsula
  (Campeche,
  Quintana Roo,
  Tabasco)
Yukon Territory

CENTRAL AMERICA (9)
Belize (British
  Honduras)
Cocos Island
Costa Rica
El Salvador
Guatemala
Honduras
Nicaragua
Panama
San Blas Islands

SOUTH AMERICA (16)
Argentina
Bolivia
Brazil
Chile
Colombia
Ecuador
French Guiana
Guyana
Juan Fernandez
  Islands
  (Robinson
  Crusoe)
Malpelo Island
Paraguay
Peru
San Felix & San
  Ambrosio Islands

Suriname
Uruguay
Venezuela

CARIBBEAN (42)
Anguilla
Antigua
Aruba
Aves Island
Bahamas
Barbados
Barbuda
Bonaire
Cayman Islands
Cuba
Curacao
Desecheo Island
Dominica
Dominican
  Republic
Grenada
Grenadines,
  Grenada
  (Carriacou, etc)
Grenadines, St.
  Vincent (Bequia,
  Canouan,
  Mustique, Union,
  etc.)
Guadeloupe &
  Deps.(Marie
  Galante)
Guantanamo Bay
Haiti
Jamaica
Martinique
Montserrat
Navassa Island
Nevis
Puerto Rico
Redonda
Saba

San Andres &
  Providencia
St. Barths
St. Croix
St. Eustatius
St. Kitts
St. Lucia
St. Maarten
St. Martin
St. Vincent
Tobago
Trinidad
Turks & Caicos
  Islands
Virgin Islands,
  British (Tortola,
  etc.)
Virgin Islands, U.S.
  (St. John, St.
  Thomas)

ATLANTIC OCEAN (15)
Ascension
Azores Islands
Bermuda
Canary Islands
Cape Verde Islands
Falkland Islands
Faroe Islands
Fernando do
  Noronha
Greenland (Kalaallit
  Nunaat)
Iceland
Madeira
St. Helena
St. Peter & St. Paul
  Rocks
Trindade & Martim
  Vaz Islands
Tristan de Cunha

EUROPE & MEDITERRANEAN (94)
Aland Islands
  (Mariehamn)
Albania
Alderney
Andorra
Austria
Balearic Islands
  (Mallorca,
  Minorca)
Bear Island
Belarus
Belgium
Bosnia &
  Herzegovina
  (Sarajevo)
British Sovereign
  Base Areas,
  Cyprus
Bulgaria
Büsingen
Campione d'Italia
Catalonia
Corsica
Crete
Crimea
Croatia
Cyprus, Republic
Cyprus, Turkish
  Fed. State
Czech Federated
  Rep.
Denmark
Dodecanese Is.
  (Rhodes)
England
Estonia
Euskaldunak
  (Basque
  Territory)

439

Finland
France
Franz Josef Land
Galicia
Germany, Eastern
Germany, Western
Gibraltar
Greece
Guernsey
Herm
Hungary
Ionian Islands
(Corfu, etc.)
Ireland (Dublin)
Ireland, Northern
(Belfast)
Isle of Man
Istria
Italy
ITU HQ (Geneva)
Jan Mayen
Jersey (Channel
Islands)
Kaliningrad
Karelia
Kosovo
Lampedusa
Latvia
Liechtenstein
Lithuania
Llivia
Lundy
Luxembourg
Macedonia
Malta
Malyj Vysotskij
Island
Market Reef
Moldova
Monaco
Montenegro
Mount Athos

Netherlands
Norway
Orkney Islands
Poland
Portugal
Rockall
Romania
Russia
San Marino
Sardinia
Sark
Scilly Isles
Scotland
Serbia
Shetland Islands
Sicily
Slovakia
Slovenia
Sovereign Military
Order of Malta
Spain
Srpska Republic
Svalbard
Sweden
Switzerland
Trans Dniester
Turkey in Europe
(Istanbul)
Ukraine
Vatican City
Wales

**ANTARCTICA &
SUB-
ANTARCTIC
ISLANDS (26)**
Amsterdam & St.
Paul Islands
Antipodes Islands
Argentine Antarctic
Claim (to S. Pole)
Auckland Islands

Australian Antarctic
Claim (to S. Pole)
Balleny Islands
Bounty Islands
Bouvet Island
British Antarctic
Claim (to S. Pole)
Campbell Islands
Chilean Antarctic
Claim (to S. Pole)
Crozet Islands
French Antarctic
Claim (Terre
Adelie – to S.
Pole)
Heard & McDonald
Islands
Kerguelen Islands
MacQuarie Island
Marion & Prince
Edward Islands
New Zealand
Antarctic Claim
(Ross
Dependency – to
S. Pole)
Norwegian
Antarctic Claim
(Dronning Maud
Land – not to
South Pole)
Peter I Island
Scott Island
Snares Islands
South Georgia
South Orkney
Islands
South Sandwich
Islands
South Shetland
Islands

Llewellyn M. Toulmin

AFRICA (66)
Algeria
Angola
Annobon Island
Benin
Bioko Island
(Malabo)
Botswana
Burkina Faso
Burundi
Cabinda
Cameroon
Central African
Rep.
Ceuta
Chad
Democratic
Republic of
Congo
Djibouti
Eastern Cape
(Bisho, Port
Elizabeth)
Egypt
Eritrea
Ethiopia
Free State
(Bloemfontein)
Gabon
Gambia
Gauteng
(Johannesburg,
Pretoria)
Ghana
Guinea (Conakry)
Guinea-Bissau
Ivory Coast
Kenya
Kwazulu-Natal
(Pietermaritzburg,
Durban)

Lesotho
(Basutoland)
Liberia
Libya
Limpopo
(Polokwane)
Malawi (Nyasaland)
Mali
Mauritania
Melilla
Morocco
Mozambique
Mpumalanga
(Nelspruit)
Namibia
Niger
Nigeria
North West
Province
(Mafikeng, Sun
City)
Northern Cape
(Kimberley)
Príncipe
Republic of Congo
(Brazzaville)
Rio Muni (Bata)
Rwanda
Sahrawi Republic
São Tomé
Senegal
Sierra Leone
Somalia (Italian
Somaliland)
Somaliland (Brit.)
Sudan
Swaziland
Tanzania
Togo
Tunisia
Uganda

Western Cape
(Cape Town)
Western Sahara
(Spanish Sahara)
Zambia
Zanzibar
Zimbabwe (So.
Rhodesia)

MIDDLE EAST (23)
Abu Dhabi
Ajman
Bahrain
Dubai
Fujeirah
Gaza Strip
Golan Heights
Iran
Iraq
Israel
Jordan
Kuwait
Lebanon
Oman
Qatar
Ras Al Khaimah
Ras Musandam
Saudi Arabia
Sharjah
Syria
Umm Al Qaiwain
West Bank
Palestinian
Territory
Yemen

INDIAN OCEAN (26)
Agalega & St.
Brandon
Aldabra Islands

441

Amirante Islands
Andaman Islands
Anjouan
Ashmore & Cartier
  Islands
British Indian
  Ocean Territory
  (Chagos Arch,
  Diego Garcia)
Christmas Island
Cocos (Keeling)
  Islands
Europa Island
Farquhar Islands
  (Alphonse,
  Farquhar,
  Providence)
Glorioso Islands
Grand Comoro
Juan de Nova
  Island
Lakshadweep,
  Union Terr.
Madagascar
Maldive Islands
Mauritius
Mayotte
Moheli
Nicobar Islands
Reunion
Rodriguez Island
Seychelles (Inner
  Islands)
Soqotra Islands
Tromelin Island

ASIA (99)
Abkhazia
Adygeya (Maykop)
Afghanistan
Ajaria
Aksai Chin

Altai (Gorno-
  Altaysk)
Armenia
Arunachal Pradesh
Assam
Azerbaijan
Bangladesh
Baskortostan (Ufa)
Bhutan
Brunei
Buryatia (Ulan Ude)
Cambodia
Chechnya (Grozny)
China, People's
  Rep.
Chuvashia
  (Cheboksary)
Dagestan
  (Makhachkala)
East Timor
Georgia
Goa (Portugese
  India)
Guangxi
  Autonomous
  Province (Guilin)
Hainan Island
Hokkaido
Hong Kong
India
Indonesia (Java)
Ingushetia (Nazran)
Inner Mongolia
  Autonomous
  Province
  (Hohhot)
Irian Jaya (Dutch
  New Guinea)
Japan
Kabardino-Balkaria
  (Nalchik)

Kalimantan
  (Indonesian
  Borneo)
Kalmykia (Elista)
Karachay-
  Cherkessia
  (Cherkessk)
Kashmir, Indian
  (Jammu &
  Kashmir)
Kashmir, Pakistani
  (Hunza, Gilgit,
  Skardu)
Kazakhstan
Khakassia
  (Abakan)
Komi (Syktyvkar)
Korea, North
Korea, South
Kuril Islands
Kyrgyzstan
Ladakh
Laos
Lesser Sunda
  Islands
Macau
Malaysia
  (Peninsular)
Manipur
Mari El (Yoshkar
  Ola)
Mizoram
Molukkas
Mongolia, Rep.
  (Ulaan Bator)
Mordovia
  (Saramsk)
Mustang
Myanmar (Burma)
Nagaland
Nagorno-Karabakh
  (Artsakh)

Nakhicevan
Nepal
Ningxia
  Autonomous
  Province
  (Yinchuan)
Oecussi
Ossetia, North
Ossetia, South
Pakistan
Paracel Islands
Philippines
  (Northern/Luzon)
Philippines
  (Southern/Mindan
  ao)
Pondicherry
  (French India)

Pratas Island
Sabah
Sakha/Yakutia
  (Yakutsk)
Sakhalin Island
Sarawak
Scarborough Reef
Shenzhen
Siberia (Russia in
  Asia)
Sikkim
Singapore
Spratly Islands
Sri Lanka (Ceylon)
Sulawesi (Celebes,
  Indonesia)
Sumatra
  (Indonesia)

Taiwan. R.O.C.
Tajikistan
Tatarstan (Kazan)
Thailand
Tibet
Turkey in Asia
  (Anatolia)
Turkmenistan
Tuva (Kyzyl)
Udmurtia (Izhevsk)
Uzbekistan
Vietnam, North
Vietnam, South
Xinjiang Uygur
  Autonomous
  Province

TOTAL Count: 570

Happy travels!

Credits

Photos in this book were taken by Llewellyn M. Toulmin, with the following exceptions. These photos used courtesy of and credit to:

- Front cover photo: Terrarum Orbis, La Feuille, *Atlas*, c. 171?: Library of Congress
- Back cover photo of John Clouse: John Clouse
- Back cover photo of Charles Veley: Charles Veley

Interior black and white photos:

- "AROGANT" Telecom: International Telecommunications Union
- Around the World Rally logo: Classic Rally Association
- Bridge over the River Kwai: Atterbury Bakalar Air Museum
- Charles Veley with John Clouse: Charles Veley
- Charles Veley with Nepalese: Charles Veley
- Citadel in Haiti from above: LatinAmericanStudies.com
- Columbus bear: Teddy Travels
- Cowes sailing: Skandia
- Derek Frost portrait: Orient Lines
- Dromoland Castle: Dromoland Castle
- Eckerd College chapel: Eckerd College
- John Clouse in doorway of Shackleton hut: John Clouse
- John Clouse on Jarvis Island: John Clouse
- Haile Selassie of Ethiopia: houseofbobo.com
- Lahoree swimming pool: Lahore Metblogs
- Mangosteen painting: Onmangosteendaily.com
- Mating lions: Mcoxphoto
- Medals of Sir Henry Clinton: Buckland, Dix and Wood
- Medals of Sir Thomas Foley: Glendening's

- Medals of Thomas Wilkinson: Glendening's
- Medals of Tom Lawrence: Buckland, Dix and Wood
- Medals of William Gairdner: Glendening's
- Mullet drawing: UK Charterboats
- Mustang and old police car on track: Rally Partners, Inc.
- Mustang at US Capitol start of Great Race: Rally Partners, Inc.
- Mustang on dusty road: Rally Partners, Inc.
- Nefertari: Jimmy Dunn
- Overturned truck in India: Terraxplorer
- Papa Doc Duvalier at desk: LatinAmericanStudies.com
- Portrait of Sir Henry Pottinger: Christie's
- President Gusmao of East Timor: UNESCO
- QE2 with Statue of Liberty: Cunard
- Richard Halliburton in the Panama Canal: Sealetter
- Topkapi dagger: Topkapi Museum

Lists of countries:

- ITN: International Travel News
- Charles Veley: Charles Veley
- TCC: Travelers' Century Club

Some of the stories in this book were published previously in various magazines and newspapers in identical or similar forms. Permission was granted for reprinting here, or rights were retained by the author, for the following pieces:

- "Cowes Week: Chartering the Racing World's Historic Event," Chartering Magazine, January 1987
- "Step Aboard a Floating Museum: U.S.S. Intrepid," Army, Navy and Air Force Times, April 11, 1988
- "Seeing the Great Medals of Britain," Army, Navy and Air Force Times, May 30, 1988
- "The Panama Canal: Lock onto One of the World's Seven Wonders," Army, Navy and Air Force Times, January 9, 1989

- "Revisit the Bridge: The Real Story of the Bridge on the River Kwai," <u>Army, Navy and Air Force Times</u>, October 18, 1993
- "Marks of Courage," <u>The Peak</u>, January 1994
- "A Twentieth Century *Marco Polo* Takes a Turn Along the East African Coast," <u>TravLtips</u>, May/June 1994
- "Indian Ocean Odyssey: Sri Lanka to Kenya," <u>International Travel News</u>, March/April 1995
- "A Cruise Through 5000 Years of History," <u>TravLtips</u>, September/October 1995
- "What it Takes to Be the Most Traveled Person on Earth," <u>International Travel News</u>, June 1999
- "An Odyssey Through History with the *Marco Polo*: Jordan to Turkey via the Suez Canal," <u>TravLtips</u>, January/February 2000
- "Past Passenger Derek Frost: 58 Cruises in 5 Years," <u>Polo News</u>, 2000
- "*Marco Polo* Through the Amazing Suez Canal," <u>International Travel News</u>, September 2000
- "A Classic Car Rally Around the World," <u>International Travel News</u>, December 2000
- "South Pacific Tall Ship Adventure," <u>International Travel News</u>, March 2002
- "East Timor: Weekend Getaway," <u>The Montgomery Sentinel</u>, May 16, 2002
- "If It's 2 p.m., This Must Be Sharjah: Breaking the 100 Country Barrier," <u>The Montgomery Sentinel</u>, May 30, 2002
- "Miracle in Myanmar: Lady Leg-Rowers Leave Paddlers in Their Wakes," <u>Paddler Magazine</u>, July/August 2002
- "Swimming from Andorra to Zimbabwe," <u>The Montgomery Sentinel</u>, August 1, 2002
- "Fire When Ready Aboard *Olympia*," <u>The Montgomery Sentinel</u>, September 5, 2002
- "Papa Doc and His Colt .45 vs. My Dad," <u>The Montgomery Sentinel</u>, October 3, 2002
- "There's a Kemoy in My House," <u>The Montgomery Sentinel</u>, November 7, 2002

- "Bill Pinkney: *Amistad* Captain's Amazing Journey," The Mobile Register, November 12, 2002
- "Braving the Elements: Journey Aboard the Freedom Schooner *Amistad*," The Mobile Register, November 12, 2002
- "The Most Annoying Country on Earth," The Montgomery Sentinel, December 5, 2002
- "Trans-Atlantic Aboard *QE2*: Fit for a Queen," TravLtips, January/February 2003
- "The KGB Wanted Me," The Montgomery Sentinel, January 2, 2003
- "Quest for the Real 'Bali Hai,'" 48 Degrees North: The Sailing Magazine, February 2003
- "The World's Pinkest Pink Belly," The Montgomery Sentinel, February 6, 2003
- "Bar-Crawling with the Schoonermen," The Montgomery Sentinel, March 6, 2003
- "The Real Story of the Bridge Over the River Kwai," The Montgomery Sentinel, April 4, 2003
- "Seeing Guam the Hard Way: 28 Years in a Hole," The Montgomery Sentinel, May 1, 2003
- "Irish Emigrant Tall Ship Visits DC Waterfront," The Montgomery Sentinel, May 22, 2003
- "Running with the Bulls: The Inner Game," The Montgomery Sentinel, July 3, 2003
- "A Perfect Day Before the Mast," The Montgomery Sentinel, June 5, 2003
- "A Ship with a Story," The Providence Journal, July 17, 2003
- "An American Named Llewellyn, Ya!" The Montgomery Sentinel, August 28, 2003
- "Life of a Lady Leg-Rower," The Montgomery County Sentinel, September 11, 2003
- "Bustin' the Gamblin' at the Sunrise Bar and Pool Hall," The Montgomery Sentinel, October 3, 2003
- "The Most Traveled Man on Earth," The Montgomery Sentinel, November 5, 2003

- "Horsewhipped in 'Gypped,'" The Montgomery Sentinel, December 4, 2003
- "Ballerina, Spy, First Lady: Kirsty Sword Gusmao of East Timor," The Montgomery Sentinel, January 6, 2004
- "Sailing the South Pacific," The Montgomery Sentinel, February 5, 2004
- "Searching by Sailboat for the Real 'Bali Hai,'" The Montgomery Sentinel, March 4, 2004
- "Mongkut: King of Fruits," The Montgomery Sentinel, April 5, 2004
- "I Get the Royal Treatment," The Montgomery Sentinel, May 6, 2004
- "In the Wake of the *Bounty*: Aboard the M.V. *Discovery*," TravLtips, May/June 2004
- "Rogue's Island: on Pitcairn, Bounty Mutineers Have Ties to Providence," The Providence Sunday Journal, (RI) May 16, 2004
- "A Delightful Trip to a Comfortable Old Castle," The Montgomery Sentinel, July 1, 2004
- Comparing Fact to Fiction on a Robinson Crusoe Island Excursion," International Travel News, August 2004
- "Haiti and the Mother of All Mudholes," The Montgomery Sentinel, August 5, 2004
- "Captain Erik Bjurstedt, Giant of the Cruise Industry," The Montgomery Sentinel, September 2, 2004
- "It May Have Been the World's Worst Traffic Jam," The Montgomery Sentinel, October 7, 2004
- "The Queen and I," International Travel News, September 2004
- "The *Marco Polo*," International Travel News, October 2004
- "Captain Erik Bjurstedt: Giant of the Cruise Industry," International Travel News, November 2004
- "The Great Vietnamese Dwarf Hunt," The Montgomery Sentinel, November 6, 2004
- "The College Chapel and the Golden Calf," The Montgomery Sentinel, December 2, 2004

- "Paradise Lost: Sex Verdicts Threaten Lonely Pitcairn Island," <u>The Montgomery Sentinel</u>, January 6, 2005
- "*Queen Mary 2*: Worth the Hype," <u>The Montgomery Sentinel</u>, February 5, 2005
- "Sex Verdicts Threaten Pitcairn's Survival," <u>International Travel News</u>, February 2005
- "*Queen Mary 2*: Wow!" <u>International Travel News</u>, March 2005
- "Sailing with the Royals: Cowes Week," <u>International Travel News</u>, June 2005
- "The Great Race is Coming!" <u>The Montgomery Sentinel</u>, June 23, 2005
- "Lew's Corner," <u>Greatracer</u>, June 24, 2005
- "Lew's Corner: A Racer's Perspective," <u>Greatracer</u>, June 28, 2005
- "Lew's Corner: A Racer's Perspective," <u>Greatracer</u>, June 29, 2005
- "Lew's Corner: A Racer's Perspective," <u>Greatracer</u>, June 29, 2005
- "Lew's Corner: A Racer's Perspective," <u>Greatracer</u>, July 1, 2005
- "Lew's Corner: A Racer's Perspective," <u>Greatracer</u>, July 2, 2005
- "Lew's Corner: A Racer's Perspective," <u>Greatracer</u>, July 3, 2005
- "Lew's Corner: A Racer's Perspective," <u>Greatracer</u>, July 6, 2005
- "Lew's Corner: A Racer's Perspective," <u>Greatracer</u>, July 9, 2005
- "The Daring Darrin Duo and Their Delectable Kaiser Darrin," Great Race, Rally Partners, Inc., July 2005
- "The 12-Year-Old Genius Great Racer," Great Race, Rally Partners, Inc., July 2005
- "Total Focus for Fourteen Days Straight," Great Race, Rally Partners, Inc., July 2005
- "Hail to the Chief: The Studebaker President," Great Race, Rally Partners, Inc., July 2005

- "Band of Teenagers Rally a Ford Four Times Their Age," Great Race, Rally Partners, Inc., July 2005
- "Sail a Tall Ship to Adventure, Part 1" <u>International Travel News</u>, July 2005
- "Sail a Tall Ship to Adventure, Part 2" <u>International Travel News</u>, August 2005